THE AGE OF GREAT DREAMS

THE AGE OF
GREAT DREAMS

AMERICA IN THE 1960S

BY DAVID FARBER

ERIC FONER: CONSULTING EDITOR

HILL AND WANG

A DIVISION OF FARRAR, STRAUS & GIROUX   NEW YORK

Designed by Fritz Metsch

LIBRARY OF CONGRESS CATALOGING-IN-PUBLICATION DATA
Farber, David R.
The age of great dreams : America in the 1960s / David Farber ;
Eric Foner, consulting editor.—1st ed.
p.   cm.
Includes bibliographical references and index.
1. United States—History—1961–1969.   I. Foner, Eric.
II. Title.
E841.F37   1991   973.92—dc20   93–32266   CIP

For Beth

CONTENTS

~~~~~~

THE AGE OF GREAT DREAMS

PREFACE

~~~~~~

TORN OUT OF TIME, shorn of context, even dimmed by fading memory, images of the 1960s still haunt us, still anger us, still entrance us, still puzzle us. Even those who came of age long after the "sixties" share the collective memories: the grainy film footage of John F. Kennedy shot down in Dallas, Neil Armstrong stepping onto the moon, Martin Luther King, Jr., telling the world about his dream of racial equality, a naked girl in Vietnam running, screaming, burning with napalm. They are among the most public moments of a very public decade, looped through the mass media in prime-time TV specials, Hollywood films, music video pastiche. In those memories and others lie much of the charge of the 1960s: the possibilities, the grandeur, and always the tragedy. In the 1960s Americans dared to chance grand dreams and they paid for it.

The mission of this book is not to render the high emotions of the 1960s into neutral prose or to turn existential drama into tidy scholarship. But I do place the 1960s back into our history, which links the epochal events of that era to Americans' grand projects of the previous decades: the forging of a national system of social provision; the emergence of America as global superpower; the creation of the national security state; and the maturation of a national, consumer-driven, mass-mediated marketplace. These big, ongoing structural developments, I believe, ground most of the explosive events of the 1960s.

I am not suggesting that the events of the 1960s were inevitable or would not have been different if heroes and villains, fools and visionaries of the times had not fought their way onto the historical stage. Any history of the 1960s must paint the brilliant colors of revolt and rupture, of people desperate to make history even as others fought fiercely to stop them. But if the 1960s seemed to many who lived through them a revolutionary time awash in unanticipated and inexplicable conflict, they are, too, very much the culmination of an era that began with the Great Depression and the New Deal and continued with World War II and its aftermath.

Much of my history of the 1960s explains how Americans' rapidly developing consumer-based, expert-oriented, nationally managed and internationally integrated economic and political system affected life in the United States. On a domestic political level, the relatively new national system and the affluence that fueled it brought much of American life that had long been left to the control of local elites under national purview. Neither Mississippi's legally prescribed racism nor Bible Belt educators' practice of starting off each school day with classroom prayer, for example, were by the mid-1960s still unchecked by the federal government. And as Vietnam proved, America's vast economic and geopolitical interests, as well as the national security apparatus created to serve those interests, made every part of the globe a potential site for massive intervention.

America's economic and political journey from the dark times of the Great Depression to the go-go years of the 1960s did more than produce new government structures and burgeoning interests abroad. The new economic realities of the postwar years affected Americans' sense of values and helped produce what some have called the "culture wars" of the 1960s, which today still tear at the nation's social fabric.

By the mid-twentieth century Americans had to wrestle with two contradictory sets of values. One was necessary for efficient economic production: discipline, delayed gratification, good character, and the acceptance of hard work done in rigidly hierarchical workplaces. The other set of values justified the expansive personal consumption on which economic growth increasingly depended: license, immediate gratification, mutable lifestyle, and an egalitarian, hedonistic pursuit of self-expression. By embracing new consumer-based values, Americans, young and old, often found themselves questioning the production-oriented values of the past and the authorities who espoused them. In sociologist Daniel Bell's compelling words, Americans were caught in "the cultural contradictions of capitalism." For example, many young, middle-class, white Americans had been raised on the credo that what made America great was its people's right to decide for themselves what products brought them happiness. Not surprisingly, these same young people rejected authorities' right to tell them what music, clothes, and even drugs were culturally and morally acceptable. In the 1960s, market values—especially those that insisted on the continuous "creative destruction" of the old in pursuit of the new—ripped through American culture.

In the chaotic 1960s marketplace of new ideas, new products, and new responsibilities, a great many Americans—and not just radical protesters—were challenged to find new rules and understandings by which to live. Americans questioned the rule makers and rule enforcers who formally and informally governed their lives. Specific events in the 1960s—like those associated with the civil rights and liberation movements, the failed war in Vietnam, and the chaotic violence that engulfed America's cities—sprang from America's changing cultural values, national economic and political system, and international role. Such events also intensified many Americans' doubts about the legitimacy and responsibility of their leaders and the authority and wisdom of their cultural arbiters. And since Americans by the 1960s lived in an interconnected world, increasingly governed by national elites, challenges to the status quo were almost impossible to keep localized or out of public view. Instead, every new shock and every new outburst ricocheted throughout the national system and became an issue of collective concern. In the 1960s, issues that at one time could have been treated as local or regional or even personal and private became objects of national scrutiny, judged by national standards.

While many—both in praise and in criticism—have exaggerated the impact of the 1960s on today's America, those times were explosive and they were the source for many of the changes with which we now live. As a result of what Americans did in the 1960s our country has become a very different place. Personal freedoms have been greatly expanded—though not without causing some to lose their moral compass. Racial and gender hierarchies have been radically subverted—but not overthrown. New political players and interest groups have multiplied, increasing the nature and scope of public debate—but also fracturing and even polarizing our governing process and cultural life. What Americans did in the 1960s helped bring an earlier era to an end and begin another.

In the 1960s—a long time ago—Americans wrestled, as we do today, with fundamental issues of critical national importance. In part we need to understand their struggles because their acts continue to shape our world. Thus we need to judge their dreams and their deeds, and to recount their successes and failures, if we are to understand our own times. But more important, their confrontations, their protest movements, their resentments, their flawed leaders, and their weary martyrs offer us a spectacular drama of a democratic people caught in the grip of their epoch— as we are caught in ours—fighting hard, though with blinkered vision, to bend history to their individual and collective wills. In their rich and moving story—a tragedy, I think—we find much to stir us and much to contemplate as we struggle to make our own history.

1. GOOD TIMES

THREE HUNDRED THOUSAND Americans stood shoulder to shoulder. They had been waiting in the cold for hours. Liquor was passed from hand to hand, but the crowd remained good-natured. At last the countdown began: 10 . . . 9 . . . 8 . . . High above Times Square the illuminated globe began its descent. 4 . . . 3 . . . 2 . . . 1 . . . The crowd roared. The 1960s had begun.

Throughout the nation, millions watched the scene on American-made television sets. They sang along with Guy Lombardo: "Should auld acquaintance be forgot . . ." They drank, kissed, and banged on pots and pans, a rite whose meaning few knew: the noise was meant to scare off evil spirits.

President Dwight D. Eisenhower, member of the West Point class of 1915, made no public statement to welcome the new decade. The general celebrated the New Year privately at his favorite retreat, the whites-only, men-only Augusta National Golf Club in Georgia. There he laughed at the "nigger jokes" commonly told at places like that. One might imagine that the way the President celebrated the New Year spoke louder than any official words he might have uttered, but few Americans were looking to the President as the clock struck midnight and ended the 1950s.

Francis Cardinal Spellman, the spiritual leader of the Roman Catholic Church in America, was out of the country when the 1950s came to a close. He was touring U.S. military bases in the Middle East, and took advantage of the opportunity to broadcast a New Year's message over Radio Free Europe to the hundreds of millions of people who lived behind the Iron Curtain. "By your fortitude in a dark and desperate time," he told them, "you are cautioning the lukewarm of the free world not to take liberty for granted." The nation's leading theologians, like its politicians, saw the world cast in terms of the Cold War.

The Reverend Martin Luther King, Jr., who had recently given up his pulpit in Montgomery, Alabama, to concentrate on the growing but still unfocused civil rights movement, spent New Year's Day leading a march on the state capitol in Richmond, Virginia. The Virginia government had elected to close down the entire public school system in Prince Edward County rather than obey federal court orders to integrate the schools. King's actions in Richmond went unnoticed by the mass media, the White House, and the overwhelming majority of Americans.

Most Americans celebrated the new decade very simply, taking the day off from work, sleeping late, watching TV, doing some work around the house, sharing a meal with family or friends. It is true that the fate of the nation was unclear, the changes of the past fifteen years immense. But it is also true that tens of millions of Americans, on New Year's Day 1960, did not expect or desire anything fundamental to change in the decade to come. Many believed they were living the American dream; they saw their lives swirling with possibilities. Some, far fewer in number, had already begun to nourish the seeds of change.

In 1960, most Americans old enough to remember looked back at the fifteen years since World War II with a sense of amazement. Given the Depression before that war, America had an extraordinary postwar era. Between 1946 and 1960 every indicator of national wealth and prosperity had soared. The stock market entered the new year more than twenty times higher than it had been in the Depression year of 1932. The gross national product had increased about 250 percent since the end of World War II, and the median family income, adjusted for inflation, had almost doubled. What those numbers meant for a majority of Americans was a material life, in world-historical terms, of incredible abundance. In 1960, America was the richest nation the world had ever seen. Americans, though not without some doubts, expected that boom times would just keep on rolling. Economic wealth—coupled with the faith that economic growth would continue and the fact that for many years it did—shaped the 1960s like no other single factor.

In 1960, in a nation of fewer than 50 million families almost 60 million automobiles were registered; big, flashy cars with powerful engines, chrome grilles, fabulous tail fins. The fact that between 1930 and 1948 the number of Americans who owned cars had not increased and that as late as 1950 most working-class families did not own a car made the new "auto-mania" a powerful indicator of 1950s prosperity. And in another sign of prosperity, by 1960 an overwhelming majority of Americans could sit back in their own homes and "push a button" (as ad after commercial after billboard accurately reminded them) and watch America's greatest entertainers on television, listen to a hi-fi record, or use any one of an arsenal of electrical appliances that few in the world could command. Few adult Americans who had weathered the Great Depression expected such luxury, much less expected it to become nationwide. But by 1960, telephones, televisions, refrigerators, and the electricity to power them were accepted as an American birthright, and fast cars and cheap gas were markers of the American way of life.

The locus of this new American affluence was undoubtedly suburbia. Well-to-do Americans had been living in suburbs for generations, but it was only after World War II that relatively inexpensive suburban housing boomed. The ranch-house bonanza was fostered by government subsidies and policies, builders' clever use of mass-production techniques, and middle-class prospective homeowners' faith in continued economic prosperity. Most of all, the postwar suburban boom was driven by the pent-up demand of millions of Americans whose dreams of owning a home had been frustrated by the economic turmoil and the social dislocations of the Great Depression and then World War II. As late as 1947, before new housing could catch up with demand, 6 million American families had lived doubled up with friends or family.

Between 1948 and 1958, 13 million homes were constructed; 11 million of them were built in the suburbs. By 1960, as many people lived in the suburbs as in America's central cities. These new suburban developments—in places like Glenview, Illinois; Beech-wood, Ohio; and Levittown, New York—were often lambasted by contemporary critics for their "ticky-tacky" houses and their general ambience of bland conformity. The great urbanist Lewis Mumford wrote in 1961: "The archetypal suburban refuge: a multitude of uniform, unidentifiable houses, lined up inflexibly, inhabited by people of the same class, the same income, the same age group, witnessing the same television performances, eating the same pre-fabricated foods, from the same freezers, conforming in every outward and inward respect to a common mold." Mumford's sharp words about suburban conformity were not inaccurate but they hid as much as they revealed about Americans' love affair with the tract home subdivision.

The new suburbs were in many ways a conformist's dream—but the 1950s conformists were of a new breed and represented a major change in the American social landscape. In the new suburbs, the "melting pot" was being reinvented. By 1960, massive legal immigration to the United States had been shut down for almost forty years. In the 1950s and into the 1960s the children of European-born immigrants—many of whom had grown up in relatively parochial and exclusive ethnic communities—recast themselves, at least partially, in the nascent communities of suburbia as just plain middle-class white Americans.

Catholics and, with greater restrictions, Jews mixed with Protestants in these new communities. Farm-born people, many of whom had come to the cities during the factory labor shortages of World War II, moved next door to former city people. Even regional differences, once the greatest divide between white Americans, were moderated in the new communities, which looked nearly identical whether they were located in what had been cotton fields outside Smyrna, Georgia, or cornfields adjacent to Niles, Illinois. Many suburbanites did aim to blend in and to conform, but what the critics failed to note was that in their conformity they were inventing a new, even daring identity for themselves and their children. While many would rebel against this new identity in the 1960s, far more would find in it a sustaining vision of the good life.

In this new world, in which old differences of ethnicity and religion and region were often downplayed, the binding ties of national culture were magnified. The great events, World War II, the Korean War, and the Cold War military draft, contributed to this nationalization. So many of the dads in the new suburbia had served their country, mingling with white men of all kinds from all parts of the country. But even more, a national culture of prosperity had become the great common denominator. The car one drove, the cigarettes smoked, the TV shows watched, the products consumed became a common language signaling who one was and wanted to be.

This new identity, in which differences were deliberately submerged, depended on magnifying other differences. In forging the new identity of white middle-class suburbanites, black Americans became more surely outsiders. In 1960, 82,000 people lived in Long Island's Levittown, the most celebrated of the new suburban subdevelopments, and not one of them was African-American. Black families were told by the developers openly not to bother trying to buy a home—they were not welcome. Racial segregation, in the North and West, as well as in the South, was a well-accepted fact of life in the new suburbs.

The differences between men and women were also magnified in the new suburbia. Two factors threw gender difference into stark relief. One was military service. For the men who had fought in World War II and the Korean War, or even those millions of men who had been in the mandatory peacetime draft, military service was a powerful tie that marked them off as different from their wives. Secondly, and more obviously, men went off to work and most of their wives did not. Women kept house and watched over the children. In the suburban cultural landscape in which difference had become an unpleasant word, the obvious differences in experience between men and women loomed larger than ever.

These gender differences, in suburbia and out, were further heightened by the family patterns of most 1950s families. In the postwar era, American men and women married at an average age younger than ever before or since; the average woman married when she was twenty years old, and 70 percent of all women were married by the age of twenty-four. And reversing the declining birth rates of well over a century, fertility rates boomed, rivaling those in India. At the peak of the baby boom era, the average number of children per family reached 3.8 (it is less than 2 today).

Americans' rush to young marriage and child rearing is not easily explained. European countries had no similar long-term postwar urge to be fruitful and multiply, nor did Americans react to the end of World War I with the same rush to marriage and domesticity. Historian Elaine May argues that the combination of widespread abundance following years of social and economic dislocation, coupled with the uncertainties of the Cold War, led to the near-frenzied search for a private "haven in a heartless world." Whatever the causes of the marriage rush and baby boom, a great many Americans in 1960 saw the flight to suburbia and the widespread availability of consumer goods as sure signs that America was a nation both blessed and bountiful.

Not that America in 1960 had no poor people. About 20 percent of Americans were poor. But even America's poor, contemporary commentators noted, were different. In Harlan County, Kentucky, one of the poorest, most isolated places in the United States, 67 percent of the families owned a television and 59 percent owned a car; no populous country in the world could match that. Put another way, Harlem's per capita income would have ranked it among the five richest nations in the world. Compared to the turn of the century or to the still-vivid hard times of the 1930s, the 1950s *were* a time of shared abundance and it seemed that the number of poor would shrink steadily. The seeming indifference to the plight of the poor at the close of the 1950s was not just meanspiritedness (though racism and prejudice played powerful roles); it was also caused by a vague faith in the happy notion that "a rising tide would lift all boats."

The eminent economist and social commentator John Kenneth Galbraith titled his 1958 best-seller about postwar America *The Affluent Society*, half in praise and half in criticism. Only twenty years earlier the president of the American Economic Association had warned the nation to expect "sick recoveries which die in their infancy and depressions which feed upon themselves and leave a hard and seemingly immovable core of unemployment." How wonderfully dated such advice appeared to be. While the economy had slowed down in the last years of the 1950s and even dipped into mild recession, by current standards it was still growing robustly and Americans luxuriated in pondering the meaning and purpose of their material abundance.

America's riches stood in sharp contrast to almost all of the rest of the world, and Americans and the rest of the world knew it. In Japan in 1960, the ravages of the first atomic-bomb attacks were still being felt; bland rice porridge was still all most Japanese could rely on for nutrition. Many West Germans, much better off than their Communist-controlled sisters and brothers in the East, could not regularly afford to heat water for baths. The Chinese were in the middle of a brutal famine, caused in large part by the cruel stupidity of the Maoist state-sponsored Great Leap Forward; as many as 50 million would die. Much of Latin America was mired in poverty; and intellectuals as well as peasants wondered if the social and economic revolution in Cuba, which had resulted in the nationalization of hundreds of millions of dollars of United States-owned assets, was lodestar to their economic and political future.

Around the world people debated whether America's wealth was the cause of their problems or a symbol of what could be done. Most countries, in the eyes of the American government, were leaning the wrong way. Despite America's free-market success, few of the poor nations around the world fighting either the vestiges of European imperialism or the still-growing Western economic domination seemed convinced that the United States was or—more ominously—should be the model for their future. Few Americans had the historical knowledge to understand why they felt that way.

Richard Nixon, in one of those globe-hopping expeditions postwar Vice Presidents learned to endure, faced anti-American rage in its most visceral form while touring South America in 1958. He was taunted, jeered, and spit on by crowds who believed the

United States' long-standing economic investment and political influence in their countries to be a major source of their troubles. In Caracas, a Communist-led mob broke through indifferent Venezuelan security and almost succeeded in pulling the Vice President out of his limousine. Nixon, who'd served in World War II, kept his cool. He also came to believe that few, if any, of the poorer countries were ready for American-style freedom and democracy.

Nixon, like the leading businessmen with whom both he and most of his Democratic counterparts worked, did believe that America's free-enterprise system could and should be sold to the rest of the world. It would be good for them, most political and economic leaders believed, and it was a necessity for American economic growth and prosperity. Just months before the 1960s began Vice President Nixon was given an unprecedented opportunity to sell America's free-market vision directly to America's great postwar enemy, the Soviet Union, and indirectly to the world via international mass media. In what became known as the "Kitchen Debate" many of the key issues the American people would themselves debate throughout the 1960s emerged in sometimes farcical, sometimes poignant terms.

For many among America's economic and political elites, the battle between Premier Khrushchev and Nixon during the Kitchen Debate marked the single most important public issue of their time—the confrontation with Communism. And while the Kitchen Debate was far more about symbols than substance it was an indicative marker in the battle between what theologian Reinhold Niebuhr called "the children of light" and "the children of darkness." For in the eyes of many Americans it could be painted that starkly and that simply. The Leninist-Stalinist terrors that had bloodied the Soviet people for some four decades, the Iron Curtain that had fallen over Eastern Europe and the Siberian gulags made such a picture, in part, a realistic one. Of course, some in America knew that the paint was laid on a little thick. Beneath the broad brushstrokes of the Cold War, new nations in Asia, Africa, and elsewhere were struggling to escape imperialist webs and the superpowers' spheres of influence. And in the United States domestic injustices and inequities made any claim to moral purity a highly dubious one.

The Kitchen Debate between Nixon and Khrushchev took place at the United States Exhibition in Sokolniki Park in Moscow. The exhibition was part of a series of cultural exchanges that had been worked out in 1955, at the first major postwar superpower summit meeting since the 1945 Potsdam Conference. As historian Stephen Ambrose wrote, the exchange "reflected American optimism, the notion that anyone who knows us must love us." And what the Americans in charge of the exchange wanted the Soviets to know about American life was its material abundance.

The United States Exhibition featured a relatively modest model American home, built right in the park by a genuine Long Island builder, and its centerpiece was a full-scale typical middle-class kitchen. This kitchen was no futuristic, architecturally bold extravaganza. It was the kind of kitchen that millions of American suburban homeowners actually had: sink with hot and cold running water, full-size refrigerator-freezer, stove and oven, automatic washer, spacious counters and cabinets.

Nixon led Khrushchev to this kitchen and made it the leading exhibit central to his arguments about American superiority. The simple image flashed back to Americans seemed to say it all, the future of the world was being seriously discussed in the setting in which most of them started their day. This arena, Americans knew, was theirs. And Nixon understood this. He retorted to Khrushchev's stream of anti-American barbs not by talking about freedom or democracy but by saying calmly, "To us, diversity, the right to choose, the fact that we have a thousand different builders, that's the spice of life."

Yale historian David Potter, writing in the 1950s, captured this postwar American faith in the power of the "push button" kitchen in a series of lectures on the theme of "the American character" —a theme which obsessed postwar intellectuals. He noted that Americans had long desired to spread a democratic faith around the world. But, he argued, that mission was a failed one; what people wanted was not our freedoms but our material comforts:

"We supposed that our revelation was 'democracy revolutionizing the world,' but in reality it was 'abundance revolutionizing the world'—a message which we did not preach and scarcely understood ourselves, but one which was peculiarly able to preach its own gospel without words."

Nixon, toe to toe with the leader of world Communism, had only to wave his hand at the kitchen to call on the real power of the American dream. With a chuckle, the Vice President of the United States delivered his roundhouse right: "Isn't it better to be talking about the relative merits of our washing machines than of the relative strength of our rockets?"

If David Potter saw the ambivalences and tensions America's consumer capitalism unleashed in the world, social critic Daniel Bell, looking backward, recognized the domestic cultural changes that abundance was producing. He wrote in *The Cultural Contradictions of Capitalism* (1976): "The character structure inherited from the 19th century, with its emphasis on self-discipline, delayed gratification and restraint, is still relevant to the demands of the techno-economic system; but it clashes sharply with the culture, where such bourgeois values have been completely rejected—in part because of the workings of the capitalist economic system itself." Bell saw in the postwar abundance—and especially in the rapid rise of a credit-card and installment-buying society (by 1960 Sears alone had more than 10 million credit customers)—society caught between two contradictory sets of values, one necessary for efficient production and the other necessary to justify expansive consumption.

Business consultant Ernest Dichter put the matter baldly in the 1950s when he told his corporate clients, "One of the basic problems of prosperity, then, is to demonstrate that the hedonistic approach to . . . life is a moral and not an immoral one." Dichter meant that hardworking, decently paid factory workers should be taught that it was good, not bad, to go into debt to buy consumer goods, since general prosperity—based in large part on fruitful consumption—promised ever bigger paychecks down the road. Daniel Bell, however, understood that hedonism at home and at the new strip shopping centers might not so easily be turned off at the factory gates or the public school. A society that increasingly depended on selling an ideal of unrestrained pleasure might have difficulty defining the borders of responsible consumption, let alone inculcating an ethic of hard work, discipline, and respectability. By 1960 some Americans, especially the young, were pondering the mixed cultural messages.

Too much can be made of this purely materialist or consumerist portrait of America in 1960. Americans' materialism, like so much else in American culture, contained a core of idealism. Many Americans saw, in their rush to consume, a push toward a richer world, a limitless world in which people would be free to create themselves anew. Few realized how explosive such a vision would become for the nation.

The television commercials that Americans were by 1960 just learning to take for granted offered a fairly coherent vision of the merits of the materialist world. The commercials of the late 1950s and early 1960s featured a fantastic array of anthropomorphized products: dancing packs of Lucky Strike cigarettes, Muriel the burning "Blond Cigar," Ajax's suicidal "Bathroom Pixies," the jubilant "Speedy" Alka-Seltzer, marching Rheingold beer bottles . . . The list goes on. Defying gravity, mortality, and even morality, these happy products sang to be America's supper. "The commercials," cultural historian Beth Bailey has written, "in the world they defined and presented, always told of a power to create a world like theirs: a world where anything can happen, but where what does happen is always good." Americans in the 1950s did not so much celebrate unbounded consumption for the physical comforts it provided—as hedonistic release—as they reveled in the world of new opportunities, new possibilities, and limitless hopes that economic success seemed to promise. Consumption did offer its hedonistic joys—those gas-guzzling, chrome-tipped, winged road chariots—but it also represented to many a set of happy opportunities earned through the sacrifices of World War II, the Cold War, and just plain old hard work.

Just as American materialism had its idealistic side, America's general abundance hid its gross economic inequality. Political activist and social critic Michael Harrington tried to strip away the veil and expose America's hidden or ignored poverty in his 1962 call to arms, *The Other America*: "The other America . . . is populated by failures, by those driven from the land and bewildered by the city, by old people suddenly confronted with the torments of loneliness and poverty, and by minorities facing a wall of prejudice." These people, and others, too, made up America's impoverished minority.

By and large, they were forgotten Americans in 1960. As a sociologist noted only a few years later: "During the 1940s, the 1950s, and the first years of the 1960s, the topic of poverty was virtually nonexistent." But while academics and policymakers, along with the majority of the American population, were looking aside in the 1950s, the nature of poverty was changing rapidly. Poverty had been predominantly a rural problem before World War II, but by 1960 about 55 percent of the poor lived in cities and another 30 percent lived in small towns. In part, this demographic change was the result of new farming technologies which had driven many poor farm laborers off the land and into urban America. The invention of the mechanical cotton picker in 1943, James T. Patterson notes, within a few years displaced some 2.3 million farmworkers. Most of them were African-American. Because of the racist system under which they had lived and worked, they came into the cities with few useful vocational skills and painfully low levels of formal education. The prejudice and discrimination they discovered in the cities, combined with the handicaps they brought with them from the rural backwaters, made it very difficult for most of these internal migrants to take advantage of the general economic good times.

Even African-Americans with better educations and skills found adequate-paying jobs in white America hard to find. In the South, skilled and semiskilled jobs in the growing corporate and industrial sector remained almost completely off-limits to black men and women. Job opportunities were only slightly better in the North.

A young black woman in Camden, New Jersey, for example, learned from a white woman with whom she had graduated from high school about a secretarial position at the Campbell Soup Company. The young woman, near the top of her graduating class, applied for the posted job: "I was told that office jobs were not available, but if I wanted to work in the canning department I would be hired. I never did get an office job." In the South, she might well not even have been offered the factory job.

In the early 1960s, more whites than blacks were poor and on some form of public assistance. But a majority of poor whites (who were a very small percentage of all whites) lived out of sight in rural areas or were homebound older people. The African-American poor, while fewer in number, had become highly visible in America's inner cities and were, on average, much younger than poor whites. James Patterson writes that in the 1930s most Americans envisioned poverty in the guise of "the white yeoman staggered by circumstances"; in the 1940s and 1950s "people thought of the poor—whites as well as blacks—as a dwindling minority that would soon wither away. But by the early 1960s the stereotype was likely to evoke visions of 'hard core' black welfare mothers with hordes of illegitimate children."

America in 1960 was a place in which competing "truths" were on a collision course. Both economic abundance and racism were widespread. Suburbs were booming while inner cities festered. America's global mission seemed limitless even as its international reputation wavered. The demands of production and the ethos of consumption pushed and pulled against one another. Beneath the seeming consensus that ruled 1950s America, rival interests—most particularly Big Labor and Big Business—worked hard to resolve such competing truths in their own favor. America's corporate citizens—such as General Motors, Du Pont, General Electric, and IBM—were by 1960 the big winners in shaping the nation to their own interests. Since the debacle of the Great Depression, corporate managers and large shareholders had been working hard to fully recapture not only the nation's political agenda but also public opinion. Using their well-entrenched positions in the centers of American policymaking, and spending millions in the process, corporate interests largely succeeded in translating their excellent postwar economic performance into favorable legislation and good press.

"Engine" Charlie Wilson, who left the presidency of General

Motors to become President Eisenhower's Secretary of Defense, gave the most boiled-down version of the winning corporate credo when he told the world, "What was good for our country was good for General Motors, and vice versa." The 1950s were glory times for America's corporate men; they took, not without some justice, credit for the postwar abundance. And to a large extent, under the "hidden hand" presidency of General Eisenhower (who had never voted before becoming President) America's Big Business men ran the executive branch of government. Their truths often seemed to pass for the nation's truths.

Of course, in 1960 corporate America was no monolith. Texas oil interests and most New York financiers agreed on little and the factions and feuds among the corporate elite were as important as the general ignorance most Americans shared about their operations. Still, the most widespread patterns America's corporate giants set bear examination. Some of their truths were so much taken for granted, and shared by so many Americans, that they were essentially undiscussed matters of "common sense." And unlike the 1980s and 1990s, when economists and politicians focused on the economic vitality and job-producing utility of small businesses and entrepreneurs, during the 1950s and 1960s experts of all kinds understood America's megacorporations as the mainstay of economic progress and national wealth.

By 1960, most of America's corporate managers had moved subtly away from the conventional wisdom of pre-Great Depression Big Business. Then businessmen had insisted that the managers of the business corporation must focus all their energies on maximizing return on capital and that to do so they must not be hindered by government intervention. By 1960, many corporate executives, while far from renouncing the imperative of the bottom line, believed also in the maintenance of a rational, efficient organization able to secure its labor force through negotiated contracts and to please its shareholders by paying steadily improving dividends. In the postwar years, America's corporate giants, often in concert with the federal government, worked hard and well in using those beliefs to create what they and their allies saw as "the American Century."

America's business leaders exploded into new markets, mass-produced new goods, and rapidly sped up the restructuring of their internal organization and way of doing business. At a time when many of America's international competitors, especially in Japan and Germany, could only rebuild and regroup after the physical, economic, and social devastations of World War II, America's corporate leaders, fat from World War II "cost-plus" contracts, were diversifying, decentralizing, and moving fast into international markets. Instead of competing with each other over price and quality, most of America's biggest manufacturers raced with one another to produce new products and new marketing strategies. The result was economic expansion and massive profits.

The auto industry led the way, and GM, in terms of how it was managed and what it produced for consumers, was emblematic of the 1960 corporate vision. In 1960, it was in the middle of an astoundingly successful economic run. The company practically minted money; between 1946 and 1967, GM had average yearly profits of 20.67 percent based on net worth. According to automobile historian James Flink, GM's profitability was built on "Sloanism," the structure and style of business forged in the 1920s by organizational genius and longtime GM leader Alfred P. Sloan. Sloanism depended on three basic principles: "a car for every purse and purpose," rapidly introduced styling changes, and a corporate structure that combined decentralized management with highly rationalized financial controls.

Looking back, a 1982 National Research Council study on the U.S. auto market revealed how a winner would become a loser: "by the late 1950s manufacturing had become a competitively neutral factor. . . . [N]one of the major [auto] producers sought to achieve a competitive advantage through superior manufacturing performance." For America's corporate giants, price cutting was anathema and quality was far from "Job One." Nonetheless, when major corporations went to America's exploding financial markets to raise money, "the capital was tapped for investment," notes historian Ron Chernow, "not financial manipulation" (unlike the 1980s). While America's corporate leaders would hurt America in the long run by not more aggressively pursuing manufacturing excellence during these boom times, they succeeded in driving the domestic economy, selling American-made products internationally, and providing American workers with the highest wage scale in the world.

General Motors' economic mega-triumph in the postwar era was sweet vindication for semiretired honorary GM chairman Alfred Sloan, who could in 1960 still remember being vilified during the New Deal years; President Franklin Roosevelt had jauntily referred to America's premier corporate executive as "a low comedy figure." In 1960 America, GM represented, in the words of Alfred Sloan, the triumph of "the white-collar man."

At GM, and most other major corporations, white-collar triumph did not mean blue-collar woes. In the 1950s, America was not mired in an economic zero-sum game, nor were the wealthy pirating money from working people. The economic pie was genuinely increasing for the vast majority of Americans.

GM's unionized assembly-line workers—many without high school diplomas—drove new cars, bought cottages by the lake, and looked forward to guaranteed raises and generous pensions. High wages meant that very few UAW workers' wives worked (nor could they, by and large, get high-paying jobs, given the sexism male employers and employees took for granted). The United Auto Workers, protected by laws passed during the New Deal, had demanded and received a smorgasbord of wages and benefits; complacent management, rather than face strikes at a time of high demand for their products, went along. As auto executive Lee Iacocca recalled: "In those days we could afford to be generous. Because we had a lock on the market, we could continually spend more money on labor and simply pass the additional costs along to the consumer in the form of price increases." By 1960, only Volkswagen of Germany had really cracked the American auto market by selling the very inexpensive, stripped-down, but mechanically sound Beetle. No other country was producing cars that could compete in the American mass market (Japanese manufacturers still specialized in three-wheeled micro-trucks).

Above all, the winner's truth that emerged from the 1950s was that capitalism worked. "People's Capitalism," business boosters called it, with reason. Little attention was paid to the fact that in the 1950s a decreasing number of Americans actually gained greater control of the nation's capital assets. And outside union circles, few people contested the federal government's antipathy to furthering the national growth of labor unions, which had been pivotal in securing high wages in America's basic industries. Even less contested were the corporations' policies of racial and gender discrimination. Corporate executives and shareholders, self-described leaders in the American way of life, it was clear by 1960, were not going to do anything about racism or sexism by themselves. What stood out in the minds of most Americans in 1960 was that abundance seemed to be a national achievement and capitalism a triumphant system. Not that all Americans, even in 1960, accepted this triumph as complete. Amid general public self-congratulation, some artists and writers tried to shake things up by challenging the moral and spiritual worth of all the wealth. David Riesman's *The Lonely Crowd* (1954), Sloan Wilson's *The Man in the Gray Flannel Suit* (1955), William Whyte's *The Organization Man* (1956), John Keats's *The Crack in the Picture Window* (1957), and Vance Packard's *The Status Seekers* (1959) were just a few of the many books that challenged the status quo. The sharpest and, in many ways, most prescient attack on the net worth of People's Capitalism came from a small pack of self-proclaimed "Dharma bums," a.k.a. Beats, a.k.a. Beatniks, who'd fled corporate suburbia for a life of hard kicks and still minds. Poet Allen Ginsberg rammed home the Beats' outrage at an America grown old at midcentury: "Moloch whose love is endless oil and stone! Moloch whose soul is electricity and banks! Moloch whose poverty is the specter of genius! Moloch whose fate is a cloud of sexless hydrogen." The last had not been heard of Allen Ginsberg and his vision of a blasted America lost in its lust for money and power.

John Updike, a critic much closer to the center, wrote less rhapsodically but no less bitingly: "I drive my car to the supermarket, / The way I take is superhigh, / A superlot is where I park it, / and Super Suds are what I buy." And while few Americans at the dawn of the 1960s would have put their feelings so critically, many Americans did wonder about the larger meaning of the nation's prosperity. As historian Robert Collins has written: "During the latter part of the Ike age Americans grew increasingly fearful that the nation had lost its way in the blaze of its own prosperity. The result was an outburst of public soul-searching and numerous attempts to articulate an agenda of national goals that would be worthy of history's most powerful democracy."

President Eisenhower, sensing the public's uneasiness and committed to a "corporate commonwealth," had no ready answers and so appointed the President's Commission on National Goals. It came up with little. Nelson Rockefeller, immensely wealthy grandson of oil magnate John D. Rockefeller, fueled his presidential ambitions by using one of his philanthropic foundations to fund a grand investigation, the Special Studies Project, which aimed to "clarify the national purposes and objectives." The reports made headline news and two became best-sellers. *Life*, the most popular magazine in America, devoted a series of "think" pieces in 1960 to the problem of "national purpose." Archibald MacLeish, poet and onetime director of America's World War II propaganda bureau, told *Life*'s millions of readers what few probably wanted to hear: "We feel that we've lost our way in the woods, that we don't know where we are going—if anywhere."

At the coming of the 1960s, many Americans yearned for a greater sense of national purpose and both presidential candidates would center their campaigns on providing it. Still, a majority of Americans had good reason to look back at the 1950s with a feeling of personal triumph. America's gray flannel corporate men, well-paid labor union members, suburban homeowners, and big farmers, as well as the car customizers, country clubbers, powerboaters, Wednesday-night bowlers, and so many others, had reason to celebrate an American High as they looked forward to another decade in what many considered the American Century. The wealth-producing efficiency of the postwar American economic system—People's Capitalism—would be an ur-reality that shaped much of the political and cultural terrain of the 1960s.

2. THE WORLD AS SEEN FROM THE WHITE HOUSE 1960–1963

〜〜〜〜〜〜〜〜〜〜〜〜〜〜〜〜〜〜

WHEN THEY APPEARED TOGETHER on the television screen the night of September 26, 1960, the two men looked so different. John Kennedy was tan, his eyes seemed to sparkle, his dark gray suit fit perfectly; he was calm, and poised, and very confident. He looked presidential. The other man, Richard Nixon, did not. Exhausted from relentless campaigning, his knee sore, he looked haggard. His suit was bunched up and it was the wrong color; it made him appear to fade into the studio backdrop. And somebody had served him poorly by spreading Lazy Shave makeup over his face, which failed to cover his dark beard and just made him look worse. They looked so different but, in fact, the two presidential candidates in 1960 shared so much.

For millions of Americans, the end of the fifties and the rush of the sixties began with the presidential campaign of 1960 between Vice President Richard Milhous Nixon and Massachusetts senator John Fitzgerald Kennedy. For the first time both candidates were men born in the twentieth century.

Despite differences in party affiliation and personal style (Kennedy said privately that Nixon "has no taste"), in policy and program little of major importance divided these two men. Nixon and Kennedy, in major speeches accepting their nomination for President, employed common themes and even similar rhetorical flourishes. Both men sought to consolidate political support by decrying Soviet Communist aggression. They urged Americans to look past immediate self-interest and toward a world made safe by American might and munificence.

Richard Nixon, in his July 28 speech at the Republican convention in Chicago, lambasted the perfidy of the Soviets. He told his cheering audience that "the biggest problem confronting the next President of the United States will be to inform the people of the character of this kind of [Soviet] aggression, to arouse the people to the mortal danger it presents and inspire the people to meet the danger." Nixon claimed the high ground: "Our next President must tell the people not what they want to hear but what they need to hear." He meant that Americans must be prepared to spend more money—and possibly more blood—fighting the spread of international Communism.

John F. Kennedy, in his speech in Los Angeles before the Democratic convention, spoke in the same key, though throughout the electoral season his words were sweeter to the ear. Kennedy had already defused, though not yet removed, the question of his "character" in the primary season. "Character" meant not his personal life but his Catholic faith. In a sign that the 1950s melting pot worked for white Americans, that issue, which had been fundamental in the election of 1928 when Irish Catholic Al Smith, contending against Herbert Hoover, had gone down in flames, became a side issue. What Kennedy wanted to do in his acceptance speech was to demonstrate that, despite his youth, he had the ability to lead the country and thus the free world. Kennedy, just forty-three years old, was grandiloquent about the need to move past partisan bickering and toward promised greatness:

> . . . We stand today on the edge of a New Frontier—the frontier of the 1960s—a frontier of unknown opportunities and perils—a frontier of unfulfilled hopes and threats. . . . The New Frontier of which I speak is not a set of promises—it is a set of challenges. It sums up, not what I intend to offer the American people, but what I intend to ask of them. It appeals to their pride, not their pocketbook—it holds out the promise of more sacrifice instead of more security.

During the campaign, Kennedy accused the incumbent Republicans not of following bad policies or even of having the wrong priorities. Rather, he blasted them for not having the energy and the talent to make America even stronger and richer than it already was. As Richard Nixon noted in the first presidential debate, he and Kennedy disagreed "not about the goals for Americans, but only about the means to reach those goals."

Nixon was wed to the "Ike age." His campaign focused on his already well-tested Cold War, anti-Communist leadership. Presenting himself as successor to Eisenhower, he promised to continue the economic and international successes of the 1950s.

Kennedy, really without a choice, declared himself the candidate of change. But by "change" he meant not something different from what had come before, but a more intense version of the same thing. Kennedy vowed that he would "get the nation moving again."

In part, Kennedy ran as the candidate of economic growth. In the last two years of the Eisenhower administration the average growth in the gross national product had been just under 3 percent and the country had actually undergone a recession in 1957 and 1958. Premier Khrushchev had added salt to this minor economic wound by taunting the American people with claims that recent Soviet growth was more than twice that of the United States (which was possible but only because the postwar Soviets started so far behind the United States). The bullish Soviet Premier had told the world that his people's economic productivity would serve as "the battering ram with which we shall smash the capitalist system" of the United States. Jack Kennedy promised the American people that he would pump up the gross national product to annual gains of more than 5 percent.

In Kennedy's campaign oratory, talk of economic growth set the stage for a more impassioned rhetoric about America's role in the world. Hitting right at Nixon's supposed strength, Kennedy offered Americans an international mission to match the wonder of their grand, if worrisome, prosperity.

Kennedy told the American people that under the administration of Eisenhower and Nixon, the United States had lost its world leadership to the Soviet Union. He did not explain that the United States had lost credibility in many parts of Latin America, Asia, and Africa because the U.S. government had resisted these countries' struggles, whether for liberation from European imperialism or for freedom from American economic control, and had instead supported corrupt and pliant dictators. He did not discuss the Soviets' winning decision to throw their support behind the indigenous and often dark-skinned peoples in the wars of independence being fought around the world (even as they themselves imprisoned and murdered those who sought freedom in the nations the Soviet Union had seized after World War II). Without acknowledging this fundamental problem, Kennedy offered Americans a vision of a world secured and enthralled by American power. In his standard campaign stump speech he orated: "I ask you to join with me in a journey into the 1960s, whereby we will mold our strength and become first again. Not first *if*. Not first *but*. Not first *when*. But first *period*. I want the people of the world to wonder not what Mr. Khrushchev is doing. I want them to wonder what the United States is doing."

Kennedy blasted Nixon and Eisenhower for being asleep at the wheel. Under the Republicans, Cuba, just ninety miles off America's shore, had gone "Red." Cuba, he warned, was a "dagger" pointed at the heart of America.

Strident anti-Communism won votes and Kennedy made it his issue. He convinced Cold War America that he was an appropriate heir to the presidency. The vigor with which Kennedy promoted his anti-Communism, however, would severely restrict his foreign policy options and those of his Democratic successor; it contributed to the decisions that put American combat troops in Vietnam.

Most Americans listened and supported the Cold War histrionics of both Nixon and Kennedy. Then, too, anyone older than forty could remember a time when Americans had never considered being "first" in the world, at least in the sense of being the military champion of the "free world." Though by 1960 such a past was fast receding, before the military buildup of World War II the United States hadn't been even a second-rate military power. By some measures, in the late 1930s the United States barely made it into the top twenty military powers, ranking right around (though probably behind) Portugal. The United States had no troops permanently stationed outside its own territory, no Central Intelligence Agency, no formal national security apparatus, and no large arms industry. America's sophisticated, worldwide military and intelligence network had all sprung up in the postwar years, shattering the prewar federal governing process. By 1960, the Cold War was less than fifteen years old and the nation had not yet come to grips with what it had done to democratic government in the United States.

President Eisenhower hinted at the problem in his farewell address to the nation in January 1961. In the speech, he looked back at the political and governmental changes he and others had wrought in democratic government with a sense of foreboding. He noted that what had once been one of the smallest peacetime armies of any modern industrial nation had become a swollen "defense establishment" of three and a half million people; each year, the federal government spent more money on military security than the net income of all United States corporations. "This conjunction of an immense military establishment and a large arms industry," he warned, "is new in American experience."

> . . . We must not fail to comprehend its grave implications. . . . In the councils of government, we must guard against the acquisition of unwarranted influence, whether sought or unsought, by the military-industrial complex. The potential for the disastrous rise of misplaced power exists and will persist.

Eisenhower's warning garnered only muted interest among America's most powerful citizens. The President-elect apparently took little note of the general's parting remarks.

President Kennedy had won the election in a squeaker, winning with a margin of just 112,881 votes, the closest election in the twentieth century. Rumors flew that Kennedy's slim margin of victory had come through vote fraud; Mayor Richard Daley of Chicago, Republicans suspected with cause, had stolen Illinois for his fellow Irish Catholic pol. John F. Kennedy had won the presidency with the slimmest of victories under somewhat cloudy circumstances. His electoral coattails had been nonexistent; Republicans had gained seats in both the House and the Senate.

Kennedy had, as he knew, no clear mandate for bold new leadership.

But there he was on January 20, 1961, hatless and coatless in the bitter cold, the youngest man ever elected President of the United States, swearing to uphold the Constitution and carry out the duties of his office. As he appeared before the nation he looked every inch the nation's leader; with his election the word "charisma" entered the vocabulary of the nation's pundits. His wife Jacqueline stood beside him; her clothes, her hair, her makeup, her very posture and poise were all movie magazine perfect. Their newborn son, soon known to all as John-John, was at home, but daughter Caroline, bundled up against the cold, watched proudly. The First Family seemed a dream image of the new-style American family, secure in their economic success, vital, and charming. Tens of millions of Americans would fall in love with this doomed First Family. In some ways their symbolic importance, an adulation that was not, at its heart, political, would set the tone of the Kennedy years more than any particular program or policy.

Kennedy's ability to project an inspirational presidential persona to the American people was not unprecedented. Ever since Teddy Roosevelt had used candid photographs at the turn of the century to personalize his presidency and so promote his "bully pulpit," the drama of White House life had increasingly become a part of the American people's lives. Franklin Roosevelt cast an illusion of intimacy through his radio "Fireside Chats"; his wife, Eleanor, helped to create the modern idea of the "First Lady," in part through her syndicated newspaper column, "My Day." Television, which the Kennedy White House first successfully deployed, greatly intensified Americans' perceived contact with the First Family.

President Kennedy was well suited to the incredible political possibilities of both television mass marketing and the maturing national culture in which the electronic media played such a crucial role. He was movie star handsome, comfortable before the cameras, and he intuitively understood how to speak in a low-key, familiar style suited to television's living-room intimacy.

Kennedy, while no trained television performer like Ronald

Reagan, was the first President to use live televised press conferences, speeches, and special appearances (such as the First Lady's
guided tour of the newly refurbished White House) as a basic aspect
of his presidency. As Kennedy said to an aide, while watching a
film of one of his press conferences, "We couldn't survive without
television."

No President since Kennedy has enjoyed such control over his
TV image. Television was still in its youth and many Americans
had not yet grown wary of TV magic and manipulation. Nor had
mass-media executives and their employees become secure enough
in their newly developing power to lift the veil of secrecy that
surrounded the country's political and economic leaders. As a
result, during Kennedy's presidency the public knew nothing of
his womanizing, fragile health, or the mood-altering drugs he took
to control his ailments and to provide him with an artificial lift.
Above all, the public knew the cool, heroic family man they saw
on television and many idolized that image.

John F. Kennedy's Inaugural Address was like few such speeches
before or since. Kennedy conveyed a sense of grandeur and possibility that inspired a broad spectrum of the nation, particularly
its youth. In it could be seen the outlines of the one thousand days
he would serve and the seeds of policies that would lead America
in new directions.

Kennedy spoke about the necessity of expanding America's
world power and influence. He celebrated America's international
responsibility and in this he made an important break with his
predecessor. President Eisenhower had preferred covert actions to
bold thrusts; he had spoken of America's global deeds with great
caution, even reticence. He presented them as temporary chores
to be dutifully performed. The immense changes in America's
global role in the era that followed World War II, Eisenhower told
the American people, should in no way change what America
really was and should be. Eisenhower never offered the American
people a compelling explanation or legitimization of what they
had, as a nation, become—a global colossus championing an expanding international economic system. Instead, he offered them,
often with fractured syntax, a half-truth, well expressed in the

public persona he crafted—a simple, tough, small-town man doing his neighborly best to maintain the old virtues of freedom and liberty.

John F. Kennedy recast that national image. He trumpeted America's global mission and commitments as the true sign of a new national identity. If Americans had indeed been hungry for a message that would tell them what their newfound prosperity should mean, President Kennedy provided them with answers.

In his Inaugural Address the President argued that American prosperity allowed—even mandated—the nation to fight globally for its traditional beliefs in the rights and liberties of individuals. Americans' faith in individualism, Kennedy insisted, must be put in service to collective purpose and national will. In one of the most poetic, if also bellicose, phrasings in modern oratory, Kennedy "let slip the dogs of war":

> Let the word go forth from this time and place, to friend and foe alike, that the torch has been passed to a new generation of Americans—born in this century, tempered by war, disciplined by a hard and bitter peace, proud of our ancient heritage—and unwilling to witness or permit the slow undoing of those human rights to which this nation has always been committed, and to which we are committed today at home and around the world.
>
> *Let every nation know, whether it wishes us well or ill, that we shall pay any price, bear any burden, meet any hardship, support any friend, oppose any foe to assure the survival and the success of liberty.*
>
> *This much we pledge—and more.*

It was thrilling, sublime prose, but what did it mean? "Any price . . . any burden . . . any hardship . . . and more?" Were there really no limits to what Americans could and should do as a nation in the world in defending their ideals, beliefs, and way of life?

In this world of absolutes Kennedy offered Americans not "no new taxes" or "jobs, jobs, jobs" but the glory of sacrifice and the profundity of mission. "Ask not what your country can do for you," he insisted, "ask what you can do for your country." In final peroration, he touched the heavens, proclaiming "God's work must truly be our own."

Kennedy's marriage of American prosperity and American mission touched a resonant chord. Americans had been moving toward more militant, interventionist anti-Communism. Just before the 1956 election, less than half of all Americans thought that American soldiers should be stationed overseas to help "countries that are against Communism"; by fall 1960 some 63 percent of the American people wanted to see American troops abroad fighting "the Communist tide." (Before 1948 no pollsters had even thought to ask such a question.)

President Kennedy and most of the American people were not just imagining Red bogeymen in those first years of the 1960s. Real threats—Communist threats—were rife in the world. The Soviets did seek global victory, though their rhetoric ran far ahead of their deeds, and their erstwhile allies in China screeched for military confrontation with the West. For decades, Communist parties in France and Italy, Venezuela and Bolivia, Korea and Indonesia, the United States and elsewhere were controlled, to a degree, by Moscow. Cuba was fast developing a close relationship with the Soviets. The Soviet Union had indeed dropped an Iron Curtain over almost all of Eastern Europe and nearly half of Germany. And when Hungary had tried to break away from the Soviet empire in 1956, blood had flowed in the streets of Budapest.

The Soviets had sent the first satellite, Sputnik, into space in 1957. Premier Khrushchev had wasted no time in using Soviet superiority in space as a crude threat against the American people. And the Soviets really did have a nuclear arsenal, if not superior to the United States' own massive capability (as Kennedy had thundered during the presidential campaign), still more than capable of slaughtering tens of millions of Americans.

To most Soviet citizens the world situation would have looked quite a bit different. They would have seen their country's control over Eastern Europe and part of Germany as a necessary step in preventing yet another military attack from the West. Almost all the countries the Soviets occupied had joined in invading them during World War II or served as a highway for Nazi troops; more than 20 million Soviets had died during the "Great Patriotic War." And while Soviet leaders might have admitted to working to subvert capitalist countries and to arm Third World revolutionaries, they would have correctly pointed out that the American Central Intelligence Agency played the same game; democratically elected, independent-minded governments in Guatemala and Iran had been overthrown by CIA machinations ordered by the avuncular Ike. Finally, if Americans wanted to talk about Siberian work camps and Stalinist terrors, the Soviets could and did point a finger at the plight of the American Negro and the slaughter of the American Indian.

"The children of light" and "the children of darkness" shared some of the same sins, and often hid, ignored, or explained away, their most egregious faults. That does not mean one can draw a simple moral equivalency between the two great superpowers as they entered the 1960s. Even after the death of the murderous Soviet Premier Joseph Stalin in 1953 and his partial repudiation by reform-minded Nikita Khrushchev, the Soviet system was a closed and repressive society. It was plagued by economic problems, a low standard of living for its people, and the legacy of World War II and Stalin's purges. The United States, with a very different history, was a mainly prosperous and open society, a relatively free and democratic society. Those virtues would, in the 1960s, put its collective sins into sharp relief and make it possible for people to begin to treat, if not cure, the nation's ills and its own failures of ideals and beliefs.

But neither the nation nor President Kennedy upon entering office in 1961 was interested in a complex moral calculus. Kennedy and the American people preferred no shades of gray. By the end of the decade, the failure of Kennedy and other leaders to admit that American interests in the world were driven by motives more complex than neighborly goodwill or moral purity would radically undermine the faith of millions of Americans in their government. But in 1961 most Americans truly wanted to believe John F. Kennedy when he told them that they were the ones destined to carry out God's work on earth. Otherwise, what did the arms race, the millions of men stationed abroad, the National Security Council, the National Security Agency, the Pentagon, the Strategic Air Command, the Central Intelligence Agency, the Defense Department, and all the other agencies and departments and secret bureaucracies which had sprouted up like a field of mushrooms after a long hard rain mean to the real needs and hopes of the American people? The answer to that question—or at least the beginnings of the formulation of that question, the point at which many Americans began to see that such a question needed to be asked —came not with some distant rumblings in Central Europe, but much closer to home.

In 1959, on New Year's Day, Fidel Castro and a small army of guerrilla irregulars overthrew the corrupt President of Cuba, who had served American interests for better than twenty-five years. Castro made his intentions clear, at least in the minds of most American foreign policy makers, in his first speech as leader of Cuba: "The revolution begins now. . . . It will not be like 1898, when North Americans came and made themselves masters of our country. . . . For the first time, the Republic will really be entirely free and the people will have what they deserve."

Cuba had "fallen." At the very first, it was not completely clear that Fidel meant to join the Soviet camp. But it was clear that, like the Venezuelan mob that had attacked Vice President Nixon in 1958, Fidel Castro and his closest advisers had stored up a great deal of anger at the Yanquis.

Castro and his supporters had cause for their anger and distrust of the United States. American businessmen had largely controlled the Cuban economy. American interests, including American mobsters associated with Havana's wide-open vice district, had manipulated the repressive Cuban government to their own ends while dictator Batista and his cronies stole millions and left the great majority of Cubans to live in misery.

Cuba figured prominently in President Kennedy's first major intelligence briefing. Weeks before he was to be inaugurated, the newly elected President was informed by CIA director Allen Dulles that he must quickly decide what to do about Communist Cuba, which was being aided and armed by the Soviets. Richard Bissell, CIA deputy director for operations, told the President-elect that Cuban exiles were being trained and armed by the CIA to overthrow Castro. Soon, the men would be ready.

Ironically, given how he had blasted the Republican administration for letting Cuba go "Red," Kennedy came into office with the CIA's Cuban invasion plan almost operational. Thousands of Cuban exiles waited in Florida and Guatemala for their war to begin. To stop the operation, begun under another President's watch, would not have been easy, even if Kennedy had not wanted to overthrow Castro. As Kennedy told several of his key advisers, "If we decided to call the whole thing off, I don't know if we could go down there and take the guns away from them."

In preparing for the invasion, Congress had been bypassed. The CIA funded the Cuban exiles through its own secret funds. The American people, of course, knew nothing of the highly classified invasion plans. *The New York Times* did get wind of the story, but President Kennedy personally persuaded *Times* publisher Orvil Dryfoos to abort coverage. The invasion plan was hatched, developed, and discussed among a small circle in the executive branch. The Cold War had, years before, made a casualty of open democratic government.

Kennedy, in the first chaotic weeks of setting up his administration and gaining a semblance of control over the sprawling executive branch of government, chose to trust his CIA advisers. He gave the CIA the go-ahead to invade Cuba at the Bay of Pigs. Kennedy possibly (the record still remains murky) was strengthened in his decision by the CIA's assurance that their invading forces would be welcomed and even joined by other anti-Communist Cubans. Kennedy possibly knew that the CIA planned to assassinate Fidel Castro; "terminating" Castro's leadership would certainly strengthen the anti-Communist forces. President Kennedy, however, feared that an overt American action in Cuba would severely damage U.S. credibility in Latin America and cause the Soviets to move on Berlin; thus, to assure plausible deniability, he ordered that American assistance in the invasion be kept to a bare minimum.

CIA director Dulles, despite what he said to the President, knew that without extensive American air support the Cuban exiles stood little chance of success. But in the face of his President's pre-invasion concerns he did not inform him fully, fearing that the President would stop the plan if he understood that major American combat assistance would be necessary. Dulles later wrote: "We felt that when the chips were down, when the crisis arose in reality, any action required for success would be authorized rather than permit the enterprise to fail." But the President did not understand this reality, nor did the Joint Chiefs of Staff of the armed forces make it clear when he consulted with them.

Kennedy had come into the presidency with an overriding desire to act decisively in the battle against global Communism and to somehow bypass the ponderous bureaucracies of the national security apparatus created to manage the Cold War. Unlike President Eisenhower, whose experiences in the Army had accustomed him to the slow but careful processes of large-scale organizations, Kennedy felt he could personally weigh the risks and rewards of foreign policy adventures. One of his first administrative acts as President was to abolish the committee of experienced foreign policy hands Eisenhower had organized to vet his covert operations. Ex-President Eisenhower thought the move foolish. White House staffer General Maxwell Taylor was appalled to discover that the President "had little regard for organization and method as such . . . He found it far more stimulating to acquire information from the give-and-take of impromptu discussion." In the Bay of Pigs operation this method proved disastrous for Kennedy.

Despite the grand rhetoric of the Inaugural Address just a few weeks before the April 1961 invasion, President Kennedy refused to use American air power to save the anti-Castro forces he had put onto the beach at the Bay of Pigs. He believed that he had signed on to a covert operation by the CIA, and despite the world's awareness that the United States had actively launched and supported the invading forces, he would not make the action an overt American military operation. The well-armed and loyal Cuban armed forces ripped apart the 1,400 brave men of Brigade 2506.

Around the world, people protested the American government's involvement in the invasion of Cuba. Ex-President Eisenhower scolded Kennedy in a post-invasion meeting. The world knew that the invasion was a U.S. operation; Kennedy's attempt to hide America's role was a dismal failure. Either go in with whatever it takes to win or don't go in at all, Eisenhower lectured the new President. This lesson would be a hard one to learn for both Kennedy and his successors.

The Bay of Pigs invasion had failed and in failing had resolved little. Rigid anti-Communism remained at the heart of American foreign policy. National security issues and foreign policy continued to be managed by a bewildering and chaotic mélange of bureaucracies, presidential appointees, and freewheeling experts, all for the most part out of sight of the American people. President Kennedy and his administration remained obsessed with Cuba. The CIA, with at least tacit approval of the President, continued to try to assassinate Castro and sabotage the Cuban economy, at times in collaboration with American mobsters. Castro's Cuba became further intertwined with the Soviet Union and Castro's regime became more repressive. The CIA intensified efforts to fund, arm, and train thousands of anti-Castro Cuban rebels, most of whom operated in southern Florida. These men, many of them bitter over Kennedy's failure to provide the invasion with sufficient air support in its hour of need, would haunt the American body politic, resurfacing in "off-the-shelf" clandestine roles during the Watergate burglary, the Iran-Contra affair, and elsewhere.

John Kennedy had little time to remain focused on the details of U.S.-Cuban relations. Shortly after the debacle at the Bay of Pigs he met with Khrushchev in a superpower summit in Vienna. Khrushchev, riding high over American failure in Cuba and the U.S.S.R.'s success in putting the first person into outer space (Yuri Gagarin), lectured Kennedy about Soviet superiority. While some small progress was made on de-escalating Soviet-American tensions arising from the Laotian civil war, on the heated issue of the superpowers' policy toward the divided Germany nothing was accomplished.

More than fifteen years after the end of World War II, Germany swarmed with hundreds of thousands of soldiers: Soviets in the puppet state of East Germany and Americans, British, and French in West Germany. Both sides recognized in Germany the greatest possible flash point for World War III. The focus of Soviet-American tensions lay in the divided city of Berlin, which stood well within the Soviet-controlled East Germany. Kennedy—and West Berliners—feared, with reason, that the Soviets meant to grab the entire city and hold it hostage to a new agreement on the disposition of Germany more favorable to the Soviets.

On August 13, 1961, the Soviets closed the border between East and West Berlin. The concrete-and-barbed-wire Berlin Wall—a physical manifestation of the Iron Curtain, a phrase introduced by British Prime Minister Winston Churchill some fifteen years earlier—arose, 110 miles long. Anyone caught trying to cross the wall into West Berlin was shot.

Most specifically, the Soviets built the wall to stop the flow of professionals and skilled people out of East Germany. Their migration to West Berlin had put a severe economic strain on the already weak command economy of East Germany. But many in Germany saw the wall as a signal of further aggression to come.

As historian David Burner notes, President Kennedy saw the wall, at least in private, as a stabilizing if cruel act. Kennedy argued, "Why should Khrushchev put up a wall if he really intended to seize West Berlin? . . . This is his way out of his predicament. . . . A wall is a hell of a lot better than a war." Despite Kennedy's correct reading of the situation, for the next several months Soviet and American troops stood at the ready at the border of East and West Germany. Nuclear threats were made by both sides. Neither blinked but neither took the next step. Month after month, Kennedy held firm, refusing to back down or to attack, a courageous stand for which critics from both ends of the political spectrum lambasted him.

Some twenty-two months after the stalemate began, Kennedy, in a defining moment of his presidency, appeared in West Berlin. Before thousands, the men and women who had stood as nuclear hostages to a war of nerves, Kennedy made a speech which stands out as one of the most powerful and compelling of the Cold War:

There are some who say that Communism is the wave of the future. Let them come to Berlin. And there are some who say in Europe and elsewhere, "We can work with the Communists." Let them come to Berlin. And there are even a few who say that it is true that Communism is an evil system but it permits us to make economic progress. Let them come to Berlin. . . . All free men, wherever they may live, are citizens of Berlin, and therefore as a free man, I take pride in the words "*Ich bin ein Berliner.*"

The power and certainty Kennedy displayed in his speech in Berlin in June 1963 was earned painfully, months earlier, when he and Soviet Premier Khrushchev engaged in an even more tense and terrible nuclear confrontation which would become known as the Cuban Missile Crisis.

Throughout the spring and summer of 1962, the Soviets had been dramatically increasing their military presence in Cuba. In September, Khrushchev ordered that Soviet ballistic missiles be added to the island's arsenal. In part, the Premier hoped to redress Soviet strategic inferiority. Khrushchev also feared that the United States was about to invade Cuba, and had decided to secure Communist Cuba, the Soviets' sole ally in the Americas, with the ultimate defense.

President Kennedy learned of the missiles' arrival in Cuba on October 16, 1962. He was shown air surveillance photos which revealed not yet operational SS-4 medium-range ballistic missiles (MRBM). He hurriedly convened a group of select senior advisers, the Executive Committee of the National Security Council (ExCom). This time the President would not allow himself to become dependent on any one sector of the national security apparatus. He would have candid debate and examination of options and contingencies.

At the first meeting of ExCom, General Maxwell Taylor, Chairman of the Joint Chiefs of Staff and Kennedy's favorite military intellectual, pushed for an immediate air strike. President Kennedy seemed convinced at the end of the meeting: "We're certainly going to do Number One—we're going to take out those missiles. The questions will be . . . what I describe as Number Two, which would be a general air strike. . . . The Third is the . . . is the general invasion. At least we're going to do Number One." Kennedy knew that any military action against Cuba very well might result in Soviet military reprisals. An escalating spiral leading even to nuclear war could be set off by an air strike against Cuba.

In a second meeting that same day, Secretary of State Dean Rusk argued against the air attack. Rusk pointed out that the Soviets knew that the United States had a superior nuclear arsenal and that the Soviets, perhaps, wanted the United States to share their fear of living under direct nuclear threat. In 1959, he reminded the committee, the United States had placed nuclear weapons in Turkey close to the Soviet border. Attorney General Robert Kennedy, the President's brother and chairman of ExCom, also opposed a surprise air attack on Cuba. He said it would be another Pearl Harbor.

Though they disagreed on tactics, all the men, especially the President, believed that the missiles in Cuba had to go. While Rusk, Defense Secretary Robert McNamara, and National Security Adviser McGeorge Bundy all rejected the Joint Chiefs of Staff opinion that the missiles had changed the strategic balance of power, none of the President's men accepted the Soviet's deception or provocation.

Kennedy felt boxed in. Only weeks before, he had, with great fanfare, warned Khrushchev against putting missiles into Cuba. America's allies and her enemies had heard Kennedy's warning: if "offensive ground-to-ground missiles" or "an offensive military base of significant capacity" were placed in Cuba by the Soviets, the President of the United States would be compelled to do "whatever must be done" to protect his country's national security. Tragically, Khrushchev had already begun just such operations. He chose not to allow Kennedy's after-the-fact rhetoric to interfere with his in-progress program; and he chose to see the word "offensive" as not really applicable to his "defensive" nuclear weapons. Khrushchev was bound by hard-liners in the Kremlin, as well as by his own inclinations, to protect the Cuban revolution.

President Kennedy saw things very differently. Despite the relative immateriality of the missiles to America's actual security, he felt that his credibility and that of his nation were on the line. The secret Soviet missiles could not remain in Cuba. The bluster and gamesmanship of the Cold War had caught up with both Khrushchev and Kennedy. The world was at risk of nuclear war.

President Kennedy spent six days with ExCom considering the possibilities. They met in secret. The missiles stayed secret as well. In this instance, secrecy allowed the President and his men time to think, to pause, and to reconsider. The crisis did not become a national and international political free-for-all. In those six days of secret meetings, the President moderated his stance. By October 22, the President, supported energetically by Defense Secretary McNamara, resolved that the United States would not, as a first measure, bomb Cuba. Instead, the Navy would blockade Cuba. If this measure did not work, then harsher measures would be deployed.

That night, without first contacting either Khrushchev or Castro, President Kennedy appeared on television to inform the American people about the missiles and his decisions. The nation watched as Kennedy spoke:

> . . . This secret, swift, and extraordinary buildup of Communist missiles, in an area well known to have a special and historical relationship to the United States, . . . is a deliberately provocative and unjustified change in the status quo which cannot be accepted by this country, if our courage and our commitments are ever to be trusted by either friend or foe. . . . We will not prematurely or unnecessarily risk the costs of worldwide nuclear war in which even the fruits of victory would be ashes in our mouth—but neither will we shrink from that risk at any time it must be faced.

Kennedy then outlined the Cuban quarantine and plans to involve American allies and the United Nations in actions against the Soviet Union. The President concluded by demanding that Chairman Khrushchev remove the missiles and so "move the world back from the abyss of destruction."

The next few days shook the world. More than sixty American ships patrolled the waters around Cuba. The Army rushed troops to southern states to be prepared in case the President ordered a full-scale invasion of Cuba. The Strategic Air Command went on nuclear alert, moving to DEFCON 2 for the first time ever. B-52 bombers loaded with nuclear weapons stood at the ready.

The American people, though overwhelmingly in support of their President, waited in horror. They stayed by their radios. Those who had air-raid shelters stocked them. People fled major cities and military and defense centers. Earl Bailey, for example, an engineer at the Lockheed aerospace plant outside Atlanta, devised an elaborate warning code for his family; he hoped that his high-security job might gain him advance word of nuclear attack. His family and hundreds of thousands of others assembled survival kits and planned what they would do when the bombs came.

The bombs did not come. Soviet ships did not fight when intercepted by the American Navy. They turned around. Khrushchev and Kennedy had stepped back from the abyss. Khrushchev agreed to remove the missiles in exchange for Kennedy's promise that the United States would never invade Cuba. Secretly, Kennedy suggested that in time the United States would take its nuclear weapons out of Turkey. Both the American and the Soviet leader were able to claim victory. Khrushchev would claim, "I saved Cuba. I stopped an invasion." Kennedy could justifiably say he had stood up to the Communists and forced them to back down.

Hard-liners in the Kremlin were not so sanguine about the Missile Crisis; they were angry at Khrushchev for taking the missiles out of Cuba and angrier still that he had put the Soviet Union into such a position in the first place—a "harebrained scheme," they snapped. While the hard-liners went along with a post-crisis American-Soviet limited nuclear test ban, they began a major buildup of Soviet strategic nuclear arms. Never again, they insisted, should the United States be able to bargain from a position of nuclear superiority. The Cuban Missile Crisis contributed to Khrushchev's fall from power a year later.

President Kennedy fared much better. Because the withdrawal of the American missiles in Turkey was kept secret, he appeared to have won an uncompromised victory. American newspapers and television reports painted the President in heroic hues and the American people celebrated the withdrawal of the missiles. Kennedy's televised speech, the grand drama of the "seven days in October," those sublime moments when the Soviet ships turned back, and finally the withdrawal of the missiles, all contributed to the larger-than-life aura of the young warrior President.

Richard Ned Lebow, a leading authority on the Cuban Missile Crisis, argues that the Cuban Missile Crisis taught America's foreign policy managers some very bad near-term lessons:

> . . . that success in international crises was largely a matter of national guts; that the opponent would yield to superior force; that presidential control of force can be "suitable," "selective," "effective," and "responsive" to civilian authority; and that crisis management and execution are too dangerous and events move too rapidly for anything but the tightest secrecy.

These lessons would serve policymakers poorly in America's next great foreign policy crisis: the war in Vietnam.

As the presidential obsession with Cuba at least partly indicates, it was on Third World countries like Cuba and Vietnam that the President wanted to focus his attention. In 1961 he orated: "The great battleground for the defense and expansion of freedom today is the whole southern half of the globe . . . the lands of the rising people." Kennedy correctly saw that for purposes of American economic growth, as well as for reasons of world leadership, the real "action" was in the decolonizing and economically less developed countries of the world.

In the late 1950s and early 1960s, people throughout Africa, Asia, and Latin America struggled for independence from European imperial rule or against economic dependence on the Western industrial nations. In 1962, after years of war, Algerians won complete freedom from French rule. In 1963, the Mau Mau movement in Kenya helped end European colonialism in the broad sub-Saharan reaches of Africa. Throughout Southeast Asia chaotic and bloody civil wars raged as the final legacy of direct imperialist rule. In much of Latin America and the Caribbean, revolutionary and populist movements grew in popularity and strength. Many of these movements pointed to the United States as their political and economic oppressor. In the early 1960s, radical change was sweeping virtually the entire periphery of the industrialized world—a part of the world Europe, Japan, and the United States depended on for natural resources, export markets, and capital investments.

In his attempts to align Third World countries with American interests, President Kennedy developed two programs that well represented his larger vision: the Peace Corps and the Special Forces of the U.S. Army, also known as the Green Berets. Both programs revealed Kennedy's belief that in order to ensure pro-American development, the United States needed a long-term presence in the Third World. The United States had to develop institutional responses, both peaceful and not, to a world in political and economic flux. As Kennedy biographer David Burner wrote: "A world to be balanced and rebalanced invites an activity more extensive and exact than a world to be remade once and for all."

The idea of a Peace Corps had been pushed by congressional liberals for several years. Kennedy had extemporaneously raised the idea in a campaign speech before students at the University of Michigan: "How many of you are willing to spend ten years in Africa or Latin America or Asia?" The students roared their approval and Kennedy put the idea of a Peace Corps on his administration's front burner. In his Inaugural Address, President Kennedy had declared: "To those people in the huts and villages of half the globe struggling to break the bonds of mass misery, we pledge our best efforts to help them help themselves." The Peace Corps became the embodiment of that pledge.

The volunteers, trained as teachers, nurses, engineers, road surveyors, and agricultural experts, lived in the poorest countries in the world and did their best to make a practical difference in people's lives. Confronting immense problems such as gross economic inequality, catastrophic medical and nutritional inadequacies, and a pitiful infrastructure, the volunteers struggled to help the people with whom they worked. Still, as historian Irving Bernstein fairly notes, "probably the most significant Peace Corps accomplishment was the education of Americans. They came to understand the peoples and cultures of the Third World." Peace Corps volunteers were a significant part of a new elite who, through real experience abroad, began to break through the mental blinders Americans wore when looking at the rest of the world.

Another elite group of young volunteers, the Special Forces, represented the other long-term Kennedy response to Third World instability. Soon after taking office, Kennedy ordered the armed forces to develop counterinsurgency measures capable of stopping Third World guerrilla revolutionaries like those who had been victorious in Cuba and who were successfully operating in Vietnam. Out of this presidential decision came the Green Berets, an outgrowth of the Army Special Forces Group. The President targeted a significant part of the immense increase in the military budget for America's unconventional Ranger-type warriors. The Green Berets were charged not only with fighting guerrillas but with training and leading indigenous forces against such insurgents. The President took great personal interest in the Green Berets, offering ideas about how they should be equipped and outfitted. John Kennedy was proud of the Peace Corps but it was the Green Berets that captured his imagination.

The view from the White House during the presidency of John F. Kennedy was overwhelmingly colored by the sublime possibilities of maintaining and furthering America's global mission. That mission was cast, often in error and misunderstanding, by the actions and reactions of the Soviet Union. That the Cold War was not the central driving force in the world during the Kennedy years—that it was, perhaps, the quest for national independence or racial equality—was not something the President would have accepted. On the last day of his life, President Kennedy was preparing to make a fiery speech outlining what he saw as his major contributions to the nation's health: the largest peacetime expansion of the military budget up until that time and the immense growth in America's nuclear arsenal.

John F. Kennedy cast his presidency within a narrow Cold War frame. However, in important ways, he offered the American people more than just nuclear brinkmanship and national militarization. President Kennedy offered a vision of Americans engaged in the world, working to create a more just and decent society at home and abroad. Kennedy's rhetoric was inspirational, even if many of his policies and programs were not. In the years that followed his presidency, Americans of all political stripes took his words for deeds and used them in ways Kennedy may well have never imagined.

On the afternoon of November 22, 1963, President Kennedy was assassinated in a Dallas motorcade.

Everyday life in America stopped. Businesses closed down. People cried in the streets. And, as one woman remembers, schools let out:

> I was in Mr. Brown's poetry class when a girl named Marion Milgram interrupted the class . . . "Kennedy was shot and killed." . . . Mr. Brown, in his brown suit and spaghetti-stained tie, threw himself against the blackboard and cried, his shoulders heaving. We were dismissed, all five thousand of us in Newton High. It was a silent dismissal. The eerie part was that no one told us to be silent. The world fell apart after that.

For four days, the nation came together on the television screen. Over 100 million Americans watched John Kennedy's funeral. The three television networks went live, hour after hour, and everyone saw the same pictures. They saw the President's little boy salute his father's casket. They saw Jackie, shrouded in black, her face frozen in grief, refuse to break down. They even watched the President's killer, Lee Harvey Oswald, gunned down before their eyes. Americans searched their hearts for the meaning of their President's death.

Over a million Americans wrote to Jacqueline Kennedy, sharing their grief, offering condolences. In their letters, they struggled to explain what the President and his family meant to them. A woman in New Jersey spoke for many younger people when she wrote: "I don't know if you know how cynical most people of our generation have become about patriotism. When Kennedy spoke, he managed to instill a feeling of pride in me because I, too, was an American. . . . It takes a great man and now he's gone."

President Kennedy had spoken to the American people of a world of almost unlimited possibilities; with his death, Americans confronted a grim reality: not all of America's possibilities were good.

3. THE MEANING OF NATIONAL CULTURE

~~~~~~

PRESIDENT KENNEDY'S ASSASSINATION was, of course, a national tragedy. But his death also was revelatory of the ways in which national culture had penetrated and affected the lives of the American people. Through television Americans shared the tragedy of the President's assassination. His death and funeral became collective markers in the nation's consciousness, personal yet public, private yet shared. In the last weeks of 1963, the President's death was the central event in America's kaleidoscopic, ever expanding national public culture.

A teenage girl, in the condolence letter she sent to Mrs. Kennedy, revealed how television had altered the ways Americans experienced their public life.

> Mr. Kennedy always seemed like the kind of father I would have wanted, the perfect father. He seemed so warm, sincere, intelligent and just plain wonderful when I saw him on television. . . . You [Mrs. Kennedy] are so good looking and well dressed that I have tried to copy your hair and clothes. . . . Your children are so wonderful and so sweet it's just unbelievable. . . . I've seen all of this on TV and I feel as though I had been there.

As this teenage girl suggests in her letter, America's national culture was based in large part on shared images—Jackie's hairdo, Marilyn Monroe's pout, Marlon Brando's swagger, Willy Mays's basket catch . . . the President's funeral. These images and many others formed a set of commonly understood referents, a symbolic language shared by almost all. They were a part of an immediate, widely available, fast-changing culture which was beamed into almost every home and understood by young and old, poor and rich. Hollywood movies, national radio networks, popular music, national advertising campaigns, and professional sports leagues all played a key role in the development of this national culture. Nationally distributed brand-name products figured prominently. And a vastly improved system of national communication and transportation, which included interstate highways and jet passenger planes, contributed to the speed with which national goods, services, and celebrities rocketed around the country and helped to form a national culture.

The near-omnipresence of this new national public culture would have struck many an American not born in this century as a most startling development. Of course, a national public culture was not invented in the 1960s. America's democracy was built on shared political understandings, and national political parties had disseminated political perspectives and partisan attacks through newspapers and pamphlets since the founding of the Republic. Still, throughout the nineteenth century racial, religious, class, and ethnic lines rigidly demarcated Americans' lives. Perhaps even more profoundly, the boundaries of locale and region circumscribed Americans' sense of shared culture. Southerners and Northerners—well after the Civil War—saw themselves as peoples of two worlds; their differences were the most clearly articulated, but by no means the only important ones.

By the late 1920s more and more Americans were participating in a common national life as a result of national market integration (best seen in the mass distribution of brand-name products) and national cultural integration (nationally syndicated radio shows, Hollywood movies, national sports leagues, mass-circulation magazines). Americans from Alabama and Maine, from poor backgrounds and rich, could talk about Charlie Chaplin or Babe Ruth, the shenanigans of Amos and Andy and the latest adventures of Little Orphan Annie. Throughout the nation men drank Coke and debated the merits of Ford and Chevrolet. As one, the nation had followed the transatlantic flight of Charles Lindbergh in 1927.

By 1929, President Hoover had begun to use the radio—however inexpertly—in an attempt to form a national constituency, separate even from party or platform.

The ways in which people experienced this growing national culture, however, was complicated. A middle-class black businessman in Harlem and a white middle-class businessman in Dubuque, Iowa, a Chicano farmworker in California and a white sharecropper in Alabama could listen, simultaneously, to *Amos 'n' Andy* but they heard different things. In other words, even more than today, race, religion, ethnicity, class, region, gender, and sexual preference still radically affected how Americans participated in and perceived the growing consumer-oriented and increasingly mass-mediated national culture. What is crucial, though, is that in the first half of the twentieth century Americans were coming to recognize a common culture and were aware that it shaped their world.

This cultural and economic integration and nationalization was sped up by dramatic changes created by World War II, the Cold War, and postwar prosperity. Military service and the subsequent peacetime draft gave the majority of American men common experiences. The federal government promoted national economic, cultural, and political integration by building interstate highways, funding higher education, and promoting anti-Communist loyalty campaigns. Postwar prosperity and the world's best domestic distribution system allowed an ever larger majority of Americans to participate in the rapidly expanding consumer system which was efficiently managed by large, nationally oriented corporations. Women's magazines as diverse as *The Ladies' Home Journal* and *Mademoiselle*, read by millions, spoke in unison about the joys and tribulations of early marriages and suburban living. National advertising campaigns searched for the common touch; both Hollywood and the fledgling TV industry worked hard to discover which themes and plots would produce huge audiences. Even those unable to buy a small piece of the new American dream of consumption without limits could watch it unfold as fantasy in the intimacy of their own homes. By the early 1960s, the overwhelming majority of Americans could not help but share in a national set of experiences and an increasingly—if still very selective—shared knowledge about one another.

By the time of President Kennedy's assassination, television had emerged as the preeminent medium transmitting the nation's public life. While members of the nation's intellectual elite scorned television's offering and cheered Newton Minow, chairman of the Federal Communications Commission, which oversaw the licensing of the nation's airwaves, when he blasted TV programming as a "vast wasteland," most Americans disagreed. In 1961 (for the first time) a majority of Americans said they received most of their "news" from television. In the early 1960s, about 92 percent of all American households owned at least one television. They tuned in, on average, for some six hours a day.

For most of those six hours, Americans watched entertainment shows, typically during "prime time." When those shows touched on something enough people found engrossing they became smash hits, gathering tens of millions of Americans in front of their sets. In culture, hits rarely came in the form of a vivid portrait of a world crisis or a pressing political issue. People preferred a show that touched them where they lived.

In the late 1950s, while Cold War hysteria and corporate/suburbia conformity were hot topics among the intelligentsia, TV watchers reveled in frontier justice and the bloody individualism of the mythic Old West. In 1959, almost all the most popular shows were violent Westerns. *Gunsmoke, Have Gun Will Travel,* and *The Rifleman* led the list. (*Peter Gunn,* the fifth-rated show, was a detective drama, but still managed to work a weapon into the title.) By the early 1960s violent Westerns had begun to lose their audience, and were replaced by shows focused not on deadly confrontation between good and evil but on the humorous reconciliation of old virtues and new mores.

In the 1960s, no television show had greater appeal to more Americans than the seemingly banal spoof *The Beverly Hillbillies.* It was the number one show on television in its first two seasons (1962–63 and 1963–64) and a top hit throughout the 1960s.

The Beverly Hillbillies related the adventures of the Clampett family, "poor mountaineers" who discovered oil on their Arkansas property, became immensely rich, and, at the urging of their "kinfolk," had "moved to Beverly . . . Hills, that is." In California they met and mastered snobs and deceivers and tried to make sense of their affluent surroundings.

TV critics and commentators hated the show. The critic for the entertainment bible, *Variety*, sniffed: "At no time does it give the viewer credit for even a smattering of intelligence." Historians of television have dismissed the show as typical of television networks' insensitivity to genuine social problems. Of course, *The Beverly Hillbillies* was not about real mountain people or their problems. But the show was very much about American life. *The Beverly Hillbillies* was a humorously exaggerated commentary on the American dream as lived in the 1960s.

Most literally, the Clampetts' migration to the California of "swimming pools . . . movie stars" was a trip millions of Americans had taken in the postwar years. By the early 1960s, California had passed New York to become the most populous state in the country. Like the Clampetts, people from diverse backgrounds had uprooted themselves, left their kinfolk and community behind them, and started life anew in California.

Public opinion polls revealed that millions more wanted to make the trip; California ranked first among Americans as "best state" and "ideal place to live" and Los Angeles ranked first among cities as the "most desired place to live." The Clampetts' adventures in America's promised land resonated with other Americans who wanted to see their own dreams come true in California. California dreams and nightmares suffused American culture: the Mamas and the Papas sang "California Dreaming," the Beach Boys celebrated "California Girls," and Joan Didion, in essays collected in *Slouching Towards Bethlehem*, explained how the dream could become an anomic nightmare. Whether as a symbol of ultimate possibility or of the dream gone wrong, California was for most Americans as much an idea to be contemplated as a real place to live.

Just as important, the Clampetts' sudden wealth served as funhouse mirror for the relatively sudden prosperity millions of Americans enjoyed by the early 1960s. While few viewers could expect a Beverly Hills mansion, many who had lived through the Great Depression in urban tenements or broken-down farmhouses did find themselves living in all-electric California-style ranch houses and were aware of the distance they had traveled. A central comedic element in *The Beverly Hillbillies* was the Clampetts' misuse of the luxuries their wealth afforded them. Granny used the built-in swimming pool ("the ce-ment pond") to do the family laundry and the family sat down to the billiard table for their supper. While feeling superior to the Clampetts' ignorance and laughing at the Clampetts' innocence, the viewers might recall little mix-ups they had seen and felt at the supermarket, strip shopping centers, and auto showrooms, where they and their neighbors, in so many ways parvenus all, worked at mastering their new consumer lifestyles.

The moral implications of the new consumer lifestyles were at the heart of *The Beverly Hillbillies* and, for that matter, several of the leading television shows of the early to middle 1960s. In both *The Beverly Hillbillies* and, for example, the immensely popular *Andy Griffith Show*, the moral integrity of a consumer-based lifestyle—as against a rooted way of life—was sharply and unceasingly mocked. Jed Clampett, the wise family patriarch, refuses in every instance to give up his traditional way of life. Despite his immense wealth, he continues to wear his old country clothes, drive his ancient truck, and eat grits and possum. Granny, the family matriarch, also keeps to proven ways. She tries to teach the "young 'uns" good country manners, but the younger Clampetts, especially the dunderhead nephew Jethro, are at least sometimes sucked in by the Beverly Hills lifestyle. Jethro buys a convertible and a Sunset Strip wardrobe, and tries to be a player in the movie business. As a result, he looks the fool and is played for one by various deceivers. Jed Clampett, on the other hand, remains a paragon of common sense, integrity, and kindness. Through his rock-steady character, he effortlessly defeats every conniver's attack on his family and fortune.

Thematically, *The Beverly Hillbillies* contradicted the blandishments of every prime-time commercial sponsor and the entire thrust of the consumer capitalist system that was underwriting

American prosperity in the 1960s. *The Beverly Hillbillies* preached that character was more important than appearance, that a lifestyle one could purchase was no match for simple, traditional virtues. Of course, the Clampetts did not talk about "lifestyles" vs. traditional virtues, but every plot centered on this theme.

The idea that Americans had "lifestyles" was just emerging in the 1960s. The word first appeared in Webster's International Dictionary in 1961. As cultural historian Roland Marchand wrote: "The word *style* suggested free choice, the uninhibited search for what looked and felt right." Many Americans worried about the moral quality of this "uninhibited search" for self-expression. Did the consumer frenzy promoted by the "buy now, pay later; be whomever you want to be" ethos compromise older values of family, religion, and community?

Americans' ambivalence about what Daniel Bell called "the contradictions of capitalism"—which simultaneously demanded discipline and license, hard work and hedonism—seemed not to affect their purchasing decisions. Arguably, shows like *The Beverly Hillbillies* and *The Andy Griffith Show* were popular because they exposed these tensions but simultaneously defused them with broad humor, turning complex questions about modern society into escapist nostalgia.

Commercial television, of course, did not exist to probe the merits of consumer capitalism. The owners and managers of commercial television broadcasting were in business to make money. Television became a grand success from their perspective because the biggest players in the business world found that television commercials sold their products better than any other form of advertising.

No group of Americans responded more positively to the profound inanity of corporate America's TV commercials than young people. Young people loved their TV. Historian James Baughman argues: "Virtually everyone born during the postwar baby boom regarded television much as their parents had looked upon network radio and the picture house in the 1930s: it was their medium. Glib commentators would later dub them the TV generation." In fact, young people were not TV's heaviest viewers. The elderly actually spent more time before the screen. But young people watched television with a special avidity. From television they gained a shared world of words, images, and, of course, a desire for consumer products.

Marketing experts and behavioral scientists reported that young people were more comfortable with television than their parents or grandparents were. They, for example, saw commercials not as irritating interruptions of their favorite shows but as simply part of the television continuum. TV commercials, experts learned, sank in with children: kids could recognize the word "detergent" before they could read, and at the cusp of the 1950s and 1960s, far more children could sing the jingle "Pepsi-Cola hits the spot / twelve full ounces, that's a lot" than could sing the national anthem. Eugene Gilbert, youth marketing consultant, was believed when he announced: "An advertiser who touches a responsive chord in youth can generally count on the parent to succumb finally to purchasing the product."

The business community watched wide-eyed when the popularity of Disney's Davy Crockett shows in the 1950s sent the price of raccoon skins from 26 cents a pound to $8 a pound in weeks, as every boy in America demanded that his parents buy him a coonskin cap. What caught kids' fancy on TV moved products off the shelves. In 1959, the Mattel toy company began a massive advertising campaign on Saturday-morning cartoons and made the Barbie doll a necessity for little girls in the 1960s. Children from across the country and across class and even racial lines watched many of the same TV shows, yearned to buy the same products—though gender, here as elsewhere, played a determining role—and joined the youth division of the national consumer culture. The kids were product leaders thanks to the gleeful intensity they brought to the entire gestalt of their TV viewing.

Young people's proclivities for precocious consumption and TV connoisseurship would not alone have made them such a significant factor in the world of corporate marketing and advertising. What added potency to the fermenting mix was the sheer number of young people with money in their pockets by the mid-1960s.

Pepsi executives, for example, in trying to figure out why their adult-oriented ad campaign of the early 1960s—"Be Sociable"— was failing, discovered that teenagers bought about 55 percent of all soft drinks. The front end of the baby boom, the pig in America's demographic python, was by the early 1960s making its presence felt in that most respected of places—the bottom line.

The baby boomers, the offspring of all those twenty-year-olds who married and multiplied in the immediate postwar years, eventually included some 76 million Americans. In 1964, the largest age group in the country was comprised of seventeen-year-old youth; in 1965, 41 percent of all Americans were under the age of twenty. The social impact of this youth cohort was all the more powerful because the generation preceding them was unusually small as a result of the economic onslaught of the Great Depression and the beginning of World War II.

This swollen generation was unified by television and the television marketing campaigns aimed at them. But these were far from the only factors. Education was another. Young people were staying in school longer than ever before. In the 1920s, only one in five Americans graduated from high school. By the mid-1960s, the figure was almost three out of four. Whereas in 1940 only about 16 percent of all students went on to college, by the mid-1960s about half of all students attended college. This vast increase in matriculating students meant that a much greater percentage of young people stayed together in the same youth-centered institutional system and were taught many of the same things for far longer than any previous generation. And they did not at the age of twelve or fourteen, as had been typical for generations, leave youth behind them and begin working full-time in the adult world. By the early 1960s, young people—youth as they came to be known—had years together to develop their own world.

Marketers, educators, parents, religious authorities, and others from the older generation did their best (and often succeeded) to shape and control that world. Still, in overcrowded schoolrooms, in front of televisions, many of the young people who were raised amid unprecedented prosperity and optimism found their own ways—some acceptable to their elders and some not—to give shape and meaning to the many years they shared with one another.

One has to exercise some intellectual caution here to separate myth from truth. It is easy to run amuck with the image of Unified Youth on the March as many people did at the time. But a great deal divided young people in the 1960s—race, economic class, religious beliefs, level of education, politics, gender. "Youth," like "California," like perhaps even "President Kennedy," was an idea or an image as much as a real thing. Still, many young people self-consciously claimed common cultural referents in the 1960s and did have at least a superficial sense of being co-participants in a new world partially of their own making.

Rock 'n' roll was at the heart of that autonomous-feeling world. If television catered to young people, rock-'n'-roll music existed solely because of them. And while the music was, and would become ever more so, a packaged commodity marketed by large corporations, young musicians and youthful fans did their best to create a world in which their concerns, not those of their parents or their leaders, mattered most of all. The business leaders who ran the record companies listened to the young people because the kids' buying power in America's consumer society gave them cultural authority.

Rock music was by no means the first widely popular music. But like so many other phenomena that exploded in the 1960s, music-as-commodity (in the words of sociologist Simon Firth), as against music-as-experience, was essentially (though not completely) a twentieth-century invention. Because of the commercial development of the music industry in the 1920s, celebrity performers became increasingly central to the way most people enjoyed music. People related to music not by making it but by listening to professionals on the radio or record albums. In the 1930s, Bing Crosby crooned into the radio like no one ever had before and sold millions of records. In the 1940s, Frank Sinatra became a teen idol by using mass-marketing techniques to sell a carefully packaged personality.

By the 1950s, the music business was a rapidly expanding gold mine. This gold mine, unlike the automobile industry, did not demand a great deal of capital investment. Thanks to the postwar development of the "unbreakable" LP record and inexpensive recording equipment, an "independent" record producer could set up shop for less than a thousand dollars. Between 1948 and 1954 more than a thousand independent labels entered the record business, looking for something new, something that could catch the record-buying public's attention. If it would sell, they would produce it—old rules, ancient prejudices, traditional cultural arbiters be damned.

Accompanying the "indies" in the pursuit of whatever it was that sold music was another exceedingly un-Fortune 500-like group of players. Organized crime families in the 1950s largely controlled the placement of jukeboxes. Playing the jukeboxes became a 1950s and early 1960s youth fad; they gave just the right background to the drive-in, soda-shop, greasy-spoon courting rituals of teenagers with enough money in their pockets to blow some change. The gangsters—capitalists without moral or social constraints—who controlled the jukeboxes and, to a large extent, their playlists, like most of the up-from-nowhere "indie" record producers, cared only about the bottom line: how many nickels found their way into their machines. As rock-'n'-roll historian Marc Eliot emphasizes: "It didn't matter what label the record was on, who was singing, or what color he or she was," the gangsters put whatever music on their machines the kids paid to hear. "Eventually, the most popular R&B records made their way to the neighborhood soda shops up North, frequented by America's newly affluent teens," Eliot concludes. The popular music business, operating outside the racist horizon of white America's "traditional" values and increasingly dedicated to a national distribution system, was, at the level of cultural integration, working its magic by the early 1950s. Rock music defied region, race, and religion, and many young people saw it as defining their own separate culture.

Rock music, of course, was, in its guts and its drive, a style of music largely formulated by African-American musicians. Rock evolved out of their urbanization and electrification of the blues and gospel music. In ghetto bars and clubs, places outside "re-spectable society," black musicians had used a driving beat and uncensored lyrics to give free play to sexual longing, frenzied joy, and other emotions. Conventional radio executives, record in-dustry bosses, and official cultural arbiters found rock too out of control for white listeners. African-Americans knew the music through "race" radio stations and record stores. By the early 1950s, the profit-hunting independent producers, the "amoral" jukebox operators, and go-for-broke white disc jockeys like Alan Freed revealed black R&B to white teenagers, who gobbled it up.

By the early 1960s, white musicians, major record labels, and big-money radio stations had largely taken over the surging pop-ularity of rock 'n' roll. For the most part, they accepted the sex-uality, racial openness, and furious rhythms of the music. Elvis Presley became the most successful 1950s performer by incorpo-rating the black sounds of R&B into his own white country roots music. Presley, like the best of early white rock stars, did not merely "bleach" a black sound but had the gifts to forge a new sound out of all that he felt and saw and heard around him. Rock 'n' roll, to a degree, broke down the wall that monitors of con-ventional morality had raised between what they considered ac-ceptable and unacceptable forms of music.

Tens of millions of young people had faith in the power of rock 'n' roll to give shape to their adolescent rushes. Marc Campbell, a Navy brat born in Corpus Christi, Texas, who had lived on military bases all over the United States, expresses the excite-ment a new rock group could bring: "On the jukebox came some English-speaking voices. . . . It was the Beatles doing 'I Want to Hold Your Hand,' and I immediately heard something that changed my life. Those were my heroes . . . Rock 'n' roll was really what was happening for me. I could chart most of my evolution through rock 'n' roll."

The Beatles toured the United States for the first time in Feb-ruary 1964. They rode a wave of chart-busting successes: "I Want to Hold Your Hand," "She Loves You," and "Please Please Me," all become number one songs in rapid succession. Their American tour started with an appearance on prime time: *The Ed Sullivan*

Show. Kids across the country tuned in as the studio audience of mainly young teenage girls screamed in rapture (a side note: while women faced nearly impossible odds in becoming record producers or industry executives in the sexist music business, as consumers they often earned the right to lead). In stadium show after stadium show, the Beatles had audiences sobbing in adoration and joy. By April, the Beatles owned the hit list; their singles ranked one through five in sales. In July their inspired film *A Hard Day's Night* filled movie theaters in virtually every city and town across the country. "Beatlemania" had arrived. The Beatles, in the hyperbolic words of their co-leader John Lennon, were "more popular than Jesus" by the mid-1960s. By 1968 they had sold more than $154 million in records. For some members of the "'60s generation" the Beatles were, are, and always will be the essence of what it meant to be young and alive in the 1960s.

Like a more artistically sophisticated and successful version of hit TV show *The Beverly Hillbillies*, the Beatles' hypersuccess defined a part of what American society had become by the mid-1960s. First of all, the Beatles were working-class English—a fairly exotic commodity in the United States. That touch of the exotic was, according to Beatles press agent Derek Taylor, a significant part of the Fab Four's appeal; young Americans in 1964 had "a basic longing to find something outside themselves and their experience." The same week that "She Loves You" was released, African-American musician Stevie Wonder had the number one hit in America. The frenetic, profit-hunting music industry had exposed white Americans to a barrage of African-American musicians, as well as Chicano rockers like Richie Valens and later Cannibal and the Headhunters. British rock music was the next, the newest, and, in the mid-1960s, the hippest thing happening.

Not that the Beatles were simply just tools of some music industry sharpies looking for something different. The Beatles were brilliant innovators who successfully melded the African-American R&B sound with their own music-writing genius. As John Lennon biographer John Weiner argues: "They broke out of three-chord cock rock and four-chord teenybop. Their songs brought in minor chords and unexpected sevenths, and had many more changes than guitar players were used to. . . . The Beatles sounded new and exciting because their songs had a structure that really was new and exciting." Young people living up to the consumer ethos that was pushed at them from every direction—find the new, accept the new, buy the new!—loved the Beatles' new sound.

Young people also loved the Beatles themselves, who, despite their foreign origins, so clearly sided with the kids in their declaration of independence from their elders. Unlike Elvis Presley —the biggest thing going before the Beatles—who, despite his swiveling hips, was almost painfully polite to the "geriatric" set, the Beatles loved to give patronizing parental types a kick in their collective behinds. When Beatles drummer Ringo Starr was asked at the Beatles' first American press conference (!) by a smug reporter what he thought about Beethoven, he smiled back: "I love him, especially his poems." As 1960s historian Alan Matusow concludes in writing about this emblematic one-liner: "Treating the adult world as absurd, they told their fans to kick off their shoes, heed their hormones and have fun. . . . The frenzied loyalty they inspired endowed the Fab Four with immense potential power—power to alter life-styles, change values, and create a new sensibility, a new way of perceiving the world."

In 1964, it was still only a seed, but the Beatles—like other masters of the fast-developing rock music world—carried with them the threat of becoming more than the next big, monster record-selling act. They carried with them a power—never as strong as it seemed either to their friends or to their enemies, but real nonetheless—to define, alongside their fans and followers, just what the new, increasingly transatlantic American dream of consumption without limits would, should, and could mean to young people born in an age of both unprecedented affluence and potential global nuclear annihilation.

The Beatles and rock 'n' roll were far from universally loved by Americans. There were those who dreaded the capacious, race-crossing, gender-bending, tradition-breaking offerings of the rock-'n'-roll culture. Many of those people saw the African-American roots of rock 'n' roll as the surest sign of its depravity.

As early as 1956, historian Jon Weiner writes, Southern white church groups organized against what they called "Negro-style" rock music. The Alabama White Citizens Council, a powerful and virulently racist anti-civil-rights group, blasted rock music as "a means of pulling the white man down to the level of the Negro. It is part of a plot to undermine the morals of the youth of our nation."

More than racism, however, was at work. A cadre of fundamentalist Christians believed that the Beatles, in particular, were "destroying youth's faith in God." By the mid-1960s millions of Americans, though a minority to be sure, looked at rock 'n' roll and saw the devil's work.

For some, rock 'n' roll was only the most manifest danger of the large-scale social changes overtaking their country. Many proudly parochial and provincial Americans observed that the stronger the pull of national culture and national rules became, the less control they had over their families and communities.

For many Christian fundamentalists, as well as other Christians, the most flagrant sign of the disregard with which national elites held their views came in 1962 when the Supreme Court ruled that children in public schools could not start their day with a class prayer. Led by Chief Justice Earl Warren, the Court was methodically establishing national standards to protect the rights of minorities, criminal defendants, and nonconformist opinion. The Court's prayer-in-the-schools decision stretched the federal government's long arm into every classroom and put a stop to a tradition that had ruled in thousands of schools for generations.

As the pro-prayer parents and their supporters saw it, their beliefs about how their schools should be run were being superseded by a distant authority that cared nothing about their morality or way of life. The federal government and the national purveyors of television and music, they believed with at least partial justification, were making it far more difficult for them to teach their values and beliefs to their children. They did not believe that the new national culture, with its emphasis on materialism, mutable lifestyle, and feel-good secularism, made for a proper Christian life. And in their own terms, they were right. The notion

of consumption without limits did not sit comfortably with fundamentalist or traditional Christian beliefs. What these tradition-
alists did not acknowledge, however, was that the market
economy most of them wholeheartedly embraced lay behind much
of the change they abhorred. As observers from Adam Smith on
have noted, the capitalist marketplace depends on the "creative
destruction" of old ways, traditional beliefs, and comfortable
patterns.

As consumer culture destroyed, it created, and its products were
complex. At its root, twentieth-century consumer capitalism stood
for a new kind of equality. In essence, this version of equality was
simply the right of every American to push a shopping cart and
to decide what brought happiness. Everyone should have the same
right to drive a new Chrysler, smoke a Camel, and wipe their
kitchen floor Mr. Clean clean. The mass market—on the purchasing side—excluded no one by virtue of race, religion, ethnicity, or level of formal education.

For example, when the executives at Pepsi decided in the first
years of the 1960s to radically revamp their product's image and
create a bigger market for their products, they broke through a
long-standing racist barrier and used black musicians for their
nationally broadcast commercials. Membership in the "Pepsi Generation," they indicated—though only in the late 1960s did
African-Americans appear on-camera—required only the money
to pay for a soda. How members of oppressed minority groups
would get that money, of course, was something the admen and
marketers failed to discuss. Still, compared to the teachings of the
White Citizens Councils or xenophobic provincials, the men and
women who wanted to see everyone inside the "Big Tent" of the
mass market promoted an inclusive vision of consumer egalitar-
ianism.

The spectacle of consumer equality was not just hype, though
like most 1960s visions it hid at least as much as it revealed. Many
Americans were able to live out their consumer dreams in their
daily lives. Tom Wolfe, writing in the 1960s, argued that America's unprecedented affluence had created a "Happiness Explosion."

In a series of influential articles—collected in the best-selling *The Pump House Gang* and *The Kandy-Kolored Tangerine-Flake Streamline Baby*—Wolfe described "new status leagues," in which "regular" Americans found "novel ways of . . . *enjoying*, extending their egos way out on the best terms available, namely their own." In a gyrating prose style meant to mirror what he saw, Wolfe played ethnographer to car customizer cults, California surfer kids, up-from-the-Bronx art collectors, Hugh Hefner's Playboy Mansion, and a host of other self-created consumer-based lifestyles. In America, Wolfe argued, people wanted to and could use the postwar prosperity to buy, not into the old status game in which middle-class values and the allure of upper-class glamour were given highest privilege, but into their own communities of value. While Wolfe publicized the most exotic of these new communities, he believed that the United Automobile Workers member who took immense pride in his powerboating adventures, as well as the middle-class suburbanite who collected antiques, also participated in a new world. In this world, cultural authority had devolved to the individual level and corporate America worked only to feed the frenzy for ever new, ever more grand ways of giving Americans what they wanted, "novel ways of . . . enjoying."

How many Americans really saw themselves in the lifestyles Wolfe and others obsessively portrayed in the 1960s? It's hard to measure. Ben Wattenberg and Richard Scammon, in a series of contemporary statistical portraits of the United States, give strong evidence of a white America overwhelmingly in love with what prosperity provided. Wattenberg and Scammon also reveal, without any doubts, that black Americans felt much less able to participate in America's affluent national culture and were angry about their exclusion.

Nonetheless, in the early 1960s many African-Americans looked at the new national culture with a sense of great hope. While white racists and fundamentalist Christians saw themselves as losers in the nationalization of American political, economic, and cultural life, African-Americans correctly perceived themselves as potential winners. When political leaders in the nineteenth century referred to the nation as *these* United States, in which Southern states were guaranteed by the Supreme Court the right to set their own standards and laws, black Americans lost the rights, privileges, and immunities America's national creed seemed to have guaranteed them. Regional authority, local custom, and the production-oriented economy of the South had for many years worked against the aspirations of African-Americans.

The national and nationalist premises of postwar American elites seemed to offer African-Americans new opportunities for equality. In *the* United States, the American people—not just some of them—were supposed to be united against the Soviet Communists. In *the* United States, the federal government—not state or local officials—was increasingly taking responsibility for guaranteeing one standard of basic social provision, justice, and equality before the law. In *the* United States, with its electronically interconnected culture, the gross mistreatment of any part of the citizenry became, more likely, visible to all the citizenry.

White Americans' treatment of African-Americans gave the lie to everything whites liked to believe about their country—that it was the land of opportunity in which freedom and democracy ruled. More and more, African-Americans understood that America's global role, the increasingly powerful role of the federal government, and the formation of a national cultural life gave them opportunities to expose the racist lie and demand that white America live up to its claims of democracy.

4. FREEDOM

~~~~~~

ON FEBRUARY 1, 1960, four students from the all-black
North Carolina Agricultural and Technical College took stools at
the "whites only" lunch counter of the Woolworth's in downtown
Greensboro, North Carolina. They were Ezell Blair, Jr., Franklin
McCain, Joseph McNeil, and David Richmond. "We'll stay until
we get served," they had vowed to one another. The young men,
acting on their own, had decided to confront Jim Crow by putting
their bodies on the line. When a reporter asked them, "How long
have you been planning this?" the young men replied, "All our
lives!" Within weeks, thousands of African-American students,
with white supporters, had begun hundreds of sit-ins at restaurants
and boycotts of segregated stores throughout the South. Up
North, black and white students staged sit-ins at local branches
of Woolworth's to protest the national chain's complicity with
state segregation laws in the South. By the end of 1960, some
70,000 people in over 150 cities and towns had participated in sit-
ins. Close to 3,600 of them had been arrested.

The sit-in movement of 1960 provided a direct and immediate
way to fight racism and discrimination. The sit-ins showed young
African-Americans that they could act without waiting for the
NAACP or other civil rights organizations to pave the way. They
could make history themselves by personally confronting racism.
Through local actions, the young protesters learned a hard lesson
they would carry with them for years. It was up to them, they
decided, not the federal government or Big Business or even their
elders, to change their country's direction. They learned through
experience that the struggle would be hard but that victories could

be won. For some, the sit-ins marked the first act of "the sixties."

The sit-in was not the first act in the civil rights movement. In many ways, it marked the crescendo of that movement, which had in its modern form begun in the mid-1950s and which would climax in August 1963 with a massive rally in Washington, D.C. But the sit-in movement also marked the beginning of a new, less organized struggle in which young people were to be propelled to the forefront of social protest, and whose goals were no longer integration but a much-expanded idea of justice, often proclaimed in the name of Black Power.

In the 1960s, African-Americans took four crucial steps that dramatically changed their nation. First, Southern blacks took a stand against racial segregation, discrimination, and their relative public submission to the racist status quo; they formed an organized mass movement. Second, African-American activists in the North and South convinced the Democratic Party and the federal government to put racial equality and social justice among their highest priorities. Third, a powerful faction of activists and their supporters convinced the federal government that remedies for centuries of racist practices based on individual relief were not sufficient and that radical solutions would be necessary. And finally, by the late 1960s, many African-Americans rejected the ideal of a color-blind, melting-pot society and began to fight the legacies of oppression and racism by organizing a multifaceted program of black nationalism or Black Power. The United States would feel the impact of these actions.

None of these immense social changes, of course, had its origins in the 1960s. African-Americans had been struggling for freedom and power since colonial times. They had fought for emancipation from slavery and then again, in the post-Civil War years, to ensure themselves of genuine freedom. Even in the first decades of the twentieth century, when hooded Ku Klux Klansmen paraded down streets across America, not only in the South, some African-Americans had (as one older 1960s activist described his father in Columbia, South Carolina) "held their ground outside on their porches, brandishing shotguns."

In the long, hard years that followed Reconstruction, African-

Americans had picketed, boycotted, and marched. Many had followed champions of black nationalism like Marcus Garvey and some, a smaller group, had paid their dues to the integrationist National Association for the Advancement of Colored People (NAACP). The movement of the 1950s and the 1960s was built on years of struggle.

To understand the development and fragmentation of the African-American movement for social justice in the 1960s, one must understand two key points. First, black America had never been, and was not in the post-World War II years, one place; Southern blacks and Northern blacks lived in very different worlds. As a partial result, the struggles for racial justice that radically escalated in the 1960s would follow different courses in the two regions. So, too, the many other divisions among African-Americans—socioeconomic, skin color, religious background, gender, age—would determine how individuals and communities participated in the dramatic change in race relations that swept America in the 1960s.

Many of the factors that divided African-Americans in the United States were for the first years of the 1960s ignored by both white supremacists and by many civil rights activists. Racists wanted to believe that all African-Americans were fundamentally the same. In the pseudoscientific gobbledygook of the white supremacists, "Negroes' " shared "blood" made them all members of the same lowly "race." But the majority of African-American activists, for completely different reasons, also championed the idea of a single black America. They saw in black unity the power to create progress for all black people. By the mid-1960s this papering over of real differences among African-Americans would result in the implosion of the civil rights movement.

Second, to understand what African-Americans and their allies did and did not accomplish in the 1960s, it is crucial to understand, even in a superficial way, the historical forces and interests they confronted. Racism is not a timeless fact; it has a history. Racism is a relationship between people, made by people, to various ends. From the end of Reconstruction (1877) until late in the New Deal, the African-American struggle was intentionally blocked by powerful interrelated interests and forces. Racism was one of their most effective tools in maintaining and expanding their own power.

By the end of World War II, the racial equation in the United States had begun a dramatic change. By 1960, many of the forces that maintained the traditional system of racial subjugation in the United States had been seriously weakened.

One fundamental change was that African-Americans had begun to vote with their feet against the South's Jim Crow system. High demand for workers in the World War II industrial buildup allowed African-Americans to migrate North and West—a process which had begun in the World War I era but which had been stopped by the economic downturn of the 1930s. By 1960 about 40 percent of all African-Americans lived outside the South.

In the North, racism was widespread but not unanswerable. In the North, black citizens voted, they had elected representatives, they served on juries. They exercised their constitutional rights by picketing stores in the black community that refused to hire African-Americans and by speaking out against discrimination. Chapters of African-American civil rights groups, most important the NAACP, met openly and raised funds aggressively. Progress was slow but the fight had been joined.

In the postwar years, the Southern economy also was undergoing a rapid transformation which had a far-reaching impact on race relations. As large landholders, who had been instrumental in creating Jim Crow laws and subjugating African-Americans, further mechanized their farms in the 1940s, millions of African-Americans were pushed off the land. While many went up North, more moved into Southern towns and cities. The social and economic dislocation was difficult to cope with, but it also created new opportunities and possibilities for struggle.

Jane Pickman, who joined the civil rights movement as a young girl in Montgomery, Alabama, explains the problem African-Americans still had in the South in the early 1950s: "Many of the jobs held by black folks were working for white folks as farmworkers or household help. So black folks usually never did things that would upset them because they did not want to lose their jobs . . . they needed them to put food on their tables and clothes on their families' backs." African-Americans' ability to find work outside the direct control of local white employers (most of whom opposed giving African-Americans their civil rights) was important to the growth of the movement. Northern job opportunities gave African-Americans some leverage on their employers even in the South—if treated too badly, they might join the mass migration—but the changes in the Southern labor market contributed directly.

In the 1950s, some African-Americans were finding work—almost always at the bottom of the wage scale—at the rapidly proliferating military bases and factories the Cold War military-industrial buildup had brought to the South. These new opportunities, as well as the large-scale movement of black Southerners from the countryside to the cities and towns, began incrementally to change relations between black and white Southerners. As historian Bruce Schulman writes, by 1960, the federal government had led the way in sowing "the seeds" of a new Southern economy linked not to plantation life but to the needs of the national market. The economic underpinnings of racism were being transformed by the South's growing participation in the national economy. By the late 1950s, the South's economic progress depended, in part, on federal programs and contracts, as well as interregional and international trade.

By 1960, the federal government had become a dynamic, intervening force in American life. The radical growth in government capacity and actions underwritten by New Deal social welfare and regulatory reforms, coupled with the centralization of power in Washington, increased by World War II and the Cold War, opened the door to a radical reappraisal of the federal government's role in protecting the basic rights and liberties of every American. By the late 1930s, federal courts committed to New Deal social and economic reforms reversed earlier decisions that had restricted federal intervention in state, local, and corporate affairs. Before 1960, the White House offered African-Americans no true champion of the civil rights struggle. But President Truman, willingly (as he proved in 1948 when he ordered the armed forces desegregated despite often hysterical protests by military leaders), and President Eisenhower, begrudgingly, found themselves increasingly caught up with the civil rights struggle. White House concerns about America's image abroad, especially in the Third World, the federal government's expanding powers, and strong lobbying and legal victories by the NAACP had begun to make the civil rights struggle a national political issue.

The only factor that really had not changed on the federal level by 1960 was the power of the very senior Southern Democratic members of Congress. Beneficiaries of the South's one-party system, they remained chairmen of the most powerful congressional committees and intractable enemies of racial equality before the law. But even their power was waning, due both to the rise of liberal Southern representatives and to the efforts of an increasingly large bloc of antiracist Northern and Western congressmen.

By 1960, Americans were rethinking the racist ideology that had passed for common sense for decades. Biological, behavioral, and social scientists, often funded by America's leading philanthropic foundations, had demolished the pseudoscientific doctrines of the early twentieth century. The battle against Nazism had caused some Americans to reconsider their own form of racism. For example, the Brooklyn Dodgers' general manager, Branch Rickey, looking to help his team but also believing that New Yorkers were ready for equal opportunity on the ball field, had signed Jackie Robinson in 1946 and so broken baseball's color line. By 1960, racist acts were still commonplace in both the North and the South, but among a majority of white Northerners, racism and racial segregation had stopped being simply a matter of uncontested common sense.

The change in racial ideology was hammered home in the series of Supreme Court rulings that was climaxed in *Brown* v. *Board of Education* in 1954. The NAACP, in a campaign begun years earlier, had found enough courageous African-American families in the South to challenge state-mandated school segregation. These black families (several of which were economically devastated as a result of bringing suit) and their lawyers argued that legally segregated schools were by definition inferior schools whose sole purpose was to isolate and exclude black children and thus denigrate and demoralize them. The Supreme Court, rejecting the narrow definition of federalism established some fifty-eight years earlier in *Plessy* v. *Ferguson* together with the racism that informed it, agreed with the plaintiffs. In a subsequent ruling, the Court decreed that states must end legally mandated school segregation and integrate their school systems "with all deliberate speed."

The Court had made a monumental ruling but it received no backing at the White House. Southern governors and state officials, unsure of what to make of the ruling, took heart from President Eisenhower's opposition to *Brown*. Approximately 250,000 Southern whites formed Citizens Councils to oppose the desegregation of schools. Even more ominous, the nearly defunct Ku Klux Klan was revived by the ruling. By the late 1950s Klansmen promoted and participated in hundreds of violent and murderous attacks on African-Americans, almost all of which went unprosecuted by Southern state and local officials. The federal government under Eisenhower did little about the violence or the flouting of the *Brown* decision. The result was that in 1960 over 99 percent of Southern black schoolchildren still attended state segregated schools.

Many African-American activists believed that while they had won a great legal battle, actual civil rights reforms and effective social justice measures would be achieved only through their own efforts. In 1955 and 1956, a powerful step in that direction was taken by the entire black community in Montgomery, Alabama, when they supported NAACP stalwart Rosa Parks, who had been arrested for refusing to sit in the back of a city bus. The successful Montgomery bus boycott did more than end seating discrimination. As boycotter Jane Pickman said: "It showed me that we black folks have the power to make a difference if we come together and combine our strength." African-Americans in Montgomery had shown the way in 1956, but until the sit-ins of 1960 the means by which a mass movement could be organized proved elusive.

Not that the last years of the 1950s were a fallow time. In 1957, the NAACP and other civil rights activists did push Congress into passing the first civil rights bill since Reconstruction. Though the bill did relatively little in practical terms—"soup made from the shadow of a thin chicken that had starved to death," in the words of NAACP lobbyist Roy Wilkins—it was a sign that even Congress, long under the control of Southern officeholders, could be moved by effective pressure. The question civil rights activists struggled to answer in the late 1950s was how to exert that pressure.

Martin Luther King, Jr., just twenty-six years old when he became leader of the Montgomery bus boycott, offered the most visionary answer. King seemed, at first, an unlikely prophet. A short, handsome man, who loved a good joke almost as much as flirting with a pretty woman, King had done little before Montgomery to suggest that he would become the nation's most powerful bearer of freedom's call. Not that Martin King, even at twenty-six, was without obvious gifts.

He had grown up in the church, son of one of black Atlanta's most prominent ministers. After graduating from all-black Morehouse College, he had gone up North to the integrated Crozer Theological Seminary, and then—taking some very questionable shortcuts—received a Ph.D. in theology from Boston University. By the time he accepted his first full-time pulpit in Montgomery, Martin Luther King, Jr., was known throughout the small world of the Negro Baptist Church as a gifted preacher capable of both erudition and a fiery rhetoric of spiritual uplift. But no one saw the young minister as a civil rights firebrand.

In Montgomery, it was E. D. Nixon, the working-class leader of the local NAACP chapter, and Jo Anne Robinson, the well-educated head of the black Women's Political Caucus, who would first organize the bus boycott. King came on as leader of the boycott only at the strong urging of the plainspoken E. D. Nixon. But it would be King, helped and counseled by many, who would find within himself the direction the civil rights movement would take.

Reverend King saw the world, above all else, through the teachings of Jesus. He believed that society could be made whole only through the power of love and suffering, and he believed firmly in the idea that every person was the child of God and could be reached through the power of love. Reverend King preached that through nonviolent protest African-Americans could change not only racist laws but racists' hearts and convince the apathetic majority of white Americans that moral right lay on the side of the civil rights movement.

King's Christian message of redemption through nonviolent resistance to evil was given political potency by the practical example of Mohandas Gandhi, whose resistance to British colonial rule of India inspired King (he even visited India in 1959 to learn more about Gandhi's practice of nonviolent protest). King was not the first civil rights leader to take inspiration from Gandhi. In 1941, A. Philip Randolph had borrowed from Gandhi in devising a mass march on Washington, D.C., the mere threat of which had forced Franklin Roosevelt to order—if not fully implement —the desegregation of war work during World War II. For several decades, in fact, civil rights leaders had quietly debated the possibility of using nonviolent techniques, including acts of civil disobedience, in their struggle.

Civil rights protesters who chose nonviolent civil disobedience as a way to fight segregation and discrimination found themselves challenging both white and black Americans' notions of respectability and political legitimacy. Taylor Branch, in his masterful history of the civil rights movement, *Parting the Waters*, explains the practical and intellectual problems prospective nonviolent protesters faced, when he describes Rosa Parks's conscious decision to be arrested: "It was not possible for her to think lightly of being arrested. Having crossed the line that in polite society divided Negroes from niggers, she had reason to expect not only stinging disgrace among her own people but the least civilized attentions of whites." Rosa Parks and those who would follow her example willingly broke laws they believed to be immoral because it was the only means available to them to challenge the *moral* legitimacy of the lawmakers. They declared that, in the case of racial decorum, respectable behavior was not to be earned by being law-abiding but by being a lawbreaker. They argued that only through disorder and disrespect for the existing civil order could a genuinely civil society be created. According to Martin

Luther King, Jr., and other civil rights advocates, in the American South the laws were unjust, the legal authorities lacked moral legitimacy, and the whole social and civil order that demanded that blacks willingly accept their own subordination was without proper authority. In this rejection of both the political legitimacy of the standing order and the cultural authority of "respectable" society lay seeds of the most explosive confrontations of the 1960s.

The four young men who started the Greensboro sit-in brought all of these grand and worthy abstractions down to the concrete, just as Rosa Parks had done. Dressed in suits and ties, always polite, they resolutely broke the law and refused to bow to racial decorum or to accept black submissiveness to white authority. "I'd like a cup of coffee, please," the protest began.

In Nashville, which became the focal point for the sit-in movement, the means by which a protester should politely refuse to accept the legal bounds set by civil society were carefully codified. James Lawson, a longtime student of Gandhian nonviolence, explained: "Do show yourself friendly on the counter at all times. Do sit straight and always face the counter. Don't strike back or curse back if attacked." With discipline, the protesters were turning American society on its head.

The ranks of the sit-ins were overwhelmingly drawn from the approximately 200,000 Southern black college students—not one of whom was yet able to attend the all-white public state universities below the Mason-Dixon line. Within the black community these young people had much to lose. As college students, they already had won a ticket to the tiny black middle class. Getting arrested and possibly beaten by white bystanders or the police threatened the respectability many of them had worked for all their young lives.

On the other hand, these young students had the most to gain. More than anyone, they were aware of how low a ceiling stood above their ambitions. To reemphasize: in the South no African-American held political office, no blacks worked as lawyers, doctors, engineers, or executives in white-owned businesses or firms. During the week of the first sit-in, the *Atlanta Constitution*, in its race- and gender-segregated want ads, offered black men exactly three jobs: car washer, custodian, and broiler cook. African-American women saw six listings for maids, and openings for a salad girl, a laundress, and a babysitter. And Atlanta prided itself on being the most "progressive" city in the South. African-American college students risked their toehold in the fragile black middle class, but they stood to gain a new world.

The Southern Christian Leadership Conference (SCLC), the civil rights organization which had grown out of the Montgomery boycott, immediately responded to the students' determination and grit. Reverend Fred Shuttlesworth, the first SCLC leader on the scene, reported that the sit-ins had the power to "shake up the world." The SCLC's executive secretary, Ella Baker, who had been a political activist before most of the protesters had been born, agreed and immediately set to work to help the young protesters explore the power they had unleashed.

Since Baker had become involved with the SCLC in 1957 she had been trying to get King and the other ministers who led the organization to move more rapidly and in a more focused fashion. She also had her doubts about the ministers' big-*man*-at-the-pulpit style of leadership. Baker wanted to organize men *and women* to become their own leaders, to become—in a word that would define much of the student activism of the 1960s—empowered. She explained: "Instead of the leader, a person who was supposed to be a magic man, you would develop individuals who were bound together by a concept that provided an opportunity for them to grow into being responsible . . . provide for a sense of achievement and recognition for many people, particularly local leadership." Baker organized a conference in April 1960 to help the young protesters to, in her carefully chosen words, "SHARE experience gained in recent protest demonstrations and TO HELP chart future goals for effective action."

Many of the younger generation's most dedicated and gifted activists attended this conference: James Lawson, Marion Barry, Julian Bond, John Lewis, Diane Nash, and many others. With Baker's support, the young people formed the Student Nonviolent

Coordinating Committee (SNCC), which would more than any other organization between 1960 and 1966 shape both white and black student protest in the United States.

As SNCC activists discovered how ingrained racism and poverty were in America, they would begin on a painful path that led many of them to espouse revolutionary violence. But in the spring of 1960, SNCC's leaders attacked the Jim Crow South with an almost romantic dream of Good triumphing over Evil through simple courage and undeniable virtue. Despite a warning speech by Ella Baker about the range of social and economic problems that confronted African-Americans, few of the young people at SNCC's founding could imagine what lay ahead. As Julian Bond, one of SNCC's most articulate organizers, wryly observed: "We were just not ready. . . . To our mind, lunch counter segregation was the greatest evil facing black people in the country and if we could eliminate it, we would be like gods."

To a small group of white college students, the SNCC activists were almost like gods—heroes certainly. Tom Hayden, editor of the University of Michigan student newspaper in 1960, was galvanized by the SNCC activists he met at a student conference: "They lived on a fuller level of feeling than any people I'd ever seen, partly because they were making history in a very personal way, and partly because by risking death they came to know the value of living each moment to the fullest. . . . I wanted to live like them." Hundreds and then thousands of white students, in the South as well as the North, sought ways to join what more and more people were calling the Movement.

Between the spring of 1960 and the summer of 1963, the civil rights movement exploded throughout the United States. While grounded in nonviolent protests against racial segregation and discrimination, the Movement became for many of the activists, both young and old, more than just a new kind of political action. It became a way of life, an embodiment, many felt, of the Christian ideal of a "Beloved Community." Much of the culture of this new community was carried through music. Songs like "We Shall Not Be Moved," "Keep Your Eye on the Prize," "This Little Light of Mine," and, most famously, "We Shall Overcome" became anthems of a people united in hope and action.

Segregationists responded to the sit-ins and subsequent protests unpredictably. In Greensboro, the first sit-in protesters were left alone. In Nashville, whites brutally abused the nonviolent protesters, putting out cigarettes on their backs and pouring ketchup over their heads. In Orangeburg, South Carolina, on a bitterly cold day, police turned fire hoses on the protesters and jailed 350 freezing young people in a chicken coop. Despite the abuse they received, the protesters maintained their nonviolent way and their dignity. Even James Kilpatrick, the segregationist editor of the *Richmond News Leader*, could not help but compare the protesting black students, "in coats, white shirts, ties," and their white antagonists, "a ragtail rabble, slack-jawed, black-jacketed, grinning fit to kill." This picture was the one the civil rights movement wanted white America to ponder.

The sit-ins became national news, forcing many whites to begin grappling with the "race issue." Too, they provided the means by which hundreds of thousands of African-Americans moved from bystander to participant. In practical terms, though, they brought limited change only in some of the towns and cities in which they had been launched. As Ella Baker had warned the young activists, more—much more—needed to be done.

In May 1961, James Farmer, of the Congress of Racial Equality (CORE), in an attempt to up the pressure in the South, organized "Freedom Rides." Supported by the NAACP and the SCLC, a small interracial group would travel by public buses through the Deep South, manifestly to test federal court orders which had desegregated interstate bus terminals. Farmer, who had been practicing Gandhian nonviolent protest tactics for many years, knew that the Freedom Riders would be met by violent whites. He wanted those confrontations, despite their grave implications for the Freedom Riders' physical safety. Only by creating a crisis, he knew, could he attract the white mass media and, more important, involve the White House.

As Farmer expected, almost everywhere the Freedom Riders

stopped in the Deep South, they were attacked. In Birmingham, the violence was particularly horrible. Birmingham police had made a secret agreement with the Ku Klux Klan to give Klansmen fifteen uninterrupted minutes to beat the Freedom Riders. The FBI knew of the arrangement and did nothing to stop it.

Stories and photos of the Freedom Riders' martyrdom flashed across the world. In Tokyo, where some of Birmingham's leading businessmen were trying to interest investors in their community, the beatings were headline news. Klan violence, Birmingham's "leading citizens" discovered, made for a terrible climate to attract investment. As *The Wall Street Journal* quoted one businessman, the violence gave the entire city "a black eye." Though few, if any, of Birmingham's leading whites believed in racial integration, the business community knew that at least some changes were going to have to be made.

President Kennedy also knew that his approach to the civil rights movement would have to change. The President was, in a general way, supportive of the goals and aspirations of the Movement. During the election campaign he had promised African-American audiences that he would work for their cause. Just before the election, he had won warm support from many for calling Martin Luther King's wife when King had been jailed in Georgia. And once in office, Kennedy did immediately improve on Eisenhower's sorry civil rights record.

Still, Kennedy resisted the civil rights activists' requests that he intensify the federal government's involvement in their struggle. He issued no significant executive orders and would not introduce any civil rights legislation. And while he appointed African-American judges in Northern courts, he also appointed a greater number of fiercely racist white judges to Southern courts. Kennedy, like Democratic Presidents before him, worried about alienating the large and powerful white Southern wing of his party. President Kennedy had his sights set on the Cold War, and he was not interested in losing support for his foreign policy initiatives over what were in his mind less important domestic issues. President Kennedy would have to be pushed into playing a forceful role in the civil rights arena by the Movement.

In Montgomery, the Freedom Riders began to push that role upon President Kennedy. Alabama governor John Patterson had assured the Justice Department's John Seigenthaler that "he had the means, the ability, and the will to preserve law and order" when the Freedom Riders arrived in Montgomery. But he had lied.

In Montgomery, the police again allowed a white mob to beat the nonviolent Freedom Riders. A dozen men knocked a white volunteer, Jim Zwerg, senseless. Then they systematically knocked out his teeth. John Lewis was clubbed unconscious. When Justice Department representative Seigenthaler tried to intervene he was hit on the head with a steel pipe and then stomped while he lay on the ground unconscious. Whites in the crowd held up their children so they could watch racial decorum being preserved.

On the basis of a little-known statute in the United States Code, an angry President Kennedy issued a finding that law and order had broken down in Montgomery. Using powers granted him by the Constitution, he ordered the Justice Department to restore order. Governor Patterson was furious and vented an argument that had helped preserve white supremacy in the South since the end of Reconstruction: "We don't want the assistance of the federal government . . . and we don't believe that the United States has any legal or constitutional right to come in here. . . . Your presence . . . will only further complicate and aggravate the situation and worsent [sic] federal-state relations." But President Kennedy had had enough violence, and despite very real qualms about increasing the federal role in the civil rights struggle, he sent U.S. marshals to Montgomery against the wishes of Alabama's elected officials. The Freedom Riders had paid a great price but they had forced the federal government to choose their side in the struggle for racial justice in the Deep South. Still, Kennedy remained a reluctant ally.

Attorney General Robert Kennedy revealed the limits of federal support when he made a secret compromise with ultrasegregationist Mississippi governor Ross Barnett. In exchange for the governor's promise to protect the Freedom Riders as they moved into Mississippi, Kennedy agreed not to involve the federal government when Barnett had the Freedom Riders arrested for trying to integrate the Jackson bus terminal. The Freedom Riders and then hundreds more who came to support their efforts—many of them SNCC activists—were jailed in Mississippi's nightmarish Parchman Penitentiary.

Angry and impatient with the Freedom Riders' version of domestic brinkmanship, the Kennedy brothers urged SNCC organizers and other young activists to stop their campaign of direct confrontation. The confrontations, Kennedy administration officials argued, were turning off white support in both the North and the South, hurting the Democratic Party, and offering little in the way of practical returns. The Kennedys knew that the violent racism the Freedom Rides exposed provided Soviet Premier Khrushchev with a propaganda bonanza.

The Kennedys argued that the Movement should turn to a massive voter registration campaign which could bring black Southerners legal and political power. Kennedy officials promised the activists financial support—through Northern philanthropic foundations—and Justice Department help.

SNCC activists had misgivings. Compared to the nonviolent strategy of confrontation the registration work seemed, to many of the activists, politically and morally compromised. Still, they decided to go ahead. Robert Moses, who had begun voter registration work in Mississippi even before Kennedy administration inducements or SNCC's collective decision, would help to convince the Movement that they had chosen well.

Robert Moses offered a vision of social change many of the Movement's young activists found even more appealing than Martin Luther King's vision. Soft-spoken, always more interested in listening than talking, Moses believed that his role was not to lead others but to help people lead themselves. He worked not from the pulpit but on the front porch, gently working with local people. He saw voter registration as a means of inspiring poor and intimidated people to fight against centuries of brutal oppression. He was far less interested in winning over the President than he was in organizing the poor black people of the Mississippi Delta.

Moses believed that ordinary people working together, not charismatic leadership, was what the Movement needed—indeed, was what the Movement existed to facilitate. Moses's practical organizing was what Ella Baker had hoped for when she urged the young sit-in activists to form SNCC. Operating out of the small, impoverished towns of the rural Deep South, Moses and hundreds of other SNCC activists fought to make the civil rights struggle a people's struggle for self-respect, social justice, and empowerment. Joined by white volunteers from the North and the South, SNCC activists focused on recruiting local African-Americans who could become effective, long-term community organizers.

While Robert Moses avoided center stage in order to make room for local leadership and participation, everyone with whom he worked saw in him a quiet exemplar of moral courage. "Bob took a lot of beatings," a McComb, Mississippi, resident observed. ". . . Sometimes I think he was Moses in the Bible. He pioneered the way for black people in McComb. . . . He had more guts than any one man I've ever known."

While the young activists increasingly worked with local people in the Deep South against Jim Crow laws and racial violence, Martin Luther King and the older civil rights leadership searched for an effective strategy. In 1962, King and SCLC tried to piggyback on a SNCC-led direct-action campaign against racial segregation in Albany, Georgia, but with little success. The Albany police chief had learned from his fellow officers' mistakes. He ordered his men to use no violence against the demonstrators and not to allow other whites to harm the nonviolent marchers. Instead, the chief just kept arresting the protesters, filling the local jail and then jails throughout the region. He refused to give the protesters the violent confrontation that would have produced national attention or White House intervention. He also gave pause to those with the moral vision that gave hope that nonviolent protests could change the heart, as well as the laws, of the white South. Chief Laurie Pritchett smilingly explained to SNCC leader Charles Sherrod the vision of social justice that informed his treat-

ment of civil rights protesters—he called it "mind over matter.
. . . I don't mind and you don't matter." It was ugly but it worked:
the Albany protest resulted in little tangible change and got little
media coverage. The Albany debacle intensified angry debates
among SNCC activists, the SCLC hierarchy, and the traditional
black leadership in the NAACP over questions of leadership and
direction of the struggling civil rights movement.

Martin Luther King and the Movement were by 1962 coming
under tremendous pressure from an unexpected source. J. Edgar
Hoover, long head of the FBI, had decided that the civil rights
movement in general and King in particular were agents of international Communism. The charge was ludicrous. No proof then,
or ever, existed to substantiate such a bizarre claim. But Hoover,
who seemed to see Communists behind every bush and tree, recognized that a campaign against King would nicely serve his agency's needs in a time of bureaucratic transition. The FBI in 1961
had a crisis on its hands: its primary mission, the destruction of
the American Communist Party, had been accomplished. Despite
the impotence of the Communist Party in the United States, in
1961 Hoover still had over 1,000 FBI agents on full-time "political
security work"—compared with just 12 looking into organized
crime (some historians have argued that Hoover left organized
crime alone because he was blackmailed by gangsters who had
proof of his secret homosexuality). Hoover, a bureaucratic
genius, knew that the FBI needed a new focal point for its anti-
Communism. The FBI director, who had made sure that at this
time not a single black person served as an FBI agent, saw the
civil rights movement as subversive to law and order in the United
States. By his logic, King, as its leader, was the number one
subversive in the nation. Having so defined King as a subversive,
it was just a short step to defining him as a Communist or Communist dupe. J. Edgar Hoover and the FBI would for the rest of
King's life do almost everything they could to destroy his reputation and tear apart the civil rights movement. Both President
Kennedy and President Johnson permitted Hoover to work his
obsessive evil—in part because they feared the Machiavellian Hoo-

ver and in part because they resented the political problems the Movement created for them. The many fiefdoms of the federal government pushed and pulled in different directions throughout the civil rights era.

While Hoover plotted, and President Kennedy worried about Communist Cuba, and Martin Luther King looked for a breakthrough, James Meredith seized the historical stage. In September 1962, the twenty-eight-year-old black Air Force veteran attempted to register at the all-white University of Mississippi. Despite a federal court order ruling that he could not be denied admission because of his skin color, Mississippi governor Ross Barnett, the scourge of the Freedom Riders, personally blocked Meredith's attempt to register at the school. The Justice Department intervened on Meredith's behalf. Governor Barnett not only fought the Justice Department's effort to implement the court desegregation order but at halftime at an Ole Miss football game led tens of thousands of students in a white supremacy rally.

In order to get Meredith into the university, President Kennedy ordered some five hundred U.S. marshals to accompany him. A thousand students, eventually joined by thousands of other whites from across Mississippi, attacked the marshals with guns, gasoline bombs, bricks, and pipes. In a battle that lasted all night, a London newspaperman and a local man were killed by the mob. In all, 160 marshals received serious wounds.

President Kennedy was at last forced to call in the Army to restore order (not surprisingly, some of the soldiers, at first, thought they were on their way to invade Cuba). But aside from forcing Kennedy to use federal power against intransigent Southern officials—and alerting the nation to the ferocity of a sizable number of white supremacists—the "integration" of Ole Miss, again, led to no real change in Kennedy's policy or the civil rights movement's agenda.

In late 1962, Martin Luther King, Jr., and the SCLC leadership were ready to take a risky gamble. The Movement was not failing—by 1963 approximately a million people had participated in about 900 nonviolent campaigns of direct action—but it was stalled. And at a personal level, King's leadership of the Movement was weakening. He and the Movement needed a concrete victory.

King and SCLC decided to stake the future of their leadership on Birmingham, Alabama, perhaps the most segregated city in the South. Between 1957 and 1963, "Bombingham" (as some of its African-American residents called their city) had suffered over 50 Ku Klux Klan cross burnings and 18 racially motivated bombings. Police commissioner Bull Connor, who'd allowed the Klan free rein in beating the Freedom Riders in 1961, used the all-white police force to terrorize the African-American community, which made up 40 percent of Birmingham's population. The city's eminent civil rights activist, Reverend Fred Shuttlesworth, assured King that in Birmingham they would have the dramatic confrontation the Movement needed to capture the nation's full attention.

Project C (C for confrontation) began slowly in April 1963. Many local black leaders resisted the campaign. Months earlier, some of them had joined with leading members of the white business community in an effort to legally remove Bull Connor and other notorious racists from office. The first protests, in fact, gained only little support.

Still, King, Shuttlesworth, and other SCLC ministers pushed forward. In mid-April, King defied a state court injunction against further protest marches and was jailed. From his cell, King wrote one of the Movement's most powerful defenses of nonviolent civil disobedience, aimed directly at the hearts of fence-sitting white moderates:

> When you have seen vicious mobs lynch your mothers and fathers at will and drown your sisters at whim; when you have seen hate-filled policemen curse, kick, brutalize and even kill your black brothers and sisters with impunity; when you see the vast majority of your twenty million Negro brothers smothering in an airtight cage of poverty in the midst of an affluent society . . . then you will understand why we find it difficult to wait. . . . I have almost reached the regrettable conclusion that the Negro's great stumbling block is not the White Citizens Council-er or the Ku Klux Klanner

but the white moderate who is more devoted to "order" than to justice.

In early May, after hundreds of adult demonstrators had been more or less peacefully arrested by Bull Connor's police, the Movement leadership took yet another tack. Running out of adult participants and, more critically, time, SCLC organized marches of schoolchildren. On May 2, 600 teenagers and children as young as six were stuffed into jammed jail cells. On May 3, 1,000 more children assembled to march. This time Bull Connor knew that his jails were full and he unleashed his forces.

First, fire hoses were turned on the children. Streams of water with enough pressure to strip bark off trees knocked schoolchildren off their feet and sent them crashing into brick walls. Black millionaire A. G. Gaston, who had been trying for weeks to get King and the protest leaders out of his city, turned on the city's white negotiator: "But, lawyer Vann! They've turned the fire hoses on a little black girl. And they're rolling that girl right down the middle of the street." Hundreds of African-Americans from Birmingham's meanest streets—who had never shown any interest in the Movement or taken any vows about nonviolence—joined the melee and began throwing rocks at the police. Black Birmingham had united. In response, Bull Connor's police sicced attack dogs on the children.

On television that night the nation watched black boys and girls set upon by German shepherds. CBS reporter Eric Sevareid described the grim reality: "A newspaper or television picture of a snarling police dog set upon a human being is recorded in the permanent photoelectric file of every human brain." Photos from Birmingham appeared in newspapers around the world.

President Kennedy, "sick" from what had happened, demanded that Birmingham's white business and political leaders stop the horrors and negotiate a settlement. Thousands of protesters increased the pressure by sitting in all over the downtown area. Overwhelmed and pressured from all sides, Birmingham's white business leaders agreed to desegregate public accommodations in

Birmingham and to make token improvements in black employment opportunities. The offer, while modest, was a genuine breakthrough, and Martin Luther King announced it to the nation as
"a great victory."

There were troubles still to come when more than a thousand
hooded Klansmen met the next night, vowed to "fight the niggers," and denounced the white businessmen who had signed the
accord. Just after their rally broke up, bombs targeted against the
civil rights leaders exploded. Some members of the black
community—few, if any, of them participants in the protests of
the previous weeks—responded to the bombings and subsequent
police brutality by rioting. Birmingham was a great victory for
the Movement but more violence lay ahead.

In the next ten weeks 758 civil rights demonstrations broke out
around the country. President Kennedy knew he had to do more
both to restore order and to assert leadership. He concluded, at
last, that the time had come to spend some serious political capital.
Just weeks after the Birmingham settlement, Alabama governor
George Wallace gave Kennedy an opportunity to announce a major
change in his civil rights position.

Governor Wallace had decided literally and personally to block
the court-ordered integration of the University of Alabama, the
last all-white state university. Kennedy, who had already played
this dangerous game with Mississippi governor Barnett, used fed-
eralized Alabama National Guard troops to face Wallace down and
safeguard the integration of the university. That night, Kennedy
went on national television to explain why he had called out troops
on a state governor and where he stood on the nation's racial
crisis:

> We are confronted primarily with a moral issue. It is as old as the
> Scriptures and is as clear as the American Constitution. The heart
> of the question is whether all Americans can be afforded equal rights
> and equal opportunities, whether we are going to treat our fellow
> Americans as we want to be treated. . . . Are we to say to the
> world—and much more importantly to each other—that this is the
> land of the free, except for Negroes, that we have no second-class

citizens, except Negroes . . . no master race, except with respect
to Negroes?

Now the time has come for this nation to fulfill its promise. . . .
We face, therefore, a moral crisis as a country and as a people.
. . . A great change is at hand and our task, our obligation, is to
make that revolution, that change, peaceful and constructive for all.

President Kennedy told the nation that he would introduce in
Congress legislation that would guarantee all Americans the right
to be served at public facilities and that would give the Justice
Department authority to bring lawsuits against school districts
that segregate students and state and local governments that restrict
black voter registration. Not since Reconstruction had a President
of the United States so strongly linked his political fortunes to the
fate of African-Americans. The civil rights movement had succeeded in enlisting the President and the head of the Democratic
Party in its cause.

As was so often true throughout the 1960s, victory by the forces
of social justice was paid for in blood. Only hours after Kennedy's
speech, Medgar Evers, head of the Mississippi NAACP, tired after
a grim meeting discussing the fate of the Movement in Jackson,
stepped out of his car. As his three children ran to greet him, an
assassin shot him in the back. "Please, Daddy, please get up!" his
children cried as they watched their father die.

5. THE LIBERAL DREAM AND
ITS NIGHTMARE

~~~~~~

ON AUGUST 28, 1963, 250,000 people gathered at the Lincoln Memorial in Washington, D.C. Movement leaders had organized a mass rally to support the civil rights legislation the President had at last proposed. More broadly, they meant to issue a sweeping call for "jobs and freedom," to remind the nation of how much still needed to be done to create genuine racial equality. Black and white together, people had traveled far to celebrate their movement and to demonstrate their commitment to a continuing struggle.

In the final moments of a memorable day no one would have predicted even three years earlier, Martin Luther King, Jr., departed from his prepared remarks and voiced a prophetic call: "I have a dream my four little children will one day live in a nation where they will not be judged by the color of their skin but by the content of their character. I have a dream today!" In simple terms, King offered the American people a vision of a color-blind society. In the powerful spiritual and moral language that marked his leadership of the Movement, he offered Americans a gift of their own best nature revealed.

As a sign of how far the Movement had come, all three television networks carried King's complete address live. Most television news executives and producers at the national level had long sympathized with the integrationist goals of the civil rights movement. By 1963, they—like President Kennedy—had chosen to risk the anger of Southern whites in the name of what they saw as a greater national good.

Before King's "I have a dream" speech few Americans had heard more than snippets of his oratory. With live coverage, millions heard King's full prophetic power and were moved. Nancy Rosenthal, a white Northerner with two small children, was galvanized by King's "dream." She called the local branch of the Urban League the next day and volunteered to do whatever she could to contribute. Public opinion polls taken in the days after the peaceful rally showed that millions of Americans, weighing recent events, looked with new favor upon the civil rights movement.

The moral charge of the Movement against the forces of white supremacy was underlined days later in Birmingham. A bomb, one in what seemed like an endless string of bombings, tore apart the 16th Street Baptist Church. It was Youth Day at the church, and four girls, preparing to lead Sunday services, dressed all in white, were killed by the explosion.

The martyrdom of the young girls revealed to many Americans the true nature of the moral forces in the battle for the nation's soul. In the minds of a growing number of African-Americans, it revealed, too, the limits of nonviolence. Writer James Baldwin spoke out in the aftermath of the bombing: "The only time that nonviolence has been admired is when the Negroes practice it."

Few Americans realized that even in the Movement's hours of greatness in Washington growing tensions were splitting the civil rights movement apart. SNCC activists, most particularly, were frustrated by what they saw as their elders' caution and co-optation by the half measures of the Kennedy administration. At the March on Washington, SNCC chairman John Lewis had planned to blast the Kennedy administration and the spirit of compromise he believed had taken hold of the civil rights leadership.

Lewis's prepared remarks, written by many SNCC hands, matched King's elevating call for national reconciliation with angry demands for "Justice Now!" He planned to attack the Kennedy civil rights bill as "too little too late," an inadequate instrument that did nothing to protect voter registration workers in the South or "young children and old women from police dogs and fire hoses." Rejecting reconciliation, Lewis meant to slap white Southern segregationists in the face: "We will march through the South, through the heart of Dixie the way Sherman did." After a bitter fight, Lewis was persuaded by the Movement's elders to moderate the speech. But the last-minute changes did not lessen SNCC's growing frustration with White House failures and the Movement's compromises.

SNCC organizers, working at the grass-roots level in the Deep South, were losing faith in the efficacy of nonviolence and, increasingly, in the integrationist agenda. They had been harassed, jailed, beaten, and shot too many times to accept the nonviolent credo that love alone could conquer hate. Working among America's poorest people—86 percent of black Mississippians lived below the poverty line—they now knew that lunch-counter integration and even the vote did not hold all the answers black people needed. They followed the revolutions fought by people of color around the world and wondered if the American capitalist system, with its built-in economic inequalities, served their people. By late 1963 most SNCC organizers were not sure what they believed in, but they knew that their faith in the American government and the moral conscience of white America was weakening fast.

After nearly two years in Mississippi, the SNCC-dominated Voter Education Project had been able to register only about 4,000 black people. Workers faced constant violent attacks, including an attempted assassination of Robert Moses in which a fellow organizer was seriously wounded. The Justice Department and the FBI offered little to no protection. While Moses and other organizers felt that they were slowly winning the trust and participation of local people, they knew by the fall of 1963 that they needed a breakthrough. They would need both strong federal support and a means by which black Mississippians could gain a tangible victory. A white visitor, Allard Lowenstein, suggested an answer to SNCC organizers: a statewide straw vote. While the votes would not elect anyone to office, they would show the nation—and the White House—that black Mississippians wanted to participate in the system. Lowenstein pointed out, too, that the straw vote would not demand actual confrontation with the increasingly violent white community and thus would help SNCC to organize more safely around the state. Lowenstein, a peripatetic organizer who was well connected to liberal Democrats and the inchoate white student movement, also promised to provide white student volunteers.

SNCC organizers worked hard on the scheme. That fall of 1963, 80,000 black Mississippians risked economic and physical retribution and turned out to vote for the "Freedom Party." In part because of the teams of white volunteers, the campaign garnered both publicity in Northern newspapers and a modicum of protection by the FBI. The small project's great success convinced Moses, in consultation with Lowenstein, to form an expanded "Freedom Summer" program for 1964. Instead of a few dozen white volunteers, Moses would bring 1,000 white students down to Mississippi to help coordinate a massive voter turnout. Moses and other backers of the plan believed white volunteers would focus the nation's attention on conditions in Mississippi. And if some of the whites were attacked—and Moses knew that was likely—then maybe the FBI, the Justice Department, and the rest of white America would finally do something about the white violence black organizers faced every day.

Some SNCC organizers protested Moses's plan. They worried that black organizers would be displaced by the better-educated white college students. They argued that local blacks, long forced into a role of racial submission, would be intimidated by the white volunteers and lose faith in their own abilities. Since black Mississippians had been deprived of a decent education and training for generations, many black organizers in Mississippi worried about the impact the upper-middle-class white students would have on black people's self-confidence.

Robert Moses disagreed: "I always thought the one thing we can do for the country that no one else can do is to be above the race issue." Despite much concern among the activists, the plan went forward.

In the summer of 1964 over 1,000 young people came to work in Mississippi. Most came from the North and an extraordinary number came from privileged backgrounds. Many saw themselves as "Kennedy's Children," called to "greatness" by the rush of world events. But where Kennedy had focused on America's international foes, these young people looked to the threat within. Warned by SNCC organizers of the dangers they faced in Mississippi, they came anyway, willing to risk their lives. Hundreds of lawyers, clergymen, and health professionals joined them. Few volunteers were unchanged by their Freedom Summer.

Freedom Summer began with a nightmare. On June 21, while investigating the burning of a church, two white workers, Michael Schwerner and Andrew Goodman, and local black activist James Chaney were grabbed by a Neshoba County deputy sheriff and then released into the hands of a Klan mob. The two whites were quickly shot and killed. James Chaney was shot three times and beaten with a chain until his bones were shattered. The bodies of the three men were not found for months, but everyone knew when they did not come home that first night that they were dead. One young volunteer expressed what many felt: "We know the blood is going to flow this summer and it's going to be our blood. And I'm scared—I'm very scared."

Four days after the disappearance of Chaney, Goodman, and Schwerner, CBS News anchor Walter Cronkite introduced an evening news story about Freedom Summer by saying that the entire nation was watching events in Mississippi. Then CBS News showed Americans the project workers, white and black together, holding hands, singing "We Shall Overcome." In 1964, America's leading newsmen made sure that Americans were aware of the Deep South's failure to create even elementary racial justice.

By the end of the summer, project workers had been arrested over 1,000 times, been shot at 35 times, suffered 30 bombings and 80 beatings; at least six people were murdered in civil-rights-related events. Despite such unremitting brutality by Mississippi's all-white police forces, the Ku Klux Klan, and other violent whites, Freedom Summer accomplished its primary goal. The project workers organized the Mississippi Freedom Democratic Party (MFDP), an integrated alternative to Mississippi's whites-only regular Democratic Party. Built by local leadership and grass-roots participation, the MFDP planned to go to the 1964 Democratic National Convention and ask to be seated and recognized as the proper representatives of Mississippi's people.

President Lyndon Johnson did not look kindly upon the MFDP plan to unseat Mississippi's Democratic regulars, issues of morality and justice notwithstanding. Johnson had just pushed through Congress the most hard-hitting civil rights legislation the nation had seen since Reconstruction. Johnson had big plans—immense plans—for his first full term in office, having only assumed the presidency in November 1963 after the assassination of Kennedy. He did not want what he saw as a recklessly idealistic, politically naive band of civil rights radicals from Mississippi seriously weakening his carefully laid plan for the convention that would nominate him.

Lyndon Johnson's desire to support the civil rights movement was genuine. Texas born and bred, Johnson saw himself—immodestly, but not without good reason—as the one man in America who could bring racial justice to the South and the South back into the nation. Just days after entering the Oval Office, Johnson had called in his old Senate mentor, the segregationist Georgia senator Richard Russell, and told him it was time for a new era in race relations. "Dick," President Johnson reportedly said, "you've got to get out of my way. I'm going to run over you. I don't intend to cavil or compromise. I don't want to hurt you. But don't stand in my way."

Though Johnson had cast racist votes early in his Senate career, he had never been a staunch segregationist. He was as much a Westerner as a Southerner, and his racial outlook was based not on bred-in-the-bone prejudice or awakened morality but above all on political calculation. As his political power increased over the years, and with his reelection more and more assured, Senator Johnson had moved away from his Southern colleagues and the white racist constituency in Texas. He believed that unless Jim Crow died, an economically resurgent South, beneficial to the vast majority of white and black Southerners, could not be developed. He also knew that no man who advocated legal segregation would appeal to the national constituency needed to win the presidency, an office on which Lyndon Baines Johnson had set his sights.

By the time Johnson had become Kennedy's Vice President he was a moderate advocate of civil rights. But once President, he became more thoroughly committed to the struggle, in part because he believed that ending legal discrimination and racism in the United States would assure his place among the greatest leaders in American history. Lyndon Johnson, unlike John Kennedy, recognized that the civil rights issue was *the* moral issue facing the nation.

John Kennedy, in his final days, had begun moving a major civil rights bill forward. Had he lived he almost certainly would have pushed a breakthrough bill, but he might well have compromised away some of the bill's full power. Johnson, using every trick he had learned as Senate majority leader, forged a coalition of Republicans and Northern and Western Democrats to defeat an eighty-two-day filibuster by Southern senators and thus pass what historian Allen Matusow called "the great liberal achievement of the decade."

The Civil Rights Act of 1964 forever changed America's racial landscape. The omnibus act contained ten titles and ran twenty-eight pages. Title II of the act essentially outlawed racial discrimination at all places of public accommodation, including hotels, restaurants, and theaters. Title VII outlawed discrimination in employment. Other titles legally bound the federal government to cut off funding to any program at any level of the government that was racially discriminatory. The act strengthened the power of the Justice Department to bring suit against segregationists, increased the investigatory power of the Civil Rights Commission, and further involved the federal government in school desegregation. Legal racism, practiced in the South for better than half a century, had now been repudiated by all three branches of the federal government. In order to address the nation's most obvious political, social, and moral failure, the federal government had greatly expanded its authority to intervene in the daily life of every American citizen.

A quick detour is necessary here. And a detour is how most participants in the battle for the passage of the Civil Rights Act of 1964 perceived the seemingly small, last-minute House amendment to Title VII of the omnibus legislation. On the House floor, Howard Smith, an ultrasegregationist congressman from Virginia, insisted that the word "sex" be added to the list of classes or groups protected against employment discrimination. Smith probably hoped the addition of "sex" to the title would prolong debate and perhaps even scuttle the bill. Few male House members had ever seriously considered, let alone condoned, equal employment opportunities for women, regardless of race. Surprisingly, Representative Smith actually had considered the matter and had been for many years a sponsor of an Equal Rights Amendment for women. Many House members, including a great many liberals, wanted to kill the proposed amendment and the "Pandora's box" they thought it would open.

Conservative Republican representative Katherine St. George disagreed with the liberal position. On the House floor she spoke sternly to her often giggling male colleagues: "We want this crumb of equality to correct something that goes back, frankly, to the Dark Ages." Supported by the House's tiny group of women members, the one-word addition survived. To turn that one word into active legal protection would take a political movement which, in 1964, was still struggling to be born.

In fact, passage of the 1964 Civil Rights Act did not end racism and discrimination in any of its forms. The Ku Klux Klan, throughout the Deep South, and often aided by the local police, rained terror on people who tried to use the freedoms the act was supposed to guarantee. Local authorities refused to stop the Klan, let alone prosecute them for the crimes they committed.

President Johnson, furious over the murder of the Freedom Summer workers, demanded that J. Edgar Hoover and the FBI take their vaunted expertise in crime solving and subversive stopping, get down to Mississippi, and produce some law and order. Johnson, who knew better than anyone how to play Washington politics, pressed Hoover by playing to the director's greatest fear, that his beloved bureaucratic turf would be trod upon. Johnson's first move was to send ex-CIA director Allen Dulles down to Mississippi. Johnson knew that Hoover would understand the message: get going or stand aside while somebody else assumes the task.

Until July 10, 1964, Hoover's role in the civil rights movement was limited to harassing Martin Luther King, Jr., and whispering into every available ear that the Movement had "Communist" ties. But some two and a half weeks after the Freedom Summer murders (and two weeks after Dulles's Mississippi mission) Hoover flew to Jackson, Mississippi, and, with much fanfare, opened a new FBI field office. Upon his return to Washington, Hoover directed the FBI to wage full-scale war on the Ku Klux Klan, using all the techniques it had developed in fighting the American Communist Party in the 1940s and 1950s. By 1965, the FBI had planted over 700 informants in the Klan and reported to the Attorney General's office that "we . . . are seizing every opportunity to disrupt the activities of Klan organization." The FBI, engaged at last, almost immediately began to make the Deep South safer for both civil rights activists and the entire African-American population. The directors of Mississippi's Freedom Summer project had, at a great price, forced the FBI to offer them and others some measure of protection. The Justice Department, in the months ahead, would also use federal statutes to bring violent segregationists in the Deep South to justice.

A caveat too important to leave out: J. Edgar Hoover never saw himself or his bureau as allies of the civil rights movement. Even as he waged war on the KKK, Hoover continued his "anti-Communist" campaign against Martin Luther King, Jr., and others in the civil rights movement. His list of subversives, under presidential pressure, had simply grown to include both sides in the fight over racial justice.

As Lyndon Johnson expected, his aggressive pursuit of a federal role in the civil rights movement made him ripe for political attack. In mid-July, the Republican Party nominated archconservative Arizona senator Barry Goldwater as their presidential candidate. The party of Lincoln had chosen an outspoken opponent of the 1964 Civil Rights Act.

President Johnson's political nightmare had come true. The night after he had signed the act, he mournfully told a trusted aide: "I think we just delivered the South to the Republican Party for a long time to come." Goldwater, while not a white supremacist, meant to capture the vote of pro-segregation Southern whites: "We're not going to get the Negro vote as a bloc in 1964 or 1968, so we ought to go hunting where the ducks are." Lyndon Johnson approached the 1964 Democratic convention in Atlantic City knowing that he'd need every ounce of his political savvy to keep the South from going Republican that November. The President and the fearless members of the Mississippi Freedom Democratic Party were on a collision course.

Civil rights stalwart Mary King revealed the moral idealism and the political naiveté at least some members of the MFDP brought with them to the 1964 Democratic convention when she wrote: "It never occurred to us that we would be turned down." As the MFDP saw it, morality and justice were completely on their side in their move to be seated as delegates to the convention. The official Mississippi delegation, which included not a single black member, openly championed white supremacy and racial segregation.

MFDP delegate Fannie Lou Hamer, who epitomized SNCC's ability to help impoverished, uneducated people become champions of their own cause, made the most powerful case for the unseating of the regular Democrats. She testified before the convention's Credentials Committee, explaining to them what happened to her when she tried to participate in Mississippi's closed electoral system. After losing her job, she was arrested. Her jailers then had her beaten by black prisoners:

> The first Negro began to beat . . . After the first Negro was exhausted, the state highway patrolman ordered the second Negro to take the blackjack. The second Negro began to beat . . . I began to scream, and one white man got up and began to beat me on my head. . . . All of this is on account we want to register, to become first-class citizens.

Hamer concluded her remarks with a challenge: "If the Freedom Democratic Party is not seated now, I question America."

Lyndon Johnson recognized the power of Hamer's testimony (he preempted television coverage of her concluding remarks by giving an impromptu press conference). And he recognized the moral claim of the MFDP. But in Johnson's world, moral claims did not change political reality. He had been warned by the South's leading politicians that if he unseated the all-white Mississippi regular Democrats, all Southern delegates—every one of them white—would stage a walkout in full view of the prime-time television audience. Johnson believed he could not allow such a political bombshell. So as he had been doing all his adult life, he tried to cut a deal.

Johnson had his prospective running mate, Minnesota senator Hubert Humphrey, whose support for the civil rights movement was unimpeachable, offer the MFDP two at-large seats at the convention. He sweetened the pot by guaranteeing that the Democratic Party would forthwith change its delegate-selection rules to stop discrimination at future conventions. The MFDP would have nothing to do with any such deals. Fannie Lou Hamer put the matter bluntly: "We didn't come all this way for no two seats." Johnson's presidential dream of creating what he had started to call the "Great Society" and the Mississippi freedom fighters' dream of justice, equality, and open democracy had collided; the effect of the confrontation would echo throughout the decade.

SNCC organizers behind the MFDP believed themselves betrayed. MFDP chairman Lawrence Guyout and Mike Thelwell of the MFDP's Washington office later observed that they had based their efforts on a "confidence in the ultimate morality in national political institutions and practices." But in the aftermath of the 1964 Democratic convention, they believed that "they"—the President and white liberals in Congress, in labor unions and elsewhere—simply did not care enough about morality to do the right thing. SNCC's Stokely Carmichael drew the lesson "not merely that the national conscience was generally unreliable but that, very specifically, black people in Mississippi and throughout this country could not rely on their so-called allies." This shattering understanding turned many of the Movement's most dedicated young activists away from the dream of racial integration and toward an as yet undefined, fiery vision of revolutionary Black Power.

Bayard Rustin, the most capable behind-the-scenes organizer in the Movement (and a special target of the FBI), had tried to keep SNCC's firebrands from taking what he saw as the wrong path from Atlantic City. "There is a difference between protest and politics," Rustin told them. "The former is based on morality and the latter is based on reality and compromise. . . . You must be willing to compromise, to win victories and go home and come back and win some more . . . That is politics." Martin Luther King, Jr., though disappointed by Johnson's Atlantic City decision and in complete sympathy with the MFDP, believed Rustin, not the young radicals, to be right.

Lyndon Johnson had no doubts that he had handled the Mississippi problem properly. Though the all-white Mississippi delegation walked out of the convention anyway, over the Democratic Party's new platform plank supporting civil rights, the rest of the Southern delegates had stayed put. Johnson felt ready to take on his erratic Republican opponent, Barry Goldwater.

Anti-Communism was at the core of Goldwater's political faith. He was a zealous advocate of an ever bigger and costlier military primed to fight international Communism. During his presidential campaign Goldwater talked freely about waging nuclear war against Communists in Europe, Asia, and anywhere else they might appear.

Goldwater believed, too, in the moral necessity of minimizing the federal government's role in the lives of America's citizens. He opposed the social security system, civil rights laws, business regulations, and most federal programs as un-American encroachments on personal liberty. During the campaign Goldwater railed against the "false prophets" of liberalism who believed that the federal government should be used to create greater equality among the citizenry. For Goldwater, individual liberty, not greater equality, was America's bedrock value. And for Goldwater, individuals' freedom to discriminate and states' right to segregate were indivisible aspects of their constitutionally guaranteed liberty. In the summer of 1964, Goldwater's ringing declaration at the

Republican convention that "extremism in the defense of liberty is no vice," though pitched to anti-Communists, amounted to a solemn wink and a nod to the forces of white supremacy.

Lyndon Johnson, in the late-summer and early-fall campaigning, tried to avoid controversy. He let Goldwater scare the voters with his big talk about nuclear war and ending the social security system. Johnson also knew that the rapidly expanding gross national product—growing at better than 6 percent in 1964—and low unemployment—just over 4 percent—left most Americans feeling satisfied with the political status quo.

Johnson did seek to shore up one vulnerable position. In May, Goldwater had attacked Johnson's indecision about fighting Communism in Vietnam. Johnson had inherited America's military involvement in Vietnam from Kennedy, who had inherited it from Eisenhower. And six months after stepping up to the presidency, Johnson had moderately increased American military involvement in the Vietnamese civil war. But like Kennedy and Eisenhower, he had ordered that American troops serve only as "advisers" to the army of the Republic of Vietnam (South Vietnam) and not be committed to any offensive role. Goldwater pointed out that the American mission in Vietnam was adrift. To stop the spread of Communism in Vietnam the military must be unleashed, Goldwater insisted, mentioning even the possibility of using tactical nuclear weapons.

In August, Johnson took advantage of dubious reports that American ships had been fired upon in the Gulf of Tonkin, off the coast of Vietnam. He ordered a limited bombing attack on North Vietnamese targets. In large part, he used the bombing run to negate Goldwater's attack on his anti-Communist credentials. Johnson also used the Gulf of Tonkin incident to win a congressional resolution giving him essentially a free hand in crafting policy in troublesome Vietnam. But in the summer of 1964 few people outside Washington's inner circles saw Vietnam as a critical area of national concern. Mainly, Johnson spoke about his Vietnam policy not in terms of a war to be won but as a sign of his moderation and Goldwater's extremism. "There are those that may say you ought to go north and drop bombs," he told an Oklahoma

audience. "We don't want our American boys to do the fighting
for Asian boys. . . . We don't want to get involved in a nation
with 700 million people [China] and get tied down in a land war
in Asia." By late fall, Johnson was seriously considering dramatically escalating America's role in Vietnam but he never publicly
mentioned this during the campaign. To the extent that the issue
came up, Lyndon Johnson ran as the peace candidate.

Despite Goldwater's attacks, President Johnson's candidacy
faced problems in only one area of the country, the Deep South.
With only a small percentage of African-Americans yet able to
even register to vote, his civil rights record had destroyed much
of his support there.

Against the advice of campaign aides who wanted him to avoid
the issue of race until after the election, Lyndon Johnson went to
New Orleans in early October to make his case for a New South.
Before a crowd of 2,000 whites, the President told a story: Years
ago, a powerful Southern senator, his health failing, came up to
young Sam Rayburn, a newly elected congressman from Texas.
The senator talked to Rayburn about the South's poverty and its
economic needs. Then he said, "Sammy, I wish I felt a little better
. . . I would like to go back down there and make one more
Democratic speech. I just feel like I have one in me. The poor old
state, they haven't heard a Democratic speech in thirty years."
Johnson then paused, his eyes fixed on his audience. He flung out
his arms and, imitating the old senator, he roared: "All they ever
hear at election time is *Nigra, Nigra, Nigra.*"

As campaign chronicler Theodore White wrote, the President
spoke "in the presence of other Southerners as a Southerner who
had come to wisdom." Johnson won over that crowd in New
Orleans: after a stunned silence, the audience gave the President
a standing ovation. For the moment, at least, they were convinced.
But Johnson lost Louisiana that November to Goldwater. He also
lost Georgia, Alabama, South Carolina, and Mississippi, where
Goldwater won 87 percent of the vote. Johnson's political genius,
the expanding economy, the memory of JFK, the ingrained alle-
giance of many white Southerners to the Democratic Party, the
votes of Southern white liberals, and, critically, nearly every vote

from those African-Americans who'd been able to go to the polls kept the rest of the South in Johnson's column. But the future was clear. Seven Republican congressmen had been elected in the Deep South—the first since Reconstruction. Except for Johnson's home state of Texas, for the first time since the Civil War a majority of white Southerners had voted for the Republican presidential candidate.

Johnson was not pleased by the defection of the Deep South. But his displeasure was more than offset by the glee he felt in burying the inept Goldwater campaign almost everywhere else. Johnson lost only one Northern or Western state, Goldwater's own Arizona. Finally President on his own merits, with huge Democratic majorities in Congress, Johnson was ready to make his bid for greatness.

Lyndon Johnson wanted to use the power of the federal government, in his words, to "build a society where the demands of morality, and the needs of the spirit, can be realized in the life of the nation." Breaking with President Kennedy's guiding political vision of a world that needed to be balanced and rebalanced in the great struggle between East and West, Johnson saw America's great challenges as domestic, racial discrimination and poverty topping the list. He dreamed of creating the Great Society.

Johnson believed that America's economic abundance gave him the means—tax revenues, to put it bluntly—to right almost every wrong. Johnson barked at his aides: "Hell, we've barely begun to solve our problems. And we can do it all. We've got the wherewithal. . . . We're the richest country in the world. . . . We can do it if we believe it." Johnson was, in the words of historian Robert Collins, a believer in "growth liberalism."

Growth liberalism was based on two interconnected premises. First, advocates believed that federal economic policy—tax cuts and credits, targeted spending, fiscal stimulus—could significantly contribute to a robust, growing gross national product (GNP). Second, the new-style liberals believed that the increased tax revenues produced by the rising GNP could and should be used by the federal government to enlarge its role in both foreign and domestic affairs. Liberalism, in the hands of President Johnson, became an understanding that the federal government had the responsibility, power, and ability to reduce inequality, protect historically oppressed minorities, champion American interests and values around the world, and balance the private sector's singular focus on making money with a broad concern for the nation's long-term good. The Johnson administration rivaled the New Deal in the sheer number of bills passed, including consumer protection acts, mass-transit aid, antipoverty programs, health measures, the creation of the National Endowments for the Arts and Humanities, consumer and workplace protection acts, aid to higher education, and pathbreaking antipollution, conservation, and beautification measures.

Joseph Califano, White House staff assistant for domestic affairs in the Johnson administration, put the best face on the Great Society:

> We simply could not accept poverty, ignorance and hunger as intractable, permanent features of American society. There was no child we could not feed, no adult we could not put to work, no disease we could not cure, no toy, food or appliance we could not make safer, no air or water we could not clean.

Liberals in the Johnson administration had grand dreams of what they could use the federal government to accomplish.

John Kennedy laid the foundation for what became the centerpiece of 1960s liberalism in action: the War on Poverty. In early 1963, Kennedy had the chair of his Council of Economic Advisers, Walter Heller, study possible antipoverty measures. Just days before his assassination, Kennedy had seemingly decided to make a poverty program a major component of his 1964 legislative agenda. That he would have publicly declared a War on Poverty as Johnson did, however, is unlikely.

The difficulty with declaring a War on Poverty was that proven generals, proven strategies, and proven weapons for such a battle were few. Before the mid-1960s, policy planners and social scientists had spent little time (in part because of lack of interest among those who fund research) studying the poor or poverty itself. The politics of poverty ran ahead of politicians' knowledge of what to do to end poverty, but that did not slow down the Johnson administration very much.

President Johnson did not want to be told that an antipoverty campaign should start slowly with small-scale pilot programs. Johnson "wanted to set world records in politics as a star athlete would in sports," and for a politician records came in the number of programs created, money spent, legislation enacted. Harry McPherson, a key White House aide, argued that one of the President's biggest problems was that he was "a Washington, D.C., provincial . . . He thinks this world, this orbit here, is the dynamo on which the whole country runs, the only place that matters." Great Society liberals, their leader most of all, wore blinders in their pursuit of greatness.

The simplest way to have ended poverty would have been to give poor people more money. Despite certain myths about liberalism in the 1960s, this redistributive solution—increasing taxes on the rich and middle class in order to give money to the poor —was not at the center of the War on Poverty. The income tax, in fact, was not raised until late in the 1960s (to pay for Vietnam); indeed, in the heyday of the Great Society tax cuts for both corporations and individuals were duly delivered by the Democrats.

President Johnson, a traditionalist in this regard, wanted no part in simply giving people enough money to lift them out of poverty: "We want to offer the forgotten fifth of our people opportunity, not doles." The Great Society liberals believed they could, in the words of historian James Patterson, "get the poverty out of the people—and afterward the people out of poverty."

At the heart of the War on Poverty stood a radical, wonderful, untested, but unlikely notion: that the best way to end poverty in America was to have poor people themselves decide on the means by which they could create new opportunities and leave poverty behind. The government would provide the means but poor people, through Community Action Programs, would decide what would do them the most good: job training, education, cultural enrichment, political activism, or whatever. Under the rubric of "maximum feasible participation" of the poor themselves, community boards made up of activists and residents were formed in poor neighborhoods and charged with fighting their own customized "wars."

Mayor Richard Daley of Chicago, like most big-city politicians, was appalled by the idea of the poor running their own programs. In part, he resented losing control over the federal money streaming into "his" city. He observed that every federal dollar in his city that he did not control was a dollar potentially of use to his political enemies. But Daley, reasonably proud of his skill in running city government, also believed that giving the poor and neighborhood activists the say-so over poverty programming was a formula for disaster. To reporters he explained: "[It] would be like telling the fellow who cleans up to be the city editor of a newspaper." Another city official concurred: "You can't go to a street corner with a pad and pencil and tell the poor to write you a poverty program. They don't know how."

Mayor Daley and his fellow mayors were, essentially, right. That mayors like Daley, fearful of the political ramifications of poor people gaining power, also did their best to sabotage neighborhood programming didn't help matters. Nor were the poverty programs well served by local activists who saw them as essentially job bases for their followers. Corrupt individuals played an unfortunate role in some programs. With some heroic exceptions, such as the program in Springfield, Massachusetts, the Community Action Programs failed.

By 1966, the President had begun to lose faith in his war's central strategy (and increasingly events in Vietnam diverted his attention). Congressmen, always suspicious of the liberal policymakers who had planned the War on Poverty, began to earmark funds by their preferred means: the pork barrel. In 1967, despite clear signs of failure, over 1,000 Community Action Programs were still being funded.

The War on Poverty was not limited to the Community Action Programs and the strategy of "maximum feasible participation" by the poor. The Johnson administration pushed through dozens of programs aimed at changing the lot of the poor. Though most of them were larded with congressional "pork" and compromised by special-interest lobbying, many had significant impact on the quality of poor people's lives. There were housing acts, school bills, preschool programs, rent supplements, training programs, medical assistance, legal aid, food and meal subsidies, rat control, delinquency prevention, supplements to social security benefits, expanded welfare programs, and much more.

The food stamps program, for example, was massively expanded. In 1965 only about 633,000 people received what was often minimum aid at a barely noticeable cost of $36 million. A decade later over 17 million people benefited from food stamps at a cost of $4.3 billion. Combined with free school meal programs and other targeted nutrition projects, Great Society reforms dramatically reduced the number of people going hungry in the United States.

In a move that would have major consequences for the United States, the Johnson administration passed the Medicaid and Medicare programs in 1965. Medicaid, which provided the poor with free health care, had been piggybacked onto the far more popular Medicare, which guaranteed almost free medical care to all people over sixty-five, regardless of income. In order to get past the American Medical Association, which spent millions fighting what they called "socialized medicine" (doctors feared that the programs would diminish their incomes), the administration had been forced into a very expensive compromise. Language was added to the legislation ensuring that the government would pay doctors and hospitals who served Medicare and Medicaid patients their "customary" rates and fees. This vague phrasing amounted to carte blanche for physicians. By 1974, Medicaid alone served 23 million people at the budget-busting cost of $9 billion. Medicare costs were even more out of control. The good news was that Medicaid and other entitlement programs enacted by Lyndon Johnson and the Democratic Congress improved the quality of life and increased the life span of the poor.

America's elderly, poor and not poor, gained the most from the Great Society reforms. In a huge government-mandated transfer of income from the young to the old, senior citizens received almost free medical care, more social security payments (benefits increased at almost twice the rate of the national income from 1965 to 1969), special housing programs, and other measures. In 1959, about 40 percent of the public over sixty-five lived below the government's official poverty line. By 1970 only 25 percent of them remained poor, and by 1974, due to still greater social security benefits, the numbers had fallen to just 16 percent.

The program most Americans associate with helping the poor, Aid to Families with Dependent Children (AFDC), commonly called welfare, also grew greatly under Johnson and in the years just after his administration. Between 1960 and 1975 the basic welfare caseload quintupled, with the largest increases coming between 1965 and 1970. This huge increase proved to conservatives, then and now, that despite the large overall decline in the numbers of poor Americans in the 1960s—from about 21 percent of the population in 1959 to about 12 percent in 1969—the War on Poverty failed abysmally.

While the federal government did create a more generous welfare benefit formula, the growing number of recipients was mainly due to a complex change in attitudes of the poor, the courts, and government administrators. The biggest change seems to have come from the ranks of the poor. In the early 1960s about one-third of those eligible signed up for welfare. By the end of the 1960s, some 90 percent of the poor chose to accept welfare. In part, more ready acceptance was made possible by War on Poverty activists and lawyers who used the courts and pressured government bureaucrats to ease many restrictive, sometimes racist, and often demeaning rules that had discouraged participation in the AFDC program. As a result, people found it both easier and less humiliating to sign up for welfare. But even more important, those in poor communities saw welfare, in the words of historian James Patterson, not as a privilege but as a right:

The role of the civil rights movement was undoubtedly vital. It enlisted militant leaders who campaigned to improve the legal and then socioeconomic position of the poor. It trained a cadre of activists who apprised poor people of their rights. Most important, though hardest to pinpoint, the civil rights movement quickened the sense of inequality and relative deprivation that affected all low-income people, whether black or white.

This change in attitude described by Patterson had implications far greater than simply increasing the welfare rolls. Many poor African-Americans in America's largest cities were becoming angry. They believed the immense successes of the Movement in fighting Jim Crow laws and enfranchising black people to be irrelevant to their lives in Northern cities. The War on Poverty, they felt, did nothing to provide them with real opportunities or better lives. In August 1965, the nation could see both the civil rights movement triumphant and the African-American urban poor furious, and most white people, polls showed, felt somehow betrayed.

The Movement's last great triumph came in March 1965. Martin Luther King, Jr., led protests against Selma, Alabama, officials' refusal to register black voters. After a series of dramatic confrontations, including the murder of a minister by white extremists, President Johnson seized the political opportunity King and the Movement had created for him.

Before a joint session of Congress, on national television, Johnson proselytized for a strong national voting rights act. His speech brought tears to the eyes of Martin Luther King. "Their cause," said the President to the American people, "must be our cause, too. Because it is not just Negroes but really all of us who must overcome the crippling legacy of bigotry and injustice." The President showed how far the Movement had taken America by closing his speech with the watchword of those who had marched and boycotted, been beaten and shot: "And we shall overcome."

On August 6, 1965, Johnson signed the Voting Rights Act. The act mandated Justice Department intervention to provide federal examiners anywhere voter registration discrimination occurred. It had easily passed Congress. Bowing to the inevitable, to reason, and in a few cases to a slow but steady increase in their black constituency, 37 Southern House members and 6 Southern senators voted in favor of the act. The President's speech and Martin

Luther King's campaign in Alabama, which had been thoroughly covered by the mass media, had swung the American people solidly behind the bill. Only a hard-core minority in the South remained intransigent about African-Americans' right to vote.

Five days after President Johnson signed the Voting Rights Act and more than a year after he had announced his War on Poverty, Los Angeles' black ghetto, Watts, went up in flames. By the time order was restored, six days and nights later, 34 people had been killed, 864 hospitalized with injuries, and more than 4,000 people arrested. Whole city blocks had been torched and property damage exceeded $45 million. A chilling chant was born: "Burn, baby, burn!"

The specific flash point for the riot was a confrontation between white police and a young black man pulled over for a traffic violation on a crowded street. A crowd watched the police manhandle first the young man—who was drunk and uncooperative —and then his abusive brother. In a matter of minutes rocks and bottles were being thrown at the police. Overnight, rumors flew, anger turned into violence, and looting, arson, and terror spread over 150 square blocks.

Watts was the first major riot of the 1960s. Hundreds more would follow in the next three years. Many of the most devastating riots between 1965 and 1967 began with a police incident.

Most big-city policemen saw themselves as agents of street justice, quick to use their hands, feet, batons, and even guns to maintain order in "the jungle." That Northern city police departments were still overwhelmingly white, despite the rapid influx of African-Americans since World War II, often made the police in black neighborhoods seem like occupying armies. In Watts, in 1965, 200 of the 205 police in the 98 percent black area were white. Many white officers in Northern cities were admitted racists. Still, police brutality was not new; it was seemingly in decline by the mid-1960s; and in almost every major Northern city, the number of black officers was increasing. Other factors, however, were making some African-Americans less willing to accept the police's traditionally brutal role in black neighborhoods.

Lou Smith, a onetime worker for CORE, the group that had sponsored the Freedom Rides, tried to explain the larger forces he held responsible for Watts:

> What happened was that people had sat there and watched all the concern about black people "over there." And there wasn't a damn soul paying one bit of attention to what was going on in Watts. So the black people in Watts just spontaneously rose up one day and said, Fuck it! We're hungry. Our schools stink. We're getting the shit beat out of us. We tried the integration route. It's obvious the integration route isn't going to work. Now we've got to go another way.

In some ways, Smith's assertion—"We tried the integration route . . . [it] isn't going to work"—seems astounding. The Watts riot occurred less than a year after passage of the 1964 Civil Rights Act and days after the Voting Rights Act. Integration, as a nationally mandated policy, was just beginning. But Smith understood that those acts were not really aimed at Los Angeles or the North. The politicians had aimed those bills at the South, where black people had confronted legal segregation and discrimination for generations. Black people had come North, and West, to avoid old Jim Crow and to find a better life.

Some did find better lives up North. Many streets in Watts were lined with comfortable bungalows in which black families prospered. But even those families that had captured a part of the American dream faced increasingly difficult circumstances. In the years just before the riot, about 30,000 African-Americans annually streamed into Watts and other overwhelmingly black neighborhoods. Housing discrimination kept even many solidly middle-class African-Americans from moving into "white neighborhoods." When, for example, a few black families in Chicago in the 1950s tried to move into working-class "white neighborhoods," they were attacked and some had their homes burned. Locked into ghettos by discrimination, African-Americans paid higher rents than whites for worse housing in far more densely packed areas. Banks and savings and loans contributed to the problem by refusing to give mortgages in black neighborhoods, arguing that they were too densely crowded and unstable to be good investments. Lack of capital for home purchases and improvements meant that many shady landlords refused to maintain their properties. Housing segregation was worse in the North than in the South.

Housing problems were compounded by school problems. Overcrowding and poor schools were endemic in black neighborhoods in Northern and Western cities. These factors, particularly grossly inferior schools, North and South, caused many African-Americans to lose faith in the usefulness of education to lead them out of poverty. More than two-thirds of all adults in Watts lacked a high school diploma—which meant they could offer their children little educational enrichment at home. Nearly two-thirds of Watts high school students failed to graduate.

Lack of education made it hard to compete for better-paying jobs. Additionally, the low-skilled, decent jobs that had served urban migrants for generations as stepping stones to better lives were declining in areas close to where African-Americans lived in Los Angeles. To the degree that such jobs were being created, they were mainly distant from Watts in white suburban areas that LA's poor public transportation system did not serve. Since 40 percent of Watts residents had no cars, getting to these new jobs was extremely difficult. In 1965, black unemployment in LA was about three times that of whites. Even as legal discrimination declined, blacks in LA saw few new opportunities.

Some people responded to the difficulties of ghetto life, at a time when the mass media, politicians, and many African-American leaders were proclaiming that better times had come, by exploding. Social scientists in the mid-1960s talked about the phenomenon of "rising expectations." They argued that people rarely tend to rebel when their lives seem hopeless. Rather, people tend to act when conditions are improving too slowly. As French political philosopher Alexis de Tocqueville observed, "Evils which are patiently endured when they seem inevitable become intolerable when once the idea of escape from them is suggested."

Martin Luther King, Jr., found another answer when he and

Bayard Rustin walked the streets of Watts just after the riot. A gang of teenagers ran up to King, shouting, "We won!" King responded angrily, asking how death, destruction, and the alienation of white support could be called winning. One young man answered: "We won because we made them pay attention to us."

In more than twenty years the *Los Angeles Times* (which had not one black reporter or editor) had run only two major stories on the black community in LA. After the riots, angry urban blacks were headline news.

Godfrey Hodgson, a British observer of the United States in the 1960s, argued that at least some rioters were looking for a very specific kind of "attention." They wanted white Americans to see the power of their anger. He wrote:

> It was no longer a matter of what whites could be persuaded to concede . . . it was a question of what degree of attention angry young blacks would demand. . . . It was a question of how much they could make white people respect them and therefore also a question of self-respect. It was a question of "consciousness."

Taking a page from a book increasingly discussed by black radicals, Frantz Fanon's *The Wretched of the Earth*, Hodgson suggested that for some rioters violence was a means of redefining their relationship to their "oppressor." Violence directed at the oppressor, Fanon argued, was cathartic for poor and oppressed people: it liberated them from feelings of powerlessness. A young rioter offers support for the thesis:

> I felt invincible. . . . Honestly, that is how powerful I felt. I'm not too proud of what I did, looking back. But I held nothing back. I let out all my frustrations with every brick, every bottle that I threw. . . . Many people ran around looting the stores. . . . My only thought about the stores was something like "Those store owners will be furious, but who cares. They aren't black. They don't know what furious really is." Then I picked up a bottle and tried to destroy a TV in the window display. I remembered feeling completely relieved. I unleashed all the emotions that had built up inside, ones I didn't know how to express.

Of course, a great many rioters simply saw a good thing and looted out of self-interest. But the almost orgiastic destruction and firebombing waged by so many sprang from a river of emotions much deeper than simple criminality or a desire for material possessions.

The summer after Watts, some forty-three urban ghettos exploded in what some black radicals were calling "rebellions." In 1967 some 167 cities reported riots. Detroit was the hardest hit. After a routine police raid (97 percent of the Detroit police were white) on an unlicensed bar, almost three square miles of city streets were set ablaze by rioters. Forty-three people were killed. Most of them were killed by the police or National Guardsmen who shot wildly and often without cause.

A great majority of ghetto residents did not participate in the riots. They were appalled. One middle-aged Detroit woman concluded: "I don't see where the riot accomplished nothing myself but a lot of burnt-up buildings. . . . People couldn't buy a loaf of bread or a quart of milk nowhere in the neighborhood after those riots." Many poor black urban neighborhoods even twenty-five years later have not recovered from the riot years.

Despite the destruction, some black leaders saw the riots as necessary, and even useful. A grass-roots activist in Detroit argued: "After the rebellion was over, there was a strong sense of brotherhood and sisterhood. We saw a very strong sense of camaraderie in the community. . . . We enjoyed that feeling." Many of the organizers associated with SNCC saw the "rebellions" as a sure sign that the days of peaceful protests in hopes of racial integration were dead. They and others saw a new spirit of resistance in the black community, and many activists did their best both to fan the flames of violent anger and to organize their people in the name of what they came to call Black Power.

Most whites responded to the riots, and to those who argued that the riots were somehow justified, with fear and their own anger. In 1966, faded movie actor Ronald Reagan won the California governorship by blaming the Watts riot (and university protests) on liberal policymakers. The incumbent governor, Pat Brown, said in his concession speech that "whether we like it or not the people want separation of the races." Alabama governor George Wallace, who had once barred black students from the University of Alabama and proclaimed "segregation now, segregation tomorrow, segregation forever," began stumping the country in 1967, preparing for a presidential bid. In Michigan, Ohio, Indiana, and elsewhere whites responded to his calls for law and order. Millions of whites angrily turned away from the fragmenting civil rights movement because of the riots, black radicals' advocacy of violence, and the Movement's failure to categorically condemn rioters. Even liberal whites felt confused. After riots tore apart his city, one white Movement sympathizer said, "We didn't know what to believe and that made everything that happened that much scarier."

For President Johnson, the riots were not simply frightening; they were heartbreaking. His dreams of a Great Society were literally going up in smoke. After the Detroit riots, polls showed that his public approval rating had plummeted to just 37 percent. But the riots were just one part of the nightmare President Johnson found himself in. Step by step, one decision leading to another, President Johnson had drawn the American people into a land war in Asia.

6. VIETNAM

~~~~~~

PRESIDENT JOHNSON'S DECISIONS in 1964 and 1965 to escalate American military involvement in Vietnam seemed to most Americans and most policymakers so seamlessly a part of the grand Cold War adventure of the United States that they required only perfunctory explanation and legitimation. President Johnson told the American people that Vietnam was the newest front in the global war against Communist aggression that Americans had been fighting since the defeat of Germany and Japan in 1945. America's involvement in Vietnam, the American people were told, was unavoidable, necessary, and just. In 1964 and 1965 few voices in Congress, in the mass media, or in the universities challenged the escalation of American military involvement in Vietnam. And in the mid-1960s the Marines and soldiers ordered to fight the war overwhelmingly accepted their destiny.

In *Tour 365*, a booklet the U.S. Army handed out to its Vietnam troops (on a 365-day tour of duty), a litany of presidential quotations were used to explain America's involvement in Vietnam's civil war. Eisenhower—dateline 1959—asserted: "The loss of South Vietnam would set in motion a crumbling process that could, as it progressed, have consequences for us and for freedom." John F. Kennedy told them in 1961: "The United States is determined to help Vietnam preserve its independence, protect its people against Communist assassins, and build a better life through economic growth." In 1965, Lyndon Johnson hammered home the official message: "The central issue of the conflict . . . is the aggression by North Vietnam. . . . If that aggression is stopped, the people and government of South Vietnam will be free to settle their own future—and get on with the great tasks of national development." It sounded so reasonable. But beneath this proud and certain-sounding Cold War boilerplate, as the men who fought in Vietnam would learn, was a maddening swirl of deception, confusion, and delusion.

America's war in Vietnam developed in the administrative, often secret bureaucracies that both incorporated and serviced the web of interests—public and private—that pushed American power into every corner of the globe. President Johnson could not have decided to escalate American military involvement in Vietnam if he had not believed that the intelligence agency analysts, Pentagon strategists, military contractors, State Department area specialists, university-linked contract experts, and White House staffers had both the ability and the power to achieve American objectives in Southeast Asia. This system of power, an aspect of the "military-industrial complex" that President Eisenhower had warned about in his 1961 farewell address, made the war seem logical, winnable, even seductive.

While America's involvement in Vietnam grew in the secret, undemocratic recesses of the government's post-World War II national security apparatus, other developments in American society made certain that Vietnam became America's most visible war. American government and corporate investment in television, satellite communications, and other advanced information and communication technologies, in combination with the material prosperity that allowed most Americans access to this mass media culture, brought the war "home" to Americans more dramatically than any previous military conflict. Vietnam became the first war Americans watched daily on television—"the living-room war," some called it.

Living-room intimacy, however, was counterbalanced by how remote most Americans felt from the war effort. The managers of American intervention in Vietnam chose to minimize the war's reach into the lives of the American people. During World War I and World War II, government officials had created bond drives, rationed goods, organized scrap drives, and conjured up hundreds of other roles for Americans "at home" to play in the war effort.

Very few of these efforts were critical, or even necessary. Those charged with managing the war, however, believed that the best way to maximize America's commitment to it was to involve all Americans in the war effort, even if they did nothing more than plant a "victory garden" in their backyard. Domestic mobilization was matched by a system of near-universal wartime service for America's young men.

Vietnam was different. The war in Vietnam was never seen by its managers as a total war. Though the managers saw American involvement in Vietnam as serving different purposes at different times, they never defined it as a contest demanding total commitment from the American people. Vietnam was less a war to be won than a demonstration project illustrating how the United States could reshape a Third World revolutionary struggle.

As this "demonstration project" went awry, it became increasingly difficult to explain the strategic purpose and even tactical limits of the war, either to the American public or to the men charged with fighting it. The difficulties of maintaining and explaining a war evolved in secret, which was viewed so openly, greatly contributed to the most sustained mass resistance to any war in American history. Such difficulties also go far to explain why America lost the war in Vietnam.

America's involvement in Vietnam began long before Lyndon Johnson became commander-in-chief. The war in Vietnam, with and without direct American military involvement, lasted for some thirty years. Without understanding the decisions other Presidents and their advisers, consultants, agents, and operatives made in regard to America's role in Vietnam, the actions of Lyndon Johnson and then of President Richard Nixon make little sense.

For a handful of American government operatives, the war in Vietnam began during World War II. In secret, agents of the OSS—the wartime intelligence agency that preceded the CIA—joined forces with the Vietnam Doc Lap Dong Minh Hoi (League for the Independence of Vietnam), known as the Vietminh, against a common foe, the Japanese. The Vietminh, a largely Communist organization, was the latest incarnation of an underground political and military force that had been trying to win Vietnamese freedom and independence from foreign occupiers for generations. Japan meant to make Vietnam a part of its "Greater East Asian Co-Prosperity Sphere"—at gunpoint.

Japan had taken over imperialist rule of Vietnam from the French. The French had seized control of Vietnam, as well as Laos and Cambodia, almost a hundred years earlier and renamed the region Indochina. The French maintained their control of Indochina through a regime of brutality, and exploited Indochina's economic resources and the Indochina market for the benefit of the French empire. The Japanese government started the war in the Pacific, essentially, to kick France and other European imperialist powers out of Asia. Japan's motives were not altruistic; it meant to take their place.

When America defeated Japan in August 1945, the Vietminh called for a grand rally to celebrate their liberation from Japanese rule and the beginning of a free and independent Vietnam. Before half a million people in Hanoi, Ho Chi Minh declared Vietnamese independence in terms taken directly not from the *Communist Manifesto* but from the American Declaration of Independence. A Vietminh band struck up a rousing rendition of "The Star-Spangled Banner." A representative of the U.S. Information Agency, which would play a key role in the global propaganda battles of the coming Cold War, reported back to Washington on the Vietnamese people's enthusiasm for the United States: "Nowhere did the coming of Americans, in this case a mere handful of them, mean so much to a people as it did to the people of northern Indochina . . . our coming was the symbol of liberation not from Japanese occupation but from decades of French colonial rule." In 1945 the Vietnamese people joined with many colonized nations in believing that the United States—the first colonial nation to successfully defeat European imperialism through armed struggle—would champion their fight for independence from European powers.

At first, President Franklin Roosevelt seemed sympathetic to the anti-imperialist struggle in general and to the cause of Vietnamese independence in particular. But by early 1945, Roosevelt had begun to modify his views in the face of concerted British and French pressures.

FDR's successor, Harry Truman, went further. Coached by foreign policy experts, Truman placed the needs and desires of America's main allies in the world—the governments of Western Europe—well above the nationalist dreams of the subjugated peoples of the Third World. Western European nations insisted that they needed their colonies—both the economic wealth of those countries and the geopolitical power and status such colonies conferred upon them—to rebuild from the destruction of World War II. As a result, between 1945 and 1954, the United States supported France's reestablishment of colonial control over Vietnam.

American military planners and international relations experts saw other reasons—independent of French demands—to keep Vietnam out of Communist hands and under Western control. First of all, the United States had economic interests in the resources and markets of Southeast Asia. Communist governments in Asia, America's internationally oriented financial and industrial elites argued, almost certainly would make American business development of the region difficult, if not impossible. In addition, State Department experts pointed out that Japan (a pivotal ally of the United States in the postwar world) had invaded East and Southeast Asia for rational reasons: Japan needed access to the region for economic development. If Vietnam and other parts of the area went Communist, the Japanese might reach out to the Soviet Union as a way to assure continued access to the Asian mainland; such a relationship between Japan and the U.S.S.R. clearly would not be in the best interests of the United States. Pentagon planners also weighed in by emphasizing the prominence the Japanese had placed on Vietnam as a strategic building block in their war effort: Vietnam had an excellent deep-water harbor and was well situated as a staging ground for attacks on the resource-rich countries to the southwest. Losing this strategically valuable area to a potential aggressor nation could create dangers throughout the region.

Overwhelmingly, America's foreign policy managers in the State Department, and the Department of Defense, National Security Council, and Central Intelligence Agency (all three of which were formed in 1947), did not see the Vietminh struggle to win independence from France as an updated version of George Washington and a ragtag army of freedom-loving patriots taking on the redcoats. The United States, most internationally minded members of the financial, business, and government elites believed, had its own "national interest" in developing new markets abroad and maintaining its geopolitical and national security interests. And in the immediate postwar years, with American power and opportunities in the world at an unprecedented level, the foreign policy concerns of America's internationally minded economic and political elites were the very engine of American state policy.

Secretary of State Dean Acheson explained the big-picture logic that must govern the U.S. policy in Vietnam: "[Whether] Ho Chi Minh is as much nationalist as Commie is irrelevant. . . . All Stalinists in colonial areas are nationalists." Vietnam could not be seen in isolation, foreign policy managers explained. Vietnam was, they told themselves, one piece in a bigger game that must be managed according to America's global battle with the forces of Soviet Communism for control of the world's fate. Vietnam, they began to say, was a domino, which if tipped over could take all the other dominoes down with it.

In 1950, this logic dictated equivocal, if publicly almost undiscussed, American support for French imperialism. American opposition to any kind of Communism in Asia was underscored by Communist North Korea's attack on American-supported South Korea and America's subsequent armed intervention in support of their distant client. In this "Red" versus "White" world, Ho Chi Minh's request for American support, his statements that Vietnam would be a "fertile field for American capital and enterprise," and even his offer of an American naval base at Camranh Bay were all ignored by American officials. In the minds of America's foreign policy managers, Vietnamese particulars were outweighed by concerns about global possibilities. Instead, the Americans begun funneling, first indirectly and then directly, increasingly large sums of money to the French war effort even though the French, as the Americans knew, had almost no support among the Vietnamese people.

In 1954, despite billions in financial assistance from the United States and some half million troops in the field, the French lost their war against the Vietnamese. The last act of the fading imperialists came at Dienbienphu, where the Vietnamese overcame their technological inferiority by mobilizing hundreds of thousands of people in support of Vietminh troops. Vietnam's leading military strategist, General Vo Nguyen Giap, said of his French counterpart: "He could not visualize the immense possibilities of a people's army and the entire people who were fighting for independence and peace."

Whether or not the Vietminh independence movement was a front for ruthless Soviet-directed Communism (as senior American officials increasingly argued) or a nationalist organization dedicated to economic reform (as Ho Chi Minh insisted), what was clear in 1954 was that a large number of highly motivated people in Vietnam had ended French imperial rule of their country. In the eight years of fighting, 95,000 French Union forces and close to 300,000 Vietminh were killed. As many as a million civilians had died in the fighting. The French had won the battle of the body count but they had lost the war. Once again, as in 1945, Ho Chi Minh prepared to lead an independent Vietnam.

In the last weeks of the siege at Dienbienphu, President Eisenhower had tried to build a multiforce coalition to help the French snatch victory from defeat. The British, however, more experienced in fighting colonial wars than either the Americans or the French, would have no part in what they saw as a losing struggle over a less than vital part of the world economic system—and one that most directly benefited France.

While the President negotiated, he used a news conference (he was the first President to hold "live" news conferences) to prepare the American people for the possibility of American military intervention in Vietnam. If Indochina fell to the Reds, Ike told the American people, the rest of Southeast Asia would "go over very quickly" like a "row of dominoes." In an almost unique display of candor, Eisenhower enumerated the problems these fallen dominoes would cause for American interests in the area. He concluded:

". . . the possible consequences of the loss are just incalculable to the free world."

Following Eisenhower's saber rattling, Congress jumped into the fray. The Democrats, who had taken a beating from the Republicans over the Truman administration's inability to successfully resolve the Korean War and the "loss" of China to the Communists, saw a chance to get in some blows of their own. The junior senator from Massachusetts, John Kennedy, blasted Eisenhower's failed policy of supporting French imperialism. Senate Democratic leader Lyndon Johnson was more outspoken. He went on the record as opposing any policy that would send "American GIs into the mud and muck of Indochina on a bloodletting spree to perpetuate colonialism and white man's exploitation in Asia."

In this first real public debate about America's role in Vietnam, a critical paradox in Americans' self-identity as it related to the role of the American state in the world had surfaced. President Eisenhower had laid the possible groundwork for direct American intervention in Vietnam by presenting a rare discussion of America's complex global interests. He had outlined the effect Vietnam's "fall" to Communists might have on American economic interests in the region and on our allies' economic and security needs. He had also mentioned the fate of the people of Southeast Asia under Communism, but considering what the European nations had done and hoped to continue doing to the people of Asia this was not an issue Ike had thought it politic to stress. Senators Kennedy and Johnson did not focus their public remarks on America's newly perceived national security goals and international economic interests in the region—matters which most Americans did not believe to be central to what their country stood for in the world. Instead, the senators focused on more "traditional" American values of independence and freedom—the values Ho Chi Minh (who used them very differently than most Americans) had hoped would carry the day in his discussion with American intelligence and foreign policy operatives in the immediate postwar years. By focusing on these values instead of on our allies' needs or on American business corporations' interests in the region, these two future

Presidents made Ike's support of French imperialism seem almost un-American. For a few brief days, the French war in Vietnam had publicly opened up serious discussion about what America's role in the world was and should be.

Ironically, the French defeat in Vietnam and the victory of a Communist (if also a popular and nationalist) force made a forthright American intervention in Vietnam's affairs more possible. The Vietminh, by winning and ending French claims on their country, made the situation in Vietnam much cleaner—ideologically—for American foreign policy managers. As Secretary of State John Foster Dulles confided to a friend: "We have a clean base there now without a taint of colonialism. Dienbienphu was a blessing in disguise." With imperialism no longer an issue, Vietnam might be more perfectly reduced to an issue of Communism versus Freedom—the frame that had been successfully used in explaining to the American people their government's expensive and extensive involvement in the affairs of Europe after World War II. Unfortunately, as most Americans who had looked carefully into the situation knew, making Vietnam fit this picture demanded a great deal of poetic license.

According to the peace agreement the French and the Vietminh signed in Geneva in 1954, Vietnam was to be temporarily divided into two regions. In two years' time, the Geneva Accords stated, elections would be held and the country reunified.

The United States had strongly backed the creation of a non-Communist Vietnamese region at the Geneva peace talks. Neither Eisenhower nor Dulles had in any way given up hope that Communism could be defeated in Vietnam. With the French out of the way, the Eisenhower administration saw a remarkable opportunity. The United States would, somehow, create a stable, legitimate government in the newly created South Vietnam, and that government would win the support of the Vietnamese people and defeat Ho Chi Minh's Communist forces. American money and American know-how would help build a South Vietnamese Army that would give the American-created government sufficient time to develop indigenous support. American money and know-how would provide non-Communist solutions to the economic difficulties a century of French misrule had bequeathed to the Vietnamese people. American money and know-how would mold a non-Communist, independent nation in Vietnam where none before had existed.

Many American officials doubted the wisdom of this audacious experiment in nation building. Secretary of Defense "Engine" Charlie Wilson, while never claiming to be a foreign policy expert, brought his organizational genius to bear on the issue and voted thumbs down on the scheme. The Joint Chiefs of Staff believed that building an army where there was no "strong, stable civil government in control" was a "hopeless" mission. Despite these and other concerns, Ike chose to move forward and put the CIA, the National Security Council, the Department of Defense, and other executive branch bureaucracies to work figuring out how to build a Vietnam the Vietnamese would accept and American interests in the region would allow.

As internal American critics argued in the mid-1950s, the main problem was that there was no legitimate government in South Vietnam. South Vietnam was essentially a fiction created by the Geneva Accords which served after the French-Vietnamese war as a basis for the puppet government set up by the French.

As a first step in establishing a legitimate South Vietnamese government, the Americans believed they needed to give the Vietnamese a strong, respectable leader. The Eisenhower administration, at the urging of CIA operative Edward Lansdale, and with the support of powerful Catholic leaders in the United States, threw their money and support behind Ngo Dinh Diem. Diem was a genuine nationalist, committed to an independent, non-Communist Vietnam. He was also an upper-class devout Roman Catholic in a nation primarily composed of poor Buddhist peasants. A terrible politician who did not believe in democracy or land reform, Diem would prove to be a tough sell to the Vietnamese people.

As the United States replaced France in South Vietnam, Ho and the Vietminh consolidated their hold over North Vietnam. While they had a legitimate base among the peasants of Vietnam, they too had to create a stable government and economy out of the chaos, poverty, and misery a century of French exploitation and a decade of war had produced. Ho's first foray into major economic reorganization brought about both genuine land reform and a chaotic, murderous—and brief—state-sponsored reign of terror that pitted villager against villager. Some one million Vietnamese fled the Communist rulers of the north. Most of them were Catholics who had been convinced to flee, in part, by wildly creative, occasionally plausible CIA PsyOp propaganda campaigns. Then, too, Catholics, small and big businessmen, ex-members of the French bureaucracies, and many others had good reason to fear the bloody hand of the Vietminh. No more interested in political democracy than Diem, the repressive Vietminh brooked no opposition in their pursuit of a revolutionary Vietnam built on Communist principles. Overwhelmed with governing the north of Vietnam, Ho and the Vietminh gave the Americans time to build a new nation in the south.

Despite the Geneva Accords (which the United States had never signed), and the protests of the Vietminh, no real elections were held in Vietnam in 1956. In South Vietnam, Diem, with American approval, held a plebiscite on his popularity. He won 98.2 percent of the vote. Considering that in Saigon alone, where 450,000 people were registered to vote, Diem received 605,000 votes, the election was indicative not of Diem's popularity but of his and his American handlers' cynical approach to democratic politics.

To build their new nation, Americans poured money and resources into the country. The Pentagon worked to create a viable army in South Vietnam out of the corrupt, demoralized force the French had left behind. The CIA contracted with the Michigan State University School of Police Administration to organize and train a Vietnamese paramilitary police force capable of controlling dissidents. The CIA employed American academics and government economists to engineer and monitor a land-reform program. A variety of executive branch agencies and departments contributed to the billion-dollar commercial-import program which was designed to stabilize a South Vietnamese currency while propping up the new nation's economy. Congress and the vast majority of the American people were largely irrelevant to the forward development and implementation of these projects. The bureaucracies and agencies and contract experts of the national security apparatus, watched over by the commander-in-chief of the United States, were in charge.

When John F. Kennedy took over the White House in 1961, the men involved in building a new nation in South Vietnam could point to one towering achievement. The Republic of Vietnam, led by Ngo Dinh Diem, still existed. Despite almost no support in the countryside, where approximately 90 percent of the Vietnamese people lived, the Diem government had hung on. While the Army of the Republic of Vietnam (ARVN) was still corrupt and demoralized, it had prevented the Communists of the north and the many enemies of Diem in the south from taking power. Diem, by means of a reign of terror that included mass imprisonment without trials and wholesale torture, rape, and murder, had severely reduced the number of active Vietminh supporters in the south of Vietnam. Within Saigon, many people, if by no means a majority, enjoyed a high standard of living due to American largess. The American planners, against the odds, had gained time in their battle to form an independent, anti-Communist Vietnam. Their battle with time, though, was about the only victory they had won. And time, they knew, was running out.

Diem was proving to be a disaster. He treated the Buddhist majority with contempt and worse. His brutal authoritarian measures, while useful against Vietminh sympathizers, were employed so capriciously and corruptly as to make new enemies. Indifferent to the fate of the peasantry and in sympathy with the upper classes, he had refused to aggressively implement even the modest land-reform programs his American advisers had created for him. As the CIA knew, Diem's main source of support came from the United States.

Diem was able to hang on, in part, because the government in North Vietnam had its own problems. Ruling and developing a poor country, even half a country, was a monumental task, made more difficult by Communist principles which had caused many in the north's business and administrative classes to flee or be imprisoned, and by the regime's repressive, authoritarian measures which alienated many peasants who had expected greater autonomy in running their own affairs. Economic development was also made more difficult by the sustained American efforts to subvert the north's economy. Further complicating the Vietminh's plans was the failure of China and the Soviet Union to supply them with the military assistance they needed to take on the army of South Vietnam which was well armed and financed by the United States. Despite such severe internal problems, by the time President Kennedy took over the White House, the Vietminh had begun to turn to reunifying an independent Vietnam.

By the late 1950s, Vietminh supporters in the south, targeted for extermination by the Diem regime, and impatient for Vietminh assistance, had begun systematically to slaughter civilian Diem government officials as a way to stop any possibility of political consolidation in the south. In 1960 alone, and by then operating under the more direct orders of the north, the Vietcong (a label Diem fixed on the rebels—"cong" means "Commie") assassinated 2,500 officials. The previous year, the Vietminh had begun to send arms and advisers to South Vietnam and to resume formal control of the efforts to bring down the American-created South Vietnamese government. With increasing numbers of soldiers from the north in the southern countryside, the Vietminh began full-scale military operations against ARVN troops and started taking over villages. By late 1960, the Vietminh directed their forces to form the National Front for the Liberation of South Vietnam (NLF), which was to be a Communist-controlled coalition of anti-Diem forces, dedicated to an independent, unified Vietnam. By October 1961 much of the South Vietnamese countryside was under the full or partial control of the NLF, which received support, with varying degrees of enthusiasm, throughout the south.

President Kennedy came to office dedicated to the belief that America could and should shape the destiny of the world's developing countries. At the first meeting of his National Security Council in 1961, he read his advisers passages from a speech his Soviet nemesis Nikita Khrushchev had made proclaiming support for all national liberation movements in the colonial world. Kennedy told them he did not intend to allow the Soviets' spreading influence in the Third World to stand.

Vietnam, however, was not primarily what Kennedy had in mind. Vietnam was not on the new President's list of priorities, nor was it on the list of key issues departing President Eisenhower discussed with Kennedy at their transition meetings (though neighboring Laos was). Indeed, Kennedy remarked in the middle of his administration, when the fate of Vietnam had become more clearly an urgent issue, "You know, Eisenhower never mentioned it, never uttered the word Vietnam."

President Kennedy believed that the instability of the developing countries demanded new approaches. Kennedy was particularly taken by the analysis of MIT economist Walt W. Rostow, who had begun advising Kennedy during his Senate days. Rostow believed that all nations followed the same general path of economic and social development. As nations began the phase of development he called "modernization" they became unstable. A Third World country guided through this period, Rostow argued, was far less likely to become Communist.

In essence, Rostow's model was only a more polished version of the nation-building dream that had motivated the Eisenhower administration. Rather than focusing on nation building as it was specifically working in South Vietnam, Rostow merely made the general idea more attractive.

Guided in part by this modernization model (Rostow himself served as Deputy Special Assistant for National Security Affairs), the Kennedy administration considered how it might protect South Vietnam while helping guide it through the requisite stages of economic growth. Vietnam's concrete realities, its history, faded in comparison with the vivid dream of creating a modernized Vietnam secured by its people's patriotism. Of course, time would be needed to reach this goal, and to gain this time, the Communist threat would have to be repelled.

Here, too, the Kennedy administration moved with more sophistication down the path the Eisenhower administration had laid out. Kennedy and his main military adviser, General Maxwell Taylor, observed that Americans were training for the wrong kind of war in the Third World. In Vietnam, Taylor warned, America had spent over a billion dollars preparing the ARVN for a conventional troop invasion from the north. America needed a military strategy of "flexible response" capable of delivering nuclear weapons against the Soviets and a campaign of counterinsurgency against guerrilla forces in the jungles of the Third World. Like Rostow's more targeted form of nation building, Taylor's sophisticated ideas about creating a counterinsurgency force offered the Kennedy administration new and better methods for pursuing a struggle in Vietnam which they refused to understand in terms of Vietnam's history and its struggle for independence. Rather than accept Vietnamese realities, they meant to make reality conform to their vision.

Throughout Kennedy's first year in office, as historians Randy Roberts and James Olson well describe, the President and his advisers debated America's role in Vietnam. Secretary of Defense Robert McNamara, a Ford man replacing a GM man as head of the nation's single largest organization, observed that "North Vietnam will never beat us. They can't even make ice cubes." Secretary of State Dean Rusk saw the battle against Communism in Southeast Asia in general and in Vietnam in particular as central to America's mission in the world. He pushed for escalation.

Only one of Kennedy's key advisers spoke out strongly against the war. Under Secretary of State for Economic Affairs George Ball, unlike any of the other key players in the debate, had been following the Indochina situation from the early 1950s. He had been counsel to the French embassy in Washington in the early 1950s. He learned from the French that Vietnam was not a place of abstractions but a land where hundreds of thousands had died fighting for independence. He warned the President that Vietnam could not easily be bent to America's will. He stressed that success in creating a legitimate government in South Vietnam was highly unlikely. To maintain the fiction of an independent South Vietnam, Ball insisted, would mean that in "five years there will be

300,000 American soldiers fighting in Vietnam." To this prophecy, President Kennedy had snorted, "George you're crazier than hell."

More tempting advice was offered by McGeorge Bundy, Kennedy's Special Assistant for National Security Affairs. Bundy came to the White House from Harvard and was a brilliant man who relished putting ideas into action. A firm believer in Maxwell Taylor's strategy of flexible response, he saw Vietnam as an ideal site for testing America's new military capacity. Walt Rostow, Bundy's ally in this regard, put the matter most cogently: "It is somehow wrong to be developing these capabilities but not applying them in a crucial theater. In Knute Rockne's old phrase, we are not saving them for the junior prom."

In May 1961, Kennedy sent 500 more American advisers to Vietnam, bringing American forces there to 1,400 men. The military wanted more, arguing that with 13,000 troops, they could clean out the Vietcong. Kennedy didn't know what to do. Men he trusted argued both sides of the issue.

Kennedy was not deciding the fate of Vietnam in a political vacuum. Cuba, Berlin, Laos, and the bullying presence of Nikita Khrushchev all weighed on the President. As historian George Herring notes, Kennedy told his staff that the "gut issue" in Vietnam was not the relative effectiveness of the current South Vietnamese government but whether the United States of America would allow Communist "aggression" to stand in South Vietnam. "Both sides of the Iron Curtain," Kennedy argued, would watch Vietnam "as a measure of the administration's intentions and determination." America's long-shot experiment in nation building was becoming, in the minds of many of America's most powerful men, a test of American resolve. Kennedy hated the idea of failing that test. Slowly, over the next year, Kennedy escalated American involvement in the war.

At the end of 1962, the military had most of what they wanted. The United States was spending about half a billion dollars a year to keep the ARVN fighting. Some 11,300 American officers and noncommissioned officers operated at every level of the South Vietnamese army as advisers. U.S. pilots, accompanied by South

Vietnamese pilots, began flying an increasing number of missions against the Vietcong. Napalm began to rain down on Vietnamese villages suspected of harboring the Vietcong. Herbicides began to be used to clear forests. Helicopter gunships controlled the air. Vietnamese civilians in areas controlled by the Vietcong were forcibly relocated to "strategic hamlets" in order to deny the enemy support. The American military reported that the war was fast being won. Commanding General Paul Harkins told the President in early 1963 that he could begin withdrawing American troops by the end of the year and that by 1965 all Americans could be out of Vietnam.

Harkins, of course, was wrong. In fact, the war was being won by the Vietcong and the North Vietnamese. Indiscriminate bombing by the South Vietnamese air force, advised by American forces, resulted in massive civilian casualties. The Strategic Hamlet Program, which forcibly removed peasants in VC territory from their ancestral land, further angered people in the countryside. By the tens of thousands, men and women joined the Vietcong. Many of the fighters were armed with American weapons, which were being sold and turned over to the Vietcong by people in South Vietnam supposedly loyal to the Diem regime. Vietnamese from the north were infiltrating the south in increasing numbers. The situation was fast deteriorating.

Diem had become an American nightmare. Millions of dollars in American aid and military supplies were being stolen by leading members of the Diem regime. Diem ignored his American advisers. He refused to implement land-reform programs. He continued to attack Vietnam's Buddhist majority. From the American perspective he was a puppet who refused to acknowledge that he couldn't stand without American support. He was cutting his strings and he threatened to take South Vietnam down with him when he fell. Something had to be done.

By the summer of 1963, many American war managers had decided that Diem had to go if the war was to be won. The CIA was given the go-ahead to assist in a South Vietnamese army coup against Diem. Kennedy tacitly agreed to the solution. On November 2, 1963, Diem was assassinated in a successful coup d'état.

Once again, the American government hoped it had created a fresh start in Vietnam.

Kennedy still did not know what policy to pursue in Vietnam. In the weeks before and after the coup he spoke to advisers about pulling out. He had announced that he would withdraw 1,000 men from Vietnam at the end of the year and had made serious plans to take more out if there was evidence of improved ARVN capabilities. Still, Kennedy left no doubt that, at the very least, he would see the war through until he won reelection in 1964. His closest adviser, Theodore Sorensen, has argued that Kennedy "did feel strongly that for better or worse, enthusiastic or unenthusiastic, we had to stay there [in Vietnam] until we left on terms other than a retreat or abandonment of our commitment." Secretary of State Dean Rusk and Attorney General Robert Kennedy believed Kennedy would have stayed the course and not accepted a Communist victory in Vietnam. The only certainty about John Kennedy's role in Vietnam is that before he died, just three weeks after Diem's assassination, he had escalated America's military, political, and psychological commitment to the Republic of South Vietnam.

Lyndon Johnson inherited a policy in shambles. After an early briefing on Vietnam, Johnson said he felt like a catfish that had "grabbed a big juicy worm with a right sharp hook in the middle of it." Still, Johnson believed that Americans must stay the course in Vietnam; the nation's credibility, his credibility as commander-in-chief, was at stake. He told one of his closest advisers, "They'll think with Kennedy dead we've lost heart. . . . The Chinese. The fellas in the Kremlin. They'll be taking the measure of us." Then, too, at a gut level, like Kennedy, he had no intention of being the man who "lost" Vietnam to the Communists.

In his first few months in office, Johnson faced a deteriorating situation in Vietnam. The coup left the south in political chaos. Tens of thousands of South Vietnamese soldiers were deserting. At the same time, the number of Vietcong soldiers was growing rapidly.

Johnson's Pentagon advisers urged him to increase the pressure on North Vietnam by bombing their industrial base and allow direct American involvement in the ground war. No one in government expected such efforts alone to end the war. One report that Defense Secretary McNamara had commissioned simply argued that bombing the north would "demonstrate U.S. power and determination, along with restraint to Asia and the world at large" and would provide "some time and opportunity by the government of South Vietnam to improve itself." CIA officials and high-level Defense and State Department officials also knew, by this time, that attacks on the north would not affect "Communist capabilities to continue that insurrection" because "the primary sources of Communist strength in South Vietnam are indigenous." But American war managers hoped that attacking the north might weaken the "will of the DRV [North Vietnamese] leaders." In other words, despite the bloody history of the Vietnamese war against the French, the Americans hoped that if the United States fought a limited war against the people of the north, Ho Chi Minh and others who had been struggling for an independent nation for decades would suddenly give up. The Americans had to further hope that the Vietcong, without the support of the Ho regime, could be exterminated by the corrupt South Vietnamese government. At this point, total American casualties in Vietnam numbered about 750 men.

Johnson, like Kennedy, had a very difficult time signing on to his defense experts' arguments that by incrementally increasing the pressure on North Vietnam the war could be won and a stable government, friendly to the United States, could be maintained. Still, Johnson gave the go-ahead for a series of covert attacks on the north's infrastructure, bombing runs against North Vietnamese supply lines that crossed through neighboring Laos, and air and naval surveillance of the north. In general, policy drifted. South Vietnam was sinking. By the summer of 1964, 20,000 American military advisers were in Vietnam.

Republicans in the House and Senate began to attack Johnson's policy, hoping to make Vietnam an issue in the upcoming election. The Republican presidential candidate, Senator Barry Goldwater, called for air attacks on North Vietnam. While Vietnam still remained for most Americans an issue of only minor importance,

Johnson was starting to feel the political heat. His military and civilian advisers urged him to act, to do something as soon as an opportunity arose to show his enemies at home and abroad that American interests were being actively defended.

On August 4, 1964, the American destroyers *Maddox* and *C. Turner Joy*, sailing in the Gulf of Tonkin, after a run-in two days earlier with North Vietnamese patrol boats, reported that though no damage had been sustained or enemy ships sighted, they believed they were under North Vietnamese torpedo attack. The President, under pressure to demonstrate American resolve in Vietnam, had his provocation. He ordered an immediate retaliatory attack. The Air Force bombed torpedo-boat bases and oil-storage dumps in North Vietnam. No conclusive evidence then or now indicates that the destroyers had actually been fired upon, as Johnson's key advisers knew.

At 11:36 p.m. in Washington, D.C., as the Air Force made its bombing runs, President Johnson went live on all three television networks. He calmly told the American people that "aggression by terror against peaceful villages of South Vietnam had now been joined by open aggression on the high seas against the United States of America." The President assured the American people that while such aggression would be met by force, "we seek no wider war." It was one more deception to add to the list.

The public was being led to believe that the U.S. role in Vietnam consisted of assisting the sovereign nation of democratic South Vietnam against Soviet-sponsored attacks by the Communist nation of North Vietnam. It was as if nothing that had happened before was real: the hundred years of French imperialism, Ho's 1945 declaration of independence after the defeat of the Japanese, the Vietminh's bloody war against the French, the 1954 Geneva Accords, America's failed attempt to manufacture a legitimate government in the south, the NLF's indigenous roots in the south.

By the next morning, Johnson began pressing Congress to pass what came to be called the Gulf of Tonkin Resolution. The resolution allowed the President "to take all necessary measures to repel any armed attack against the armed forces of the United States and to prevent further aggression." With little debate the

House approved the measure with a unanimous voice vote. The Senate did debate the issue for a couple of weeks. Alaska senator Ernest Gruening called the resolution "a predated declaration of war." He and Senator Wayne Morse of Oregon refused to support the measure. Other senators, especially George McGovern, voted yes but made it clear, on the record, that they were not in support of escalating American involvement in Vietnam. Still the final vote in the Senate was 88–2 and President Johnson had attained the appearance of near-consensus in pursuing the war in Vietnam in whatever manner he chose. As public opinion polls revealed, he had found an excellent way of defusing Goldwater's attacks on his position. As has always been true in the first weeks of war or perceived foreign threat, the American people flocked to their commander-in-chief. Johnson also believed he had found an excellent way to demonstrate American resolve to the nation's enemies abroad.

In fact, the retaliatory bombings were taken by the North Vietnamese not as a sign of American resolve but as an indication of American obstinacy. The premier of North Vietnam, Pham Van Dong, in a frank discussion with a Canadian diplomat (who carried messages to the north from the Johnson administration demanding that North Vietnam give up its efforts to take over the south; otherwise it would face an escalating war) said he was "extremely angry" about the bombing of North Vietnamese territory. As author Marilyn Young reports, Pham charged that the United States "sought to extricate itself from a failed policy in the south by expanding the war to the north." Pham told the Canadian diplomat to tell his American friends that his people would "fight a war if it came"; they would not back down before American firepower. In the next few weeks, the North Vietnamese decided to begin sending their regular combat troops to the south in force. Even as President Johnson went around the country claiming to be the "peace candidate," America's war in Vietnam was beginning to escalate out of control.

7. A NATION AT WAR

~~~~~~

ON THE GROUNDS of the Washington Monument more than 15,000 people came together for the first national protest against American policy in Vietnam. It was April 17, 1965, and the war still seemed a peripheral issue to most Americans. Paul Potter, the president of Students for a Democratic Society (SDS), the small, almost unknown group that had sponsored the protest, wanted to draw America's attention to the war and to give the public a new way to think about it. In his speech, he linked the war in Vietnam to larger problems in American society.

Potter and his young colleagues in SDS believed something had gone very wrong with America. The war in Vietnam, Potter argued that day, was a sign of the failure of democracy. It represented not the will of the people but the interests of an interlocking financial, technocratic, and military elite—the "system" —which manipulated the public in order to direct national policy for its own ends and for its own benefit.

The speech Potter gave was an early version of a standard "sixties" speech, reflective of late-night discussions taking place among young people throughout the country. Inspired by the civil rights movement, Potter and the others who belonged to what was beginning to be called the New Left dreamed of forging a new democracy in which all Americans could, and would, have a voice in their own communities and play a role in shaping their nation's destiny. That was what protest that day was all about—one small step, it was hoped, in taking back the governance of their country.

"The incredible war in Vietnam," Potter said that day, "has provided the razor, the terrifying sharp cutting edge that has finally severed the last vestiges of illusion that morality and democracy are the guiding principles of American foreign policy." Behind that illusion, Potter argued, stands a "system" of power that managed the American government for the benefit of its own narrow interests. Potter did not claim to understand exactly how that "system" worked or what ends it pursued. He only knew, he later said, that "something new [was] afoot in the world." He hoped that by raising sharp questions about how the nation was managed "from on high," he, in company with many others, could somehow begin to change it:

> What kind of system is it that justifies the United States or any country seizing the destinies of the Vietnamese people and using them callously for its own purpose? What kind of system is it that disenfranchises people in the South, leaves millions upon millions of people throughout the country impoverished and excluded from the mainstream and promise of American society, that creates faceless and terrible bureaucracies and makes those the place where people spend their lives and do their work, that consistently puts material values before human values—and still persists in calling itself free and still persists in finding itself fit to police the world?

In closing his impassioned speech, Potter offered a brief analysis of the Vietnamese struggle for independence and outlined the work that lay ahead for the demonstrators and all who would challenge the American "system." He observed: "In both countries there are people struggling to build a movement that has the power to change their condition. The system that frustrates these movements is the same. All our lives, our destinies, our very hopes to live, depend on our ability to overcome that system."

Paul Potter, that day, expressed much of the spirit that would animate a small but vital part of the antiwar movement. Potter—in a radicalized but not unrelated update of President Eisenhower's farewell address warning against "the military-industrial complex"—meant to expose the nature and purpose of the nondemocratic, extraconstitutional, elite-controlled government bureaucracies and apparatuses that ran American foreign policy. At a time when few Americans knew anything about CIA covert operations, or about the massive influence America's giant corporations and banks had on Pentagon procurement, foreign aid programs, and overall international policy, or about the sheer extent and reach of the secretive national security apparatus, Potter's vague but compelling jeremiad against the "system" was inspiring and influential.

Most people participated in the antiwar movement because they wanted to see American troops get out of Vietnam. Theirs was a single issue. Millions of others, however, learned through their opposition to the war in Vietnam (and for some, their experiences in the civil rights movement, too) to work toward both a more open government and a new role for America in the world. They also learned to be suspicious of conventional thinking about "international Communism" and "national security"—and much more. Many people, in a phrase from the time, learned to "question authority." They started with their national leaders but extended their questioning to those who produced the "news," who ran their schools, who claimed to teach them about values and morality. The faith of many Americans in their society's complex web of cultural authority and political legitimacy was weakened, even destroyed, by the government's failed policies in Vietnam.

Paul Potter's attempt to "name the system" that orchestrated American policy in Vietnam was almost certainly beneficial to the democratic aspirations of the American people. Potter's simplistic characterization of the struggle in Vietnam, however, encouraged a darker impulse that would run wild in a small but vocal sector of the broad, multifaceted antiwar movement. In Potter's speech, the North Vietnamese and the National Liberation Front were made to seem similar to American student activists and civil rights organizers. That the Vietcong slaughtered innocent village officials and that Ho Chi Minh exterminated his political rivals and that Communist rule in Vietnam was and would be repressive and antidemocratic, all of these hard truths were left unsaid—mainly because Potter and many later antiwar activists knew little about the realities of Vietnam. Too many of the radicals dreamed of a world neatly divided between bad elites and the good "people."

They came to believe that if the American government was pursuing the wrong policy in Vietnam, the American government was bad and thus, almost by definition, the Vietnamese guerrillas must be right and good.

These radicals were, more than they would have acknowledged, the children of the Cold War and of John F. Kennedy's bipolar world, in which Light and Dark warred for the soul of humanity. And to be fair, the experiences of some of the early antiwar advocates in the civil rights movement had given real credence to this "black" and "white" worldview. Most people in the 1960s, both those for the war and those against it, were largely ignorant of and indifferent to the realities of societies so different from their own. Few Americans were prepared for a world in which moral ambiguity could be accepted as the basis for policy.

Between the summer of 1964, when the Johnson administration achieved passage of the Gulf of Tonkin Resolution, and the April 1965 antiwar rally, the American combat role in Vietnam had escalated greatly. Vietcong attacks on Americans in South Vietnam had contributed to this escalation. Before the Gulf of Tonkin bombing raids, NLF forces had not targeted the American soldiers who were advising the South Vietnamese army. The NLF had gone so far as to sneak into American positions at night and leave VC flags or messages indicating both that they could have killed the occupants and, more importantly, that they had chosen not to. But after the bombing of North Vietnam, the Vietcong began shelling the American advisers. In direct response to one of the more effective VC attacks on an American base at Pleiku, where seven Americans were killed and a hundred wounded, Johnson told the American people that he had ordered a limited bombing of North Vietnamese targets.

Despite what Johnson had told the nation, the VC attack was only the most proximate cause for beginning a sustained bombing attack on the north. A more important factor, which had already prompted the managers of the war to have bombing plans at the ready, was that the war was again in danger of being lost.

McGeorge Bundy advised the President: "Without new U.S. action defeat appears inevitable—probably not in a matter of weeks or perhaps even months, but within the next year or so." The South Vietnamese government had once again failed; another military coup had taken place. Once again, time would have to be bought. Only now, time would have to be bought not just with the blood of the Vietnamese people but also with that of America's fighting men.

President Johnson and his advisers had a serious problem by early 1965: what it meant to "win" the war by this time was both too simple and too complicated. According to Assistant Secretary of Defense John McNaughton, writing to his boss, Secretary of Defense Robert McNamara, the United States was in Vietnam only "10%—to permit the people of SVN to enjoy a better, freer way of life." By 1965 the main goal of U.S. policy in Vietnam ("70%," reported McNaughton) was "to avoid a humiliating US defeat." Victory in Vietnam, then, simply meant stopping the Communists from bringing down the American-backed South Vietnamese government.

The American war managers did not have as their objective the conquest of North Vietnam or the destruction of Ho's Communist regime in the north. The legitimacy of that regime was not questioned; taking and occupying the territory of the north was a mission no one thought could be accomplished without costing hundreds of thousands of American casualties. In 1965, General Earle Wheeler, Chairman of the Joint Chiefs of Staff, estimated that 700,000 to one million Americans fighting for seven years would be needed to completely pacify Vietnam. Destroying North Vietnam from the air with either conventional or nuclear weapons (as Senator Barry Goldwater and other "war hawks" advocated) would be an act of genocidal barbarism and seemed to offer little chance of achieving the cessation of hostilities against South Vietnam.

Ambassador to South Vietnam Henry Cabot Lodge explained why reducing the north to rubble would not advance American interests:

If you lay the whole country to waste, it is quite likely that you will induce a mood of fatalism in the Vietcong. Also there will be nobody left in North Vietnam on whom to put pressure. . . . What we are interested in here is not destroying Ho Chi Minh (as his successor would probably be worse than he is) but getting him to change his behavior.

Lodge and the other war managers knew that the Vietcong and the North Vietnamese regulars, unfortunately, were not "foreign" aggressors from the north under the control of a Communist Central located in Moscow or Beijing. The enemy were just Vietnamese people, many indigenous to the south, dedicated to a unified, independent country. The trick was to get Ho to use his power over the NLF and over his own army to make them stop fighting against the American-backed government in the south and to accept two Vietnams, or, at the least, to stop long enough for the United States to *create* that dreamed-of legitimate government.

The administration's difficulty was in putting enough military pressure on Ho to force him to give up designs on the south without pushing him against the wall, where he might well feel compelled to fight until the apocalyptic end. Then, too, the war managers believed, if too much pressure was brought to bear on the North Vietnamese, the Chinese or the Russians or both might feel obligated to support their Communist ally. In retrospect, it seems almost certain that neither the Russians nor the Chinese would have sent in their armies, but no one in the Johnson administration had that information at the time. President Johnson explained his strategy in this regard to a worried Senator McGovern: "I'm watching that very closely. I'm going up her [North Vietnam's] leg an inch at a time. . . . I'll get to the snatch before they [China] know what's happening." Preventing Vietnam from becoming a major battleground between American troops and either Chinese or Soviet forces seemed a war objective not to be taken lightly.

By mid-1965, President Johnson ordered sustained but limited bombing of the north. Since the American command, with excellent reason, did not believe the South Vietnamese army capable of protecting American air bases, Marines were dispatched in increasing numbers to provide a perimeter defense. Quickly, in accordance with good military tactics, the defensive posture of the Marines became an offensive one. The commitment of American ground forces for the first time in nonadvisory, combat roles marked a major change in the American position, a position almost unremarked upon publicly by the President.

General Maxwell Taylor, the architect of Kennedy's military strategy of "flexible response" and ambassador to South Vietnam in 1965, protested the introduction of American combat troops in a strongly worded cable to the State Department:

> Once this policy is breached it will be very difficult to hold the line . . . one may be very sure that GVN [government of Vietnam] will seek to unload other ground force tasks upon us. . . . White-faced soldier armed, equipped and trained as he is [is] not a suitable guerrilla fighter for Asian forests and jungles. French tried . . . and failed; I doubt that US forces could do much better. . . . Finally there would be the ever present question of how foreign soldier would distinguish between a VC and friendly Vietnamese farmer . . . I am convinced that we should adhere to our past policy of keeping ground forces out of direct counterinsurgency role.

Taylor's protest was ignored. General William Westmoreland, in charge of the military in Vietnam, believed American forces needed effective security. He further believed that unleashing America's well-trained and superbly equipped combat forces on the enemy—despite the French failure—would lead to quick victory: "We're going to out-guerrilla the guerrilla and out-ambush the ambush . . . because we're smarter, we have greater mobility and firepower; we have endurance and more to fight for . . . and we've got more guts." In June, Westmoreland requested an additional thirty-four battalions. In July, President Johnson, fearful of further attacks on American positions and of South Vietnam's

capitulation to the Communists, agreed to most of Westmoreland's suggestions on how to execute the war.

Johnson would not, however, allow Westmoreland to launch
an offensive on North Vietnam, believing that the immense cost
in American lives was too high a political price to pay. He believed
that a display of America's awesome military power would be
enough to force the Communists to give up and after hearing of
the Marines' first successful deployment gloated: "Now I have Ho
Chi Minh's pecker in my pocket." In the short term, the ground
forces guaranteed that the air offensive could continue to escalate
and that the corrupt South Vietnamese government would not
fall. In the long term, as George Ball and then Maxwell Taylor
had warned, the introduction of ground troops marked the rapid
takeover of the war by the American armed forces.

In mid-1965, Johnson tried to induce America's main allies to
join in the struggle. The British refused to help, arguing that the
war was a lost cause and that Johnson should seek a negotiated
settlement. The French, who had started America down the road
to war in Vietnam, were more blunt. "The United States," French
leader Charles de Gaulle warned, "cannot win this war. No matter
how far they push it in the future, they will lose it." The old
colonial powers in Asia had seen enough. Only Australia and New
Zealand sent combat troops—7,000 all told—in support of America's efforts. (American-paid Korean troops also fought in Vietnam.) In the eyes of the world, Vietnam would be an American
show.

John Kennedy had called George Ball crazy when he said that
there would be 300,000 Americans in Vietnam if policy did not
change. But Kennedy had also told one of his advisers, "They [the
military] want a force of American troops. . . . Then we will be
told we have to send more troops. It's like taking a drink. The
effect wears off, and you have to have another." Kennedy was
wrong about Ball's prophecy but he was right about the military's
escalating demands for more troops. In 1961 there had been 3,200
American advisers; in 1963 there were 16,300; in 1964, 23,300. By
the end of 1965 there were 184,300 American troops in Vietnam.
In three years, 550,000 U.S. military personnel would be serving

there. And by the end of 1968, 30,610 American servicemen had been killed in action. Despite General Westmoreland's assurances of progress, and despite hundreds of thousands of dead Vietnamese, the war was still not being won. It had become a quagmire.

By the time U.S. troops left Vietnam in 1973, over 2 million American fighting men had served in the war. They fought two wars, one in the air and one on the ground. The air war aimed to kill the enemy, to stop the flow of arms, supplies, and men from the north into the south, to deprive the enemy of cover, to pressure the Communist government, and to support American ground troops. The air war took place in Vietnam, Cambodia, and Laos. Over 7 million tons of bombs were dropped; some 4 million tons fell on South Vietnam alone. (In all of World War II, the United States dropped 2 million tons of bombs and munitions.) About 1 million tons of death and destruction rained down on North Vietnam. Over 1.5 million tons fell on the Ho Chi Minh Trail, the main supply route from the north to the south. Every industrial, transportation, and communication facility the North Vietnamese had built since defeating the French was obliterated. North Vietnamese agriculture was decimated, petroleum stocks were blown up, and cities were smashed. Hundreds of thousands of Vietnamese soldiers and civilians died in the air attacks. But supplies and arms kept coming from the Chinese and the Soviets. Enough trucks (it took only a few each night) came down from the north on roads and bridges rebuilt after every bombardment. And each year new soldiers and guerrillas came of age to replace those the Americans killed. The war continued.

On the ground, in its second war, the military fought a war of attrition. Marines and soldiers went out from secure bases to find the enemy and kill him in "search and destroy" missions. Progress was measured by counting the enemy dead, "the body count." Late in the war, the ground war spread to Cambodia and Laos, and even earlier a few men made clandestine across-the-border raids on North Vietnam. But for most of the war, the killing ground was in South Vietnam. The air war was fought on American terms. The ground war was overwhelmingly fought on the terms of the National Liberation Front and the North Vietnamese regulars.

In late 1968, with U.S. forces in Vietnam at over half a million, the CIA reported that American combat patrols were only able to find and engage the enemy, on average, less than one time in a hundred. When they did engage, especially in large groups, the Americans ground up the enemy. But most of the time the troops just walked through villages and the countryside, on edge, waiting, bored, scared, angry. As Marine officer Philip Caputo wrote: "Without a front, flanks, or rear, we fought a formless war against a formless enemy who evaporated like the jungle mists, only to materialize in some unexpected place."

The American fighting men and the 11,000 women who served in Vietnam came from every part of the country. But disproportionately they came from America's small towns, farms, and inner cities. Young men from America's well-to-do suburbs and fashionable city neighborhoods chose not to enlist. This war, unlike World War II, failed to evoke their patriotic ardor. And, unlike the years of the Korean conflict, most of America's more affluent young men sought exemptions and deferments from the draft. About 80 percent of the enlisted men who fought in Vietnam were from working-class and poor families. Most of them had made it through high school but had not gone on to college because they were either uninterested or unable. On average, the men who went to Vietnam were nineteen years old (in World War II the average age was twenty-six). Of those who died for their country in Vietnam, only a few hundred were older than thirty. The war was generally fought by those baby boomers whose families' hold on the postwar prosperity was weakest.

About two-thirds of the men who fought in Vietnam in the 1960s volunteered to serve in the Army or the Marines. For many of the volunteers, historian Chris Appey has argued, enlisting in the military had seemed their best option: "the draft was on their necks, school was a boring hassle, jobs all seemed dead end, family

life was becoming unbearable, conflicts with authorities were turning serious and dangerous."

A small group of men joined up, often with the Marine Corps,
out of a sense of adventure and out of a desire to serve their
country. As one decorated Special Forces officer who had first
fought in the Central Highlands of Vietnam in 1965 recounted: "I
wanted to go to Vietnam . . . people like myself go into a situation
like that because it's exciting, it's the ultimate challenge."

Many other working-class men joined the armed forces because
they saw it as a good employer and because they did not think
they would end up fighting in Vietnam. An airborne trooper who
arrived in Vietnam in April 1965 explained: "You never thought
you was going over to Nam. . . . I always heard, you know, go
into the service, learn a good trade and get to see the world."

African-American men, in particular, saw military service as a
means of improving their status and opportunities in life. Less well
educated than their white counterparts and discriminated against
by the military, a disproportionate number of these young black
men ended up not on Cold War duty in Germany or Korea or
learning new skills Stateside but in Vietnam in combat roles. As
a result, 24 percent of the soldiers killed in Vietnam in 1965 were
African-American men (as the war continued, the Department of
Defense reduced the number of black men in combat in order to
bring down their casualty rates).

A large percentage of the volunteers surveyed, 37.6 percent in
1964 and 47.2 percent by 1968, said that they enlisted to avoid
being drafted. By volunteering they hoped to have at least some
control over the timing and type of their military service.

About one-third of the men who fought in Vietnam were draft-
ees. But for every man who was drafted more than seven men
were exempted from service by their draft boards. A 1965 Selective
Service policy statement explained that "channeling manpower by
deferment" into a variety of pursuits and careers vital to "the
national defense" was a central aspect of the system. As a result,
all college students (until 1973) were automatically deferred. Until
1968, all graduate students were automatically deferred. Most
teachers, engineers, scientists, and many other college-educated

professionals received draft deferments. So did most "supervisors" of four or more workers. Then, too, many apprentices in well-paying trades like plumbing and electrical work could receive job-related deferments.

Local draft boards had a great deal of leeway in deciding who would be given deferments. Since Vietnam was not treated by the federal government as a total war demanding complete mobilization, there were far more baby boomers of draft age than were necessary for the war effort. Young men who made the case to their draft boards that they had a productive or vital or important job were often exempted from service.

Many middle-class and upper-class men, who for whatever reasons did not want to be drafted, once they used up their student deferments found myriad other ways to stay out of the armed forces. Many of them were able to draw on their families' financial resources or connections, as well as the increasingly antiwar culture of college campuses, to find the people and the information they needed to help them receive a deferment. Through friendly doctors and psychiatrists they received medical and psychological deferments. Some half a million young men, mainly in earnest, became conscientious objectors to the war and then did alternative national service. Many joined the military reserves knowing full well that the odds of being called up to active duty were very slim. Young men learned from the rapidly expanding corps of "draft counselors" to fake symptoms at their pre-induction exams, to claim to be gay, to claim to be a member of a subversive organization, to be disruptive, and so on.

As the war became more unpopular by the late 1960s, millions of young men, disproportionately from the more affluent and well-educated segments of America, actively sought to avoid the draft. Because of the war's growing unpopularity, few of these men were censured by their families, friends, or employers. Fighting the war was mainly left to poor and working-class men. William Strauss and Lawrence Baskir, somewhat cruelly, wrote: "The Vietnam draft cast the entire generation into a contest for individual survival . . . the 'fittest'—those with the background, wit, or money—managed to escape." Some 16 million young men in the Vietnam generation, a sizable majority, never served in the armed forces at all.

Early in the war, most of the men who ended up in Vietnam were uncertain about the purpose of their mission but confident that they were doing the right thing. Tim O'Brien, in his searing Vietnam war novel, *Going After Cacciato*, writes: "He didn't know who really started the war, or why, or when, or with what motives. . . . He went to the war because it was expected. . . . Because, not knowing, he saw no reason to distrust those with more experience. Because he loved his country, and more than that he trusted it." American men in Vietnam wanted to believe that "your country won't do you wrong."

Once in Vietnam, few men spent much time pondering why they were there. "Almost all of us were more concerned with staying alive and doing our job," states one veteran of the early years, "than we were with any philosophical investigation into the rights and wrongs of the war." An Army captain, Arthur Mason, explains:

> The soldiers on the field did not have a general understanding of exactly what the purpose of the war was. We did not therefore deal with those questions. We really dealt with how to help each other in extraordinarily difficult circumstances. Also, because the U.S. troops did not have a Hitler to hate, there was an attitude among the troops that they just wanted to get through the year alive and get out of there.

Almost all the men in Vietnam served a one-year tour of duty. Many soldiers worked in the rear areas handling endless paperwork, moving supplies, repairing and preparing war machinery, helping the wounded, packing up the dead. At one end of the spectrum, service in Vietnam, thanks to American affluence (in stark contrast to Vietnamese poverty), could be relatively easy duty. One rear-duty serviceman recalls: "We rode to work in air-conditioned buses, we worked in air-conditioned offices. Our bar-

racks had hot and cold running showers and flush toilets. . . .
There was a movie every night. We drank beer. You could eat all
you wanted."

But on the other end of the spectrum, Vietnam could be hell.

For almost all the men, arrival in Vietnam was a shocking experience. Most men deplaned not to the sights and smells of war
but to a seemingly chaotic, hustling world of poor Asian people
—the men called them "gooks"—few of whom seemed to regard
them as a liberating force. The men rode off to get their field
assignments in buses with windows protected by wire mesh. One
soldier wrote:

> I said to somebody, "What the hell is the wire for?" "It's the gooks,
> man, the gooks. . . . The gooks will throw grenades through the
> windows. See those gooks out there?" I look out and I see shriveled,
> little old men squatting beside the road. . . .
>
> Here we are at one of the largest military installations in the world
> and we have to cover the windows to protect ourselves from little
> old men. I didn't put it together at the time, but intuitively I knew
> something was wrong.

On patrol the sense that "something was wrong" became far
more oppressive. General Maxwell Taylor had warned his supe-
riors the troops would not be able to tell which Vietnamese were
friends and which were foes. This confusion haunted the men in
the field, who rarely saw uniformed, armed enemy soldiers. The
troops saw peasants, grim-faced and seemingly indifferent to
them. The war they fought rarely took place on set battlefields or
against enemy fortifications but in the villages and rice paddies
where the majority of Vietnamese people lived and worked. As a
result, American soldiers often died not in firefights but in ones
and twos, picked off by snipers, blown up by booby traps, emas-
culated by mines laid on paths villagers walked down every day.
Identifying the sniper or saboteur or nighttime assassin among the
blank-faced peasantry was beyond the capacity of most Americans.
The situation was infuriating, maddening, and demoralizing. Captain Mason remembers:

We really didn't know where they were, or when we would engage them, or indeed who they were. When we came to a village we couldn't tell who was or wasn't for us.

I remember walking through a village one day. One of my men tripped on a wire and was blown up. We never found very much of him. I know that the people of the village, who were standing in their doorways, knew exactly where the wire was, or else they would have hit it. They stood there passively and acted surprised. It was really the kind of thing that we could do nothing about.

Many Americans in the field, like Captain Mason and the men he commanded, resolutely, and with great courage and moral strength, did not target noncombatants, even those they knew were aiding the enemy. But some men, incensed over the ambushes and booby traps, frustrated over their inability to find the enemy, angry at the Vietnamese for forcing Americans to risk their lives in such a distant, foreign place, trained as soldiers to kill, some of the troops lost control for the second it took to kill an old man in a field, for the minutes it took to rape peasant girls and burn down peaceful villages, for the endless time it took to slaughter every man, woman, and child who had ended up in the wrong place at the wrong time.

On March 16, 1968, three platoons of Charlie Company, 1st Battalion, 20th Infantry, Americal Division, led by Lieutenant William L. Calley, descended on Xom Lang, a hamlet in South Vietnam the Army labeled My Lai-4. Not a single shot was fired at them, no enemy weapons were discovered and almost no men of military age were in the village. Nonetheless, the American soldiers slaughtered more than 450 people in Xom Lang. They gang-raped girls and then murdered them. They blew apart children with hand grenades. They lined people up and shot them. All wars have their atrocities, but in Vietnam some Americans did things that cannot be forgotten.

The occasional blind ferocity of the men in the field was exacerbated and in some sense even given legitimacy by the nature of the war America's leaders had created. The air war—napalm, cluster bombs, carpet bombing—slaughtered and maimed innocents by the hundreds of thousands. The military declared large tracts of land "free fire" zones in which every living thing was a target. The CIA and the Pentagon, in Operation Phoenix, ordered the assassination of some 20,000 civilians presumed to be local Communist officials. Officers at every level commanded their men to improve the "body count"—no questions asked. The officer corps routinely covered up atrocities. When a reporter asked General Westmoreland if he was not concerned about the number of Vietnamese civilians his war machine was killing, he replied, "Yes, but it does deprive the enemy of the population, doesn't it?"

In the first years of the war, few Americans questioned their government's Vietnam policy. President Johnson portrayed his conduct of the war as a continuation of the policies of his predecessors, emphasizing the limited nature of the conflict. The war, he asserted, was fought to stop Communist aggression against the people of South Vietnam, and if we did not draw the line against Communists in Vietnam, we would be fighting them on the beaches of California. The real history of the United States and Vietnam—dating back to the American role in financing the French—was not discussed by the American government or, for years, by the American mass media. It was as if America's combat role in Vietnam marked the beginning of the Vietnamese struggle. Moreover, the Johnson administration and the U.S. military continually told the American people that progress was being made and that the war would soon be won.

To put it bluntly, the Johnson administration and the military command—with the cooperation of the media—lied to the American people about both the nature and the development of the war. It was, therefore, very difficult for Americans to understand with any accuracy the U.S. role in Vietnam. But people who questioned the war, suggesting that it was not a simple crusade against foreign Communist aggressors or arguing that the war was not being won, were publicly accused, by self-proclaimed patriots, of lacking faith in their government, of failing to support their country and its fighting men in a time of war.

Until 1968, the mass media, with a few exceptions, mainly parroted the reports on the war given to them by government officials and military spokesmen. As television historian Erik Barnouw notes: "Reporters seldom saw the 'war' or 'the enemy.' " An Army press liaison officer in Quang Ngai, an area that saw heavy fighting, offers corresponding testimony: ". . . a lot of articles actually acted as if they were relying on either in-person sources or some sort of sources. They were relying strictly on briefings. [The correspondents] were living in the Carlisle [Hotel] in Saigon. . . . In what had to be one of the five or six most significant combat areas, there was no press at all." The briefings reporters received, not surprisingly, emphasized the enemy "body count" and successful American actions. Most of the American public, accustomed to battle lines and conventional warfare, assumed that since American firepower was grinding up the enemy the United States must be moving toward victory. Their President assured them of this victory, as did their generals and most other leading figures in American life.

The nightly news, most Americans' main source of information on Vietnam, focused on American combat missions, not on the overall strategy of the war. Network news producers believed that "talking heads" explaining the whys and wherefores of the war made for boring television; viewers wanted combat footage and progress reports. As historian Chester Pach concluded: ". . . correspondents, the editors and producers in New York who assembled the nightly newscasts were masters not of interpreting the news but of packaging it . . . It was theatrical reporting, a reflection of the nature of the expertise of television journalists." As a result, very few television news segments discussed the South Vietnamese government's endemic problems, the inability of the South Vietnamese armed forces to fight on their own, the failure of the United States to win the "hearts and minds" of the Vietnamese people, or questioned how U.S. forces expected to win the war.

But while the nightly news supplied the combat footage the public seemed to want, it almost never showed the actual results of combat. The CBS evening news producer recalled: "I had a very high 'queasy quotient.' That is to say, I felt very strongly that there was a limit to how much blood and gore we could put on a broadcast that was seen at dinnertime for most American households." News footage almost never showed dead or dying Americans, civilian casualties, enemy soldiers who had been napalmed, cut in half by helicopter gunships, or blown up. Until 1968, the most riveting pictures of the war in Vietnam appeared not on television but in magazines.

Despite newsmen's often limited knowledge of conditions in Vietnam or Southeast Asia, each year more of the people involved in reporting the war knew that victory was not forthcoming and that "official" sources were deliberately misleading. By 1968 this view was widespread among reporters, editors, and television producers. The senior producer of the CBS evening news recalls: "That the government was lying to us was obvious." Confronting the government about such lies was, however, a far more difficult undertaking. For almost all journalists covering the war, breaking with their government over the war would demand a radical rethinking of how they saw themselves and their country.

As a result of the Johnson administration's mendacity, the American people's often unquestioning, patriotic faith in their government, and most newspaper and television reporters' inability to see the war outside their own ideological and institutional blinders, few people were prepared to listen to critics of America's role in Vietnam. Despite the quagmire that Vietnam had become, opposition to the war grew slowly in the United States.

Before the rapid escalation of the war in 1965, only a few prominent people spoke out publicly against America's role in Vietnam. Walter Lippmann, the elderly dean of American pundits, argued in his newspaper column that "the price of a military victory in the Vietnamese war is higher than American vital interests can justify." Like-minded Hans Morgenthau, a prominent political scientist and policy consultant, publicly urged the government to focus on its narrow interest in the region by simply seeking to negotiate a settlement that would safeguard Vietnam from becoming a Chinese puppet state. Such dissension and, as it turned out, wise voices among the academic, media, and political elite were few and far between.

Members of what most Americans would consider to be fringe groups also spoke out early against the country's involvement in Vietnam. Pacifists, Communists and socialists, disarmament advocates, Quakers and others opposed to the war on religious grounds, a number of civil rights activists, especially those involved in SNCC, and members of several small student groups all had objected to the U.S. role in Vietnam by the summer of 1964. Their arguments and protests had little to no impact on public debate. However, their prescience and commitment did earn many activists a powerful influence on the mass movement against the war that would develop from 1965 to 1967. In addition, their alternative visions of American society gained credibility and drew adherents because of their early leadership in protesting the war.

One of the first signs of a broader movement against the war appeared on university campuses around the country in the spring of 1965. Despite the Johnson administration's attempts to deflect the American people's attention from the complex history of America's involvement in Vietnam, some intellectuals and academics had begun to have strong doubts about America's role.

In March 1965 at the University of Michigan a prestigious group of scholars, in association with a group of young instructors, organized a "teach-in" on the war. Political philosopher Arnold Kaufman had coined the phrase and helped to foster the freewheeling, participatory nature of the all-night event. Professors, instructors, and students shared information, argued, and speculated. Rather than rely on the government or the mass media for insight into America's role in Vietnam, they educated themselves. Several thousand students and faculty participated. That night, said one participant, "people who really cared talked of things that really mattered." The atmosphere was electric and many people watched the sunrise pondering what they should do about the war that was being fought in their name. By late 1965, about 120 colleges and universities had held teach-ins on the rapidly escalating war, most of them organized by faculty members and graduate students. Like the sit-in movement of five years earlier, the teach-ins showed young people that they need not simply accept what they were told by their government; they could question, they could challenge, and they could act. University campuses became centers for antiwar organizing.

Campus antiwar organizing was possible because of a fundamental shift in the nature of higher education in the United States. Before World War II, institutions of higher learning were, in the main, places of limited scholarly and scientific productivity, attended by a tiny minority. By the mid-1960s, both universities and the professors who staffed them had gained stature and security. This allowed professors to challenge the status quo with far less fear of losing their jobs; it was a significant change from the McCarthyite Red baiting that plagued higher education at the beginning of the Cold War.

By the 1960s, the most successful professors and university administrators were elite participants in America's cultural and political life. Many traded on their skills and status to serve government and corporate interests. Others strived to maintain a more independent position. America's finest professors, at the growing number of superb private and public universities, played a complex, increasingly important, and rarely discussed role in the management and oversight of American society.

The teach-ins on Vietnam at Michigan, Columbia, the University of California at Berkeley, and several other schools reflected the efforts of the most independent-minded sector of the professorate to exercise what they saw as their oversight responsibilities. Americans, these professors argued, should not just blindly follow their government's lead in foreign policy. Rejecting twenty years of Cold War thinking, they argued that it was legitimate for the American people to question their leaders' management of the nation's international role. Even as the undeclared war raged, these well-spoken authorities insisted to their young listeners that Americans had the right and responsibility to dissent.

Several factors made the more visible role professors and universities played possible. The federal government had contributed by funneling billions of dollars into the universities in the 1950s and 1960s, making them far more productive institutions able to hire larger faculties, support large graduate programs, and matriculate many more students than before. The federal government began funding higher education in a big way for three major reasons. First, Cold War managers believed that the United States as global superpower would need a dramatic increase in Americans' scientific, technological, and foreign-areas expertise. Second, a wide-ranging coterie of economic, philanthropic, political, and business elites had come to agree that a well-financed and comprehensive higher education system was essential to economic growth. Third, liberal Democratic politicians and their allies believed that making higher education available to as many as possible was a part of the New Deal–New Frontier–Great Society social compact: educational opportunity should not be a privilege but an American birthright.

In the 1960s, with generous federal loan and grant programs, state and federal subsidies that greatly reduced tuition, corporate and philanthropic gifts, and, critically, family support, a prosperous America sent its young people to colleges and universities in unprecedented numbers. Automatic draft deferments for college students helped, too. Enrollments grew from 2 million in 1950 to 7 million by 1968. This immense influx of students strongly contributed to many Americans' belief that universities had become institutions vital to national life. College students, basking in the nation's attention, also believed that they were a part of something new and exciting. But they also found the new experiment in mega-universities and mass education to be in need of reform. As they protested the war, many of this first generation to receive higher education as a near-entitlement also protested the university system that felt to some of them like a "knowledge factory" in which they were the product.

Over the next three years, campus-based protests against the war spread across the country. Thousands of graduate students, young faculty, and undergraduates had a hand in organizing the rallies, marches, and increasingly confrontational protests on nearly every campus in America. Many of the antiwar organizers had gained experience in or taken inspiration from the civil rights movement. Others began their activism in the burgeoning student rights movement that grew up in protest against overcrowded dorms, anachronistic codes of conduct, and a general feeling that they were mere "numbers" in an anonymous educational bureaucracy. Politics, they had learned, need not be confined to the ballot box or to student government—"street heat," boycotts, picketing, rallying, and sitting in were all a part of the new student politics. By 1968, antiwar protests were the most organized and active component of a fervent student movement that involved millions of young people.

Throughout the 1960s, students who protested U.S. policy in Vietnam came under attack from local politicians and conservative professors and administrators, as well as from their fellow students. Some accused the antiwar students of being naive youths, Communist dupes, even traitors. Many simply asserted that the protesters had no right to create disorder at their schools. Tony Walsh, for example, often found himself in angry confrontations with other Kent State students who found his antiwar organization a disruptive, obnoxious presence on their campus:

> In our efforts to end the war in Vietnam, he [another student] says, we scream and cry out and make a lot of noise. . . . We really do cry out and seek attention for our ideas. It is our contention that the fighting of a war in Southeast Asia is not the best way to further our vaunted American ideals of self-determination of all people and their rights to life, liberty, and the pursuit of their own kind of happiness.

As the war went on, student protesters increasingly insisted that to make their antiwar message heard amid general student apathy and the indifference of their elders, they had to shout and they had to disrupt. But overwhelmingly the angry, violent confrontations many equate with "the sixties" came at the very end of the decade and in the early 1970s. Most student demonstrators, even then, carried out peaceful protests.

Most students, like most Americans, didn't protest at all. Through the 1960s, a majority of young people supported the war in Vietnam (though not enough to volunteer for active duty). In fact, younger Americans and college-educated Americans supported the war in higher percentages than older, less well-educated Americans. However, far more college students actively protested the war than any other single group. Most older and working-class Americans who did not support the war did not dislike it enough to take action or did not consider it appropriate to publicly protest their government's policy. Most believed that politics meant voting and, perhaps, bringing their individual concerns to the attention of an elected official. Social order and civility, most Americans believed, depended on people not pushing their political views into anyone else's face. And maintaining order and proper behavior meant more to many older, non-college-educated Americans than did their discomfort with the war.

Many of the college students who opposed U.S. policy disagreed, believing that the war demanded public protest. The civil rights struggle provided them with a political model. That they or their friends faced the draft did help to motivate them into action. Also, as many prowar politicians and commentators angrily noted, college administrators and faculty encouraged student activism either by fostering it or by not punishing students who spoke out against the war. Finally, with no memory of economic hard times or Communist witch hunts, most college students felt little concern that their public protests might cause them to lose social or economic status.

Despite the attention they received, campus antiwar protests and student demonstrators were only one major component of the antiwar movement that developed between 1965 and 1967. Except for the very first national antiwar protest, almost all other national mass protests against the war in the 1960s were organized by older people. Most local groups organized against the war were also staffed by adults. By 1967, the antiwar movement included people from all backgrounds, all ages, and all regions of the country.

For example, clergymen, especially from liberal Protestant denominations, played a key role in antiwar efforts at both the local and the national level. In January 1966, Richard Neuhaus, pastor of the Lutheran Church of St. John the Evangelist in New York, helped form Clergy and Laymen Concerned about Vietnam (CALCV). This activist church group represented the coalescing of two long-term trends: a growing interdenominational, ecumenical movement in American religious life and the growing involvement of white churches with black churches in the civil rights movement and other social justice causes. At both the local and the national level this religiously oriented organization inspired peaceful, moderate protests against the war. By 1969, CALCV had almost a hundred local affiliates and a number of mainline Protestant denominations had issued statements against America's war in Vietnam.

Despite the widespread antiwar sentiments of Protestant clergymen from liberal denominations like the United Church of Christ, most churchgoing Americans supported the war effort. As *The Lutheran* reported: "Officially the churches may coo like a dove but the majority of their members are flying with the hawks." This divide between clergymen and congregants over Vietnam would cost some of the liberal denominations members in the years ahead.

White middle-aged women of the middle class also played a key role in the antiwar movement: organizing marches, running petition drives, providing draft counseling. Some of the leading women activists were members of groups opposed to nuclear testing and proliferation that had grown up in the 1950s. Many became involved through church and neighborhood groups and many drew on experience working in volunteer organizations like the PTA. Others became involved in support of their sons or other young men they knew who were eligible to be drafted. Women Strike for Peace, the most effective women's antiwar group, promoted a march on Washington, D.C., with the slogan: "Stop! Don't drench the jungles of Asia with the blood of our sons. Don't force our sons to kill women and children whose only crime is to live in a country ripped by civil war."

Many middle-aged women active in the movement saw themselves as useful symbols of respectability. Ellen Switzer trained to be a marshal at the local Unitarian Church:

A marshal made sure the peace marches stayed peaceful, that nobody started throwing rocks at the cops and nobody called the cops any names. . . . Being a female marshal was good when you had to deal with the cops. I wore pearl earrings to every march because I thought it was important to look respectable. It helped . . . I never had a problem with the cops. No one in my group ever got arrested.

By the end of 1967 hundreds of mainstream, "respectable" organizations opposed the war. Peace historian Charles DeBenedetti, in an attempt to indicate the diversity of the antiwar movement, has listed some of them: Business Executives Move for a Vietnam Peace, Washington Physicians and Other Health Workers for Peace in Vietnam, the Returnees Association (ex-Peace Corps volunteers), the Federation of American Scientists, the International Ladies' Garment Workers' Union, Americans for Democratic Action, a group of Rhodes Scholars, and a Beverly Hills group called Another Mother for Peace.

Perhaps the most influential American to speak out against the war in 1967 was Martin Luther King, Jr. King had long opposed America's involvement in Vietnam but had avoided the issue publicly at the urging of friends and advisers who feared antagonizing President Johnson and other politicians who supported the civil rights movement. But King's conscience would not allow him to maintain his relative public neutrality. In April, at Riverside Church in New York City, King focused his gifts and his influence on the war:

> I could never again raise my voice against the violence of the oppressed in the ghetto without having first spoken out clearly to the greatest purveyor of violence in the world today—my own government. We are at a moment when our lives must be placed on the line if our nation is to survive its own folly. Every man of humane convictions must decide on the protest that best suits his convictions, but we must all protest. . . . I oppose the war in Vietnam because I love America. I speak out against it not in anger but with anxiety and sorrow in my heart. . . . This war is a blasphemy against all that America stands for.

King was blasted for his antiwar speech by Vice President Hubert Humphrey and many other powerful figures in American life.

King was shaken by the response but he felt that he had done what was morally right.

By the end of 1967, many other influential voices spoke out against the war. *The New York Times* had been running stories critical of the war's management for several years; on Christmas Day 1966, the paper began a series of pieces by associate editor Harrison Salisbury which showed that the President had lied when he said that only military targets were being hit in North Vietnam. Salisbury, on the basis of his firsthand observations in Hanoi, reported that American bombing seemed only to strengthen the Communists' resolve to keep fighting. In 1967, the *Times*'s influential editorial page turned against Johnson's war. By the end of 1967, many of America's most distinguished and established academics, intellectuals, artists, and writers had joined the antiwar movement.

The mass media tended to focus attention on antiwar "celebrities" and militant protesters, but across the country people in increasingly large numbers marched and rallied, collected petitions, and counseled draft resisters. Most antiwar activities occurred at the local level and were organized by people at the grass roots. For example, a Brooklyn housewife, in early 1966, gathered together neighbors to picket offices of the nearby Witco Chemical, a company that made napalm. Over the next couple of years, similar protests against Dow Chemical (the main manufacturer of napalm) and other weapon-producing companies spread at the grass-roots level. People held silent vigils, they passed out leaflets and held public prayer meetings against the war. As historian Terry Anderson has shown, no grand ideology or overarching critique of the American system unified these protests; most people came together simply to protest the war.

National protests against the war—on which the mass media focused—also began to grow in size in the spring of 1967. On April 15, the Spring Mobilization to End the War in Vietnam held marches and rallies in San Francisco and New York City, drawing over a quarter of a million people. The planners meant to emulate the 1963 March on Washington and demonstrate not only to policymakers but also to their fellow citizens the number and commitment of Americans opposed to the war. Many of the organizers of the Spring Mobilization were the same "outsiders"—pacifists, socialists, religious dissenters, and radicals of differing persuasions—who had protested the war in tiny numbers back in 1964. By 1967 their views on the war, while still radical to most Americans, had begun to gain credibility among many more politically conventional citizens.

The antiwar movement, as it grew in size and as it included more and more prominent and mainstream participants, began to affect the Johnson administration. Mainly, the protesters infuriated Johnson and his advisers. They saw the protesters as giving comfort to the North Vietnamese. Johnson suspected—and wanted to believe—that the grass-roots antiwar movement was Communist-controlled or at least influenced by Communists taking orders from foreign governments. In hopes of proving Communist connections, Johnson gave full approval to FBI and illegal CIA surveillance, infiltration, and "dirty tricks" operations against antiwar advocates and organizations. Even if no actual Communist connections were proved, Johnson hoped such police-state tactics could be used to discredit the antiwar movement in the eyes of most Americans.

The growing antiwar movement most affected the Johnson administration's portrayal of the war—or, put more harshly, its domestic propaganda campaign. Johnson believed that antiwar critics, who now included Senate Foreign Relations Committee chair William J. Fulbright, as well as tens of thousands of people speaking out in their schools, churches, and neighborhood groups, had to be fought. The tens of millions of Americans who debated the war around their dining-room tables had to be convinced, Johnson told his men, that the war was right. The American public had to be made to believe that the war was not a quagmire, that it was being won. Word went out to every war manager to accentuate the positive. General Westmoreland was brought before the National Press Club: "We are making progress . . . we have reached an important point when the end begins to come into view. . . . The enemy's hopes are bankrupt." Westmoreland assured the nation that there was "light at the end of the tunnel."

In fact, neither President Johnson nor his key advisers were so sure of that. By the end of 1967, Johnson had lost many advisers over the war: George Ball, McGeorge Bundy, Jack Valenti, Bill Moyers, and Secretary of Defense Robert McNamara (who had been so sure that American technological might would crush the backward Vietnamese enemy). Before resigning, in an attempt to understand why the war had gone so wrong, McNamara asked a senior aide to collect the secret plans and classified reports that documented U.S. policy in Vietnam beginning in the 1940s. Reading over this secret history (called the Pentagon Papers when they were leaked to the press almost four years later), McNamara told a friend, "You know, they could hang people for what's in here."

By late 1967, Johnson was being hounded by antiwar protesters at his every public appearance. The President hated the angry words and the epithets the protesters hurled at him. At a political level, Johnson worried about public opinion polls which showed that support for his Vietnam policy was fast fading.

Searching for advice, or at least confirmation of his policy, the President met with "the Wise Men," a small group of veteran Cold War strategists and the President's most trusted advisers. All but one of these old hands told the President to stay the course. Only George Ball, the former Under Secretary of State, challenged his President. Like an increasing number of antiwar protesters, Ball reacted with fury to what he saw as the brutal and obdurate stupidity of the war makers. He stood up at the meeting and shouted: "I've been watching you across the table. You're like a flock of buzzards, sitting on a fence, sending the young men off to be killed. You ought to be ashamed of yourselves."

By the end of 1967, Vietnam had begun to tear at the nation's fabric. A minority of antiwar protesters, frustrated by their inability to move their government, had begun to move, in their words, "from protest to resistance." Many more of them had begun to see connections between policies in Vietnam and other domestic and international policies; they were becoming radicalized.

But it was not just Vietnam that was tearing at the nation's fabric. Black Power advocates screamed for justice. Black ghettos were erupting into violence. A minority of young people, bored with the legal drugs—tobacco and alcohol—and the other mass-market consumer items that were pushed at them on their TVs and radios with an energy and an expertise that surpassed anything heard at school or in church, had begun to experiment with new products and new lifestyles. In pushing past the boundary of permissible consumer behavior they had begun breaking the law and frightening their parents. As the first Black Power advocate of the 1960s, Malcolm X, had said in a very different context: "The chickens were coming home to roost." As the war raged in Vietnam, America had begun to come apart.

8. THE WAR WITHIN

~~~~~~

BY THE LATE 1960s the Vietnam War had become a prism on American society, refracting that society into bands of linked but separate realities. Americans were not simply divided politically over the war. The war had become much more: a way for Americans to vent their feelings about the values, morals, and "self-evident" truths that guided their everyday lives.

For some Americans—a minority—this national conversation felt like a blessing. Ellen Switzer, the middle-aged, middle-class, antiwar parade marshal, called it "real democracy." She argued: "In the 1960s, people seriously sat at cocktail parties and in their backyards and discussed politics. . . . The 1960s were self-critical but in a constructive way . . . people listened to each other, the First Amendment was real. There was free speech." For Ellen Switzer and many other articulate Americans, the antiwar movement offered a chance to participate in a national debate and to feel that they could, even in a small way, help guide their nation. Ellen Switzer believed that speaking out against the war in Vietnam was her patriotic duty.

Most Americans felt differently. According to a national public opinion poll taken in the fall of 1969 (by which time a majority of Americans conceded that the war in Vietnam had been a "mistake"), 69 percent of all respondents believed that the antiwar protesters were "harmful to American life." When they looked at the antiwar movement they saw people challenging the very foundations of American life: people refusing to support their nation in a time of war. "They were traitors," one Army veteran stated bluntly. "Love It or Leave It," a popular bumper sticker advised.

These self-described patriots believed that social order and national unity had to come before free speech and the right to protest. Many of these same Americans saw the antiwar movement as only the most visible sign that the traditions and values that had made their nation the greatest in the world were under attack by people who did not respect them or their way of life.

Most antiwar protesters would have denied feeling contempt for the values that sustained most Americans. And by 1969, the national antiwar movement was primarily in the hands of people who wanted to reach out to the large number of Americans who were uninterested in broader issues of social change. But people were not just imagining things. By the late 1960s, many young antiwar activists and others who were involved in a variety of social and political movements were in open revolt against what they considered "the American way of life."

They believed that the "traditional" verities and "traditional" values of American life were what had produced the war in Vietnam and racism and a lot of other ugliness and stupidity. They did not accept the stories most white Americans told themselves about themselves: that they were the best, most generous, most free people on earth. They advocated new identities, new dreams, and radical change. By the late 1960s this fight over values, morality, and the fundamental nature of American life inflamed America.

The shock troops in this "culture war," at least as most Americans saw it, were the long-haired "freaks" and "hippies" of what was then called the "counterculture." It was the counterculture, more than the antiwar movement or Black Power groups, that seemed to many older Americans to be most threatening to their families and loved ones. And they were right to be worried; far more young people would experiment with illegal drugs and counterculture lifestyles than would ever participate in the civil rights, antiwar, or student movements.

The counterculture seemed insidious. It was everywhere and nowhere, hard to define and thus difficult to stop. The closest most people, especially those in the mass media, could come to pinning the whole thing down was to say that its capital was in San Fran-

cisco and that its epicenter was at the corner of Haight and Ashbury. It wasn't but it was, too. The counterculture took root in
Atlanta's Fourteenth Street, Chicago's Old Town, the Lower East
Side of New York, in Austin, Texas, Lawrence, Kansas, Fayette-
ville, Arkansas, and dozens of other places. The counterculture
was about space, about taking over a few city blocks or a few
acres of countryside and trying to make a world out of it, a place
where all the old rules were up for grabs and where, as the saying
went, you could take a trip without a ticket. The counterculture
was a way of life, a community, an infrastructure, and even an
economy, not just a few lifestyle accoutrements like long hair and
an occasional toke on an illegal substance. While very few young
Americans made a serious commitment to forging this alternative
way of life, tens of millions of Americans, young and old, watched
the experimenters with dread, fascination, and envy. And millions
of kids, charmed by the pictures and the sounds flashed at them
from TV screens and concert halls, raised by marketing geniuses
to open their minds to new products, and finding themselves freed
from restraint by a society at war with itself over the meaning of
racial justice and Vietnam, played with the possibilities.

The Haight-Ashbury in San Francisco wasn't the only counterculture enclave, but it was the first and the biggest and the most
photogenic. It did yeoman duty as image, as inspiration, and as
horror show. It served as both a literal and, far more often, a
figurative destination for millions of young people who found
themselves in the midst of a national debate about the meaning of
the American dream that left most of them just confused.

The Diggers, operating out of a few apartments scattered around
the Haight, were the nearest thing the counterculture had to a
visionary core. Never more than a few dozen, they took their
name from a band of seventeenth-century English utopians. They
believed in a world made "free because it's yours." To make the
vision real on their few blocks of San Francisco, they set up a free
store, opened up "crash pads," organized street theater and free
concerts, kept the community wired with an instant news service,

and from the fall of 1966 until it became an impossible hassle, gave away free food every day at the park panhandle off Ashbury Street. To receive the free food—and to give ritual to the freedom—the Diggers had everyone, be they long-haired runaways or sightseeing day-trippers, pass through the Frame of Reference, a wooden thirteen-foot-square golden orange reality check that stood between the way things were and how they might be.

The Diggers wanted to break free of the money nexus and the profit motive that underwrote American society. More than anything, the Diggers acted on a dream of autonomy, of making a community where people took care of each other, lived by their own visions, and busted free from the "trips" laid on by parents, teachers, and every other authority dedicated to the proposition that life is social conformity. Influenced by artistic and theatrical movements—like Pop Art and Happenings—that broke down the barriers between performers and audience, high culture and popular culture, the Diggers saw life as a theatrical performance played for keeps, in which costumes, put-ons, and high drama were sustaining acts in a gray world. The Diggers called themselves "life actors."

The Diggers represented the counterculture at its most productive and its most fantastic. They had not run away to the Haight. They and other cultural escape artists, some of whom, like the Grateful Dead, would become famous, were just living out their dreams on a bit of real estate they had been able to claim temporarily as their own. The creative energy they spun around themselves like a whirlwind drew tens of thousands of young people, most of them far less able to cope with the freedoms the Diggers and others used as the coin of the realm.

The Diggers, like most "freaks" (the name of choice for the serious counterculturalist), were disgusted by the war in Vietnam. By their lights, the war and the war makers were the predictable spawn of a metal and plastic death culture that had organized life around the workable lie of Cadillac dreams, prime-time TV, and a forty-hour week. But marching down city streets, they argued, and shouting "No!" to the generals' "Yes!" was not the way to stop the war. To stop the war, they said, you had to fight the

mad internal nightmare of control. Gary Snyder, poet-saint to the
Diggers, grimly reported the solution in his poem "A Curse on
the Men in Washington, Pentagon," which was freely distributed
in the *Digger Papers*:

> As you shoot down the Vietnamese girls and men
> > in their fields
> > > Burning and chopping,
> > > Poisoning and blighting,
> So surely I hunt the white man down
> > in my heart.
> The crew-cutted Seattle boy
> The Portland boy who worked for U.P.
> > > that was me.
> I won't let him live. The "American"
> > I'll destroy. The "Christian"
> > > has long been dead.
> They won't pass on to my children.
> I'll give them Chief Joseph, the Bison herds,
> Ishi, sparrowhawk, the fir trees,
> The Buddha, their own naked bodies,
> Swimming and dancing and singing
> > > instead.
> As I kill the white man,
> > the "American"
> > > in me
> And dance out the ghost dance:
> To bring back America, the grass and the streams.
> To trample your throat in your dreams.
> This magic I work, this loving I give
> > That my children may flourish
> And yours won't live.

To "kill the white man, the American" that was planted deep
inside and to be reborn—gentler, attuned to the natural world—
among a community of fellow believers, that was the vision that
set the counterculture apart from a whole series of tamer thrills.

The Diggers, "freaks," and fellow long-haired true believers
scattered around the country came by their visions from sources

near and far. Gary Snyder and fellow poet Allen Ginsberg were a decade and more older than the young people who looked to them for inspiration and guidance. They had been part of a cabal of poets and writers—most of them white men, some gay—who'd come of age right after World War II and had rejected the hunt for security that motivated a large part of a generation tired of war and economic dislocation. Snyder, Ginsberg, and writers like Jack Kerouac found little nourishment in the early marriage/new car/TV/suburbs that beckoned to so many. They wanted experiences, not careers, and searched for wisdom, not success. In their hunt for alternatives they'd looked East—to China, Japan, and India—and to the black jazz scene. They probed the disciplined stillness of the Zen mind and the "Dharma Bum" rush of traveling down open highways and wilderness paths with a rucksack and eyes open. The "Beat" poets and writers—beat because they were broke and because they loved bebop and because they quested for beatitude—offered the young their rejection of American materialism, their embrace of an open sexuality, their love for "beautiful losers" like the American Indians, their appreciation of Eastern mysticism, and their respect for the land.

For young people scattered around the country, the Beat message was transmitted through cheap paperback novels—a medium first available in the postwar years—and, more rarely, independent publications like the semi-underground City Lights poem pamphlets published by Lawrence Ferlinghetti. It even came filtered through the mocking parody profiles of "Beatniks" printed in mass-circulation, fad-hungry magazines like *Time, Life,* and the youth-oriented *Mad.* Throughout the 1960s, Allen Ginsberg and Gary Snyder and a few others would offer the wisdom they'd earned to the new generation of seekers. Their words, often passed down through other minds, turned up in almost every counter-culture enclave, rap group, and drug trip.

And drug trips were a part of the message the Beats transmitted. Kerouac, Ginsberg, William Burroughs, and almost every other Beat writer taught young people that a state of intoxication and psychic exploration were requisites to a higher wisdom of the body and soul. For a generation raised to believe that the Wonderful World of Disney represented the American imagination explored, the Beats' songs of adventures earned through the consumption of something that took a little doing to score were both remarkably familiar and familiarly remarkable.

The consumption and distribution of illegal and experimental drugs, more than any other single factor, was responsible for the creation and development of America's many countercultural enclaves. Drug sales and use contributed heavily to the enclaves' economic base, social order, and cultural disposition. A heavy percentage of the very first hippies to live, for example, in the Haight-Ashbury—a kind of no-man's-land between the poor, all-black Fillmore neighborhood and the well-to-do white Pacific Heights area—sold marijuana.

The dissemination of drugs outside of these enclaves was also the single most important factor linking the small counterculture with the vast majority of going-to-school, living-at-home young people. The spread, lure, promotion, and open use of illegal and experimental drugs was also the main reason a majority of adult Americans feared and even hated the counterculture.

Cultural change rarely stems from one source or cause, or even moves in one direction. A generation of young people turned to marijuana, but for different reasons and at different times. At the most conventional level, drug use was handed down from parents to children. In the early 1960s, a majority of adult Americans used a nicotine "high" to get through the day (while prime-time TV and AM radio were ruled by alluring cigarette commercials). A vast majority of adult Americans regularly drank alcoholic beverages and many young people had seen their elders blasted more than a few times. But tobacco and alcohol were old highs.

In the postwar years, the "silent generation" parents of the kids who would get blamed for "turning on" America had embraced a legal pharmaceutical revolution of their own, aimed at curing not ailing bodies but anxious and depressed minds. By 1965, grown-up, "establishment" Americans in search of a mental state that they could not supply from their inner resources were gobbling up heavy-duty drugs, most of them far more powerful and dangerous than marijuana, in mind-numbing quantities. In 1965, doctors wrote 123 million prescriptions for tranquilizers and sed-atives and 24 million for various amphetamines. (About 3,000 Americans a year were dying of overdoses of these legal drugs by the mid-1960s.)

Drugs were not introduced to America by the hippies (a name of indeterminate origin, likely a tongue-in-cheek knockoff of the 1950s "hipster"). Hippies, however, used mind-altering sub-stances without the permission of the medical establishment, legal authorities, or the pharmaceutical industry. Many young people, who, when they rejected their parents' lifestyle choices, had been rewarded by market-happy America with product lines made just for them, decided they'd like their own drugstores and medicine chests, too. Young underground drug manufacturers and dealers, many operating out of the protected enclaves of America's coun-terculture, would at first supply the new drugs.

Perhaps most influential in specifically promoting the use of marijuana were many of the rock-'n'-roll musicians young people dreamed of emulating. The rock musicians, in turn, smoked dope at least in part because they were emulating the black jazz musicians of the preceding generation—cultural arbiters of hipness—who insisted that getting stoned made the music better.

Everyone who "got stoned" was, by the 1960s, breaking the law, although the use and sale of marijuana had not become a federal crime until 1937, when Harry Anslinger, a former prohibi-tion bureaucrat put in charge of the Federal Bureau of Narcotics, needed a new target for his anti-vice forces. Marijuana, a cheap weed (top quality sold for $6 an ounce in the 1930s) that had no powerful business sponsors and was then enjoyed mainly by pow-erless people like Mexican farm laborers, African-American city dwellers, and white hipsters, had made an easy target. Anslinger began a one-man campaign to demonize the "evil weed" in the mid-1930s immediately after the decriminalization of alcoholic beverages. He spun out articles filled with make-believe stories about innocent white boys and girls who had become dope killers, Negro-loving sex maniacs, and marijuana mother-rapers, and Hollywood made a movie, *Reefer Madness*, based on Anslinger's ludicrous charges. Just four years after re-legalizing the consumption of alcohol, Congress made smoking marijuana, for the first time, a federal crime. Very few Americans knew anything about marijuana except what they had learned from Anslinger's articles and Hollywood's fabrications.

In the early 1960s the history of the criminalization of marijuana, like the history of Vietnam, was known by very few Americans. Legal authorities and mainstream cultural arbiters rarely spoke of marijuana before the mid-1960s, but when they did it was often in terms taken directly or indirectly from the fictions of Anslinger. Marijuana, young people were taught, was a dangerous drug similar to heroin.

Young people in the music business had learned differently. Black musicians came up in a world in which marijuana was no more exotic than hard liquor and considered a far more professional high. By the early 1960s marijuana use had crossed over to the white rock scene as well. A record company executive recalled that marijuana "worked wonders in the music industry . . . [it] gave musicians that sense of heightened awareness and some produced classic hits, though not everyone used it." Jazz musicians had let their small crew of listeners know that marijuana was a kick not to miss. Rock performers did the same for a far larger audience of white middle-class kids.

One of those "kids" remembers sitting with his friends in Georgia, listening to Donovan, the Jefferson Airplane, the Doors, and the Beatles and "getting messages via the music . . . drug allusions and we wanted in on that shit." Perhaps the most powerful message came from the Beatles, who in June 1967 released *Sgt. Pepper's Lonely Hearts Club Band*. The drug imagery on the album cover and throughout the lyrics was impossible to miss. "We would all go to someone's house," he said, "and we would listen to this fucking thing nonstop and we knew we were part of a community of people, with the Beatles and the Stones being our den fathers . . . we did everything to get high."

That the men and women young people saw as their cultural arbiters—rock musicians—used drugs was an important factor in legitimating experimentation with marijuana. But as one man argues: "Did we start smoking dope because we were getting messages through the music or did we smoke dope and then the messages came? It was rock 'n' roll and pot happening simultaneously." The other factors—parents' use of "uppers" and "downers" and the mainstream-market acceptance of drunkenness and tobacco smoking—contributed greatly. Young people had been raised—like no previous generation—on sophisticated marketing messages that urged them to find happiness through ever changing consumer opportunities. The door separating the traditional capitalist virtues of thrift and discipline and the new consumer values of instant gratification and sensual delight had been deliberately slammed open by some of America's most creative and best-paid people. A small number of people, most of them African-American and Mexican-American, had been smoking marijuana for several decades; in an age of "consumption without limits" many young white people, especially relatively affluent college students (among civilians, the higher a young person's social class, the more likely he or she was to have smoked marijuana in the 1960s), felt free to buy a new pleasurable sensation, whether it was legal or not. Capping off this cultural confusion was a national political debate that severely damaged established authorities' ability to mark off the boundaries between permissible pleasures and forbidden vice.

The national debate over Vietnam and racism caused many young people to question who had the legitimate authority to tell them what was right and what was wrong. A parallel feeling existed between young people's judgments about the war in Vietnam and smoking dope. In both cases they had been told by the established authorities hard-edged "truths": the war was good and smoking dope was bad. In both cases they learned that outsiders, marginal people offered them plausible alternative answers. Anyone who tried marijuana learned that they had been lied to—dope might make you lazy and cloud your judgment but it didn't make you an addict or turn you into a rapist or a killer. By exaggerating and hiding the truth, the authorities had laid themselves open to charges of deceit and hypocrisy, which many in the 1960s had decided were the base characteristics of the people they were supposed to trust. The fact that smoking dope was illegal and that, by 1974, 445,000 people had been "busted" for marijuana, most of them for simple possession, further turned many young people against a society they saw as cruel and irrational. All dope smokers were, in the parlance of the time, part of an "illegal nation." In countercultural enclaves, student "ghettos," and concert halls, tuned into "their" radio stations, and just sitting upstairs in their rooms, young people tried to find their own truths. "There's got to be some way out of here, said the joker to the thief," cried Bob Dylan to his receptive listeners.

Marijuana was a drug particularly suited to the kinds of truths in which young people were interested. The civil rights movement and the student movement both cherished and publicized a vision of a "beloved community," a place far different from the atomized world of nuclear families in tract homes cut off from each other by moats of green grass. Many white, middle-class young people, crammed into overflowing, anonymous universities—taught that success was measured by individual achievement and private gain in a cutthroat world—wondered what it would be like to live in a world in which people could trust one another and in which cooperation came before competition.

Marijuana, used by people who were drawn to the idea of "community," seemed to break down barriers. Joints were typically passed around a circle and people who got stoned together often shared a gentle amusement over the "power trips" so many people "laid on one another." This connection helped "dope visionaries" pursue collective visions through acts of individual creativity. Many others simply found in marijuana's easy visions of American society awash in banal materialism and purposeless competition, as well as its erotic and euphoric high, in the words of one user, "an escapism from all the pressures of everything and from the world being so fucked up."

Marijuana was for most people a gentle high. You might get the giggles or the munchies, you might gain a keen insight on a book you read, experience lovemaking in a more intense way, or even see your dog in an absolutely new light, but you were not likely to see the world turned upside down and sideways. By the mid-1960s, however, a new mind drug that promised a much harder kick started to make its way around America. LSD, or acid, would change people's lives in a way marijuana rarely did.

LSD is, in part, what separated the counterculture from the thrills of the youth culture. LSD contributed to the freaks' certainty that, unlike the old-timer Beats and hipsters who dressed in black and hid in society's dark corners, they would take center stage and play their mind games in full view of a world that had forgotten how to "dream with the lights on." The politicized acid luminary John Sinclair argued that LSD convinced people that "reality" was just another illusion. Acid, said Sinclair, gave people the courage to challenge everything they had been instructed to accept and to dare to live by full-color visions of their own making. LSD produced such visions (or hallucinations from a psychiatric perspective) by chemically "unblocking" or "unlocking" the unconscious mind. According to the more spiritually inclined, acid put a person on another plane of reality in which the here-and-now physical world was given new meanings by a "higher" realm of consciousness. In places as public as the Haight-Ashbury and as private as farms in the Kansas countryside, young people dropped acid, imagined the impossible, and then tried to bring it to life. Along the way, a few people died and others lost their minds. Though LSD often just provided simple euphoric feelings and a pleasant buzz at low doses, at hallucination-producing doses of 250 micrograms or more LSD often played for keeps.

Lysergic acid diethylamide (LSD) was invented by accident in 1943 by Albert Hoffman, a Swiss chemist working for the giant Sandoz Pharmaceuticals. Hoffman was looking for a cure for migraine headaches. Instead he stumbled upon a powerful hallucinogen that in incredibly small doses produced radical reorientation, hypersensitivity, release of repressed memories, and a variety of other fantastic effects. Unfortunately for Sandoz, it was not clear what market such a product served. In deference to Say's law—supply will create demand—Sandoz began shipping LSD to America in 1949. Specifically, Sandoz sent LSD off to psychiatrists, hoping they could find a use for it in America's booming therapeutic marketplace.

Acceptance of psychiatry expanded rapidly in postwar America.

In 1940 fewer than 3,000 psychiatrists practiced in the United States; by 1956 the number had jumped to 15,000. America, quickly and with little public discussion, was becoming a "therapeutic culture" in which a psychological approach to the maintenance of a good and productive life had become a mainstream pursuit. In part this transformation was underwritten by the federal government via the National Mental Health Act (1946), which provided hundreds of millions of dollars—and legitimacy—to researchers working on neuropsychiatric disorders. By the late 1950s, as noted earlier, tens of millions of Americans—a disproportionate number of whom were women who were simply angry or sad about the course of their lives—were receiving powerful sedatives, tranquilizers, and amphetamines, prescribed by both family doctors and the hordes of newly minted psychiatrists. The underlying presumption of most of the new therapists was that their job was to accommodate "sick" or unhappy people to a sane society (an assumption many self-assured, self-medicating young people would turn on its head). Sandoz and the psychiatric community hoped that LSD would be just one more tool in the therapist's black bag.

Throughout the 1950s, LSD popped up in mental hospitals and in the private practices of psychiatrists around the country, especially in Los Angeles. People began coming to psychiatrists asking to be dosed. Among a small circle of psychiatrists and their usually well-to-do patients LSD use spread.

Acid was also used by another tight little circle interested in the inner world. In 1953, the CIA began experimenting with LSD, probing its utility as a truth drug and as a way of driving people temporarily insane. The CIA, in its secret project MK-ULTRA, surreptitiously dosed people with LSD and then watched them to see what happened. The CIA cut back on this research after an Army doctor, unaware that he was dosed, decided he'd gone insane and committed suicide by jumping out a window. The CIA classified the whole project top secret and generally kept mum about its forays into the psychedelic world. But word leaked out.

By 1960, as Jay Stephens reveals in his masterpiece, *Storming Heaven*, the small circle of LSD initiates had started to open up.

A mysterious Canadian businessman with CIA connections, Al Hubbard, began touring the United States giving LSD to famous and influential people such as author and political heavyweight Clare Boothe Luce and her husband, *Time* publisher Henry Luce. Ken Kesey, a young writer on a fellowship at Stanford, became acquainted with LSD—which he began calling acid—at a Veterans Administration mental hospital where he had volunteered to participate in a scientific study. At Harvard University, psychology professor Timothy Leary began conducting LSD experiments on students, colleagues, and himself. Expelled from Harvard in 1963 for his efforts, Dr. Leary would travel America throughout the 1960s promoting LSD as a spiritual cure-all. Leary also inspired a group of tough but psychedelically inclined young men to begin manufacturing and distributing acid around the country. Using every marketing device he could conceive of, Leary offered America a compelling—and frightening—LSD mantra: "Turn on, tune in, drop out."

A few years before Leary would take acid from the halls of academe to the pages of *Playboy* magazine, Aldous Huxley, the brilliant British writer who had moved to California, used LSD. Huxley had long been interested in exploring altered states of consciousness. He was in a long line of British and European artists and writers who had, after rejecting their own religious traditions, looked to the spiritual practices of other peoples, many of whom lived in their nation's colonial possessions. From the Middle East, North Africa, and Asia, they became familiar with a variety of mind-altering herbs and plants. In 1953, Huxley published a little book called *Doors of Perception* (from which would come the name of the rock group, the Doors) about tripping on mescaline, another synthetic hallucinogen. Huxley took his title from the poet William Blake: "If the doors of perception were cleaned / everything will appear to man as it is, infinite." The book—serious, philosophical, and spiritual—heavily influenced a small group of American fellow mind explorers.

Huxley's experiences with mescaline and LSD convinced him that only a very few people, psychologically stable, intellectually and emotionally mature, should explore the inner spaces revealed by the hallucinogens. The apostle of acid, Timothy Leary, rejected this judgment. And in the age of consumption without limits, so did hundreds of thousands of young people.

Writer Ken Kesey also believed that acid was too important an experience to be kept secret, and by the mid-1960s Kesey had the reputation to make his feelings count among young people. Kesey's first novel, *One Flew Over the Cuckoo's Nest* (1962), was a critically acclaimed best-seller. In the novel, a hell raiser named McMurphy leads a group of mental patients in a cheery rebellion against their sadistic keeper, Big Nurse. McMurphy ends up lobotomized by Big Nurse and the fury of the authorities. The novel closes with a mute giant Indian—Chief—killing the spiritless McMurphy in an act of mercy, and then pulling down the iron bars that imprison him in the mental ward. *One Flew Over the Cuckoo's Nest* became enormously popular on college campuses. Students reveled in Kesey's vision of dehumanizing authorities, trickster resistance, and a world turned upside down.

Kesey was an acid true believer, as were the swarming circle that surrounded him, known around the Bay Area by 1964 as the Merry Pranksters. Acid, in their hands, was not only a way to explore the inner world; it was a means of reinventing the one outside.

In the fall of 1965 the Pranksters began a series of public LSD parties: Acid Tests. They had secured a steady supply of acid (which was still legal) from underground hero-chemist Augustus Owsley Stanley III. Fellow acid visionaries, the Grateful Dead, became the house band for the Tests. At these acid events the music roared, strobe lights stopped motion, and people dressed in fantastic costumes, painted their faces and bodies, and tripped the light fantastic. By early 1966, the renamed Trips Festival drew 2,400 people who drank LSD-spiked punch from a baby's bathtub, dressed in whatever costumes their acid visions directed, and vibrated to the cacophony of the Grateful Dead and an auditorium full of electronic, mind-wrenching gadgetry. LSD, though criminalized in late 1966, was available wherever quality underground drugs were sold. It was openly promoted by influential and well-publicized figures like Leary, Kesey, and a number of "acid rock" musicians. In 1968 much of book-reading America learned from Tom Wolfe's profile of Kesey in *The Electric Kool-Aid Acid Test* that the vision Kesey offered in *One Flew Over the Cuckoo's Nest*, as well as the music of the Grateful Dead, was acid-driven. LSD was fast breaking out to a wider circle.

The counterculture of Haight-Ashbury, as well as of other freak enclaves, grew as acid use spread. Charles Perry, author of *The Haight-Ashbury*, argues that "psychedelic users automatically congregate with other heads . . . LSD tends to form cabals of initiates." These "initiates" then worked/played at turning their streets into expressions of their acid dreams. Going by their acid names—Wildflower, Bear, Mountain Girl, Cowboy—wearing their archetypal acid clothes—buckskin, Hindu robes, rainbow-colored tie-dyed ensembles—stripped down from the materialist, "uptight" paraphernalia of society—barefoot, hair flying, undergarments thrown away—they painted and chalked, rang bells and chanted mantras, and, yes, wore flowers in their hair. Influenced by acid's reality-bending effects, they embraced a world without rules in which the old "control systems" of science and reason squared off against the "direct spinal language" of magic and mysticism.

The freaks' public embrace of illegal drugs like marijuana and LSD was sufficient to infuriate—and scare—most Americans. "Turned-on" youths' flouting of sexual conventions widened the gulf and increased the stakes. In a nation where, as late as 1969, more than two-thirds of all people believed that premarital sex of any kind was wrong, the hippies' anthem of "Free Love!" resounded, as it was meant to, like a war cry.

John Sinclair, manager of the rock group the MC5 and dope true believer, wrote what was perhaps the most explicit paean to free love in an "editorial statement" in the Detroit underground paper, the *Sun*. "Our position," Sinclair intoned, "is that all people must be free to fuck freely, whenever and wherever they want to . . . in bed, on the floor, in the chair, on the streets, in the parks and fields." "Fucking," Sinclair argued, like dope, helps people to "escape the hangups that are drilled into us in this weirdo country."

In "crash pads" and at dope parties, young men and women promoted and observed an ethic of open sexuality. Sexual freedom was at the core of the counterculture's rejection of conventional American morality. The body's instant truths, one hippie "girl" explained, should be respected: "A guy stoned on acid and a girl stoned on acid, and we immediately wanted to fuck. We didn't say a word except 'Where are we going to do it?' " Members of the counterculture happily saw themselves at the forefront of a sexual revolution.

As in the case of drug use, no bright line separated the freaks' embrace of free love from many less committed young people's explorations of a new sexual morality. As historian Beth Bailey has argued, during the 1960s a great many white middle-class college students began to reject the sexual conventions on which they had been raised. It was not that they actually had a great deal more premarital sex than their parents' generation—the major change in sexual practices among the young and not-so-young would actually come in the 1970s—but that they spoke out publicly against the often hypocritical social norms and college rules that attempted to keep sex hidden, illicit, and "dirty." A majority of these young people were very little interested in free love. They spoke instead about "honesty," "commitment," and "family." They wanted to be open about the fact that they were having sex—as many of their parents had done before marriage—with the person they loved.

Adults, by the 1960s, were also rethinking both the public and private boundaries surrounding sexual expression. Americans' uncertainty about how to restrain or control sexual expression had become very evident in the postwar years. Between 1946 and 1967 the Supreme Court declared that most laws restricting "sexually explicit" materials were unconstitutional. The justices, like most other nationally oriented arbiters of legal and social behavior, argued that cultural issues—like what is "decent" art and what is "indecent" pornography—could not be easily codified into law or treated simply as moral issues prescribed by church leaders or even by local communities. In accordance with the transformative power of national consumer values—which mitigated against the virtue of restraint with the duty to spend—the justices ruled that cultural practices should be governed not by prior restraint but by the dictates of the open marketplace.

A wide variety of sexually explicit materials flowed into this breach. Books and movies became far more explicit (though by today's standards few would have gotten more than a PG rating). In 1953, Hugh Hefner began publishing *Playboy* as a "respectable" pornography magazine featuring bare-breasted "girl next door" centerfolds. By 1956, *Playboy* had a circulation of over one million. Hefner preached a "playboy philosophy," encouraging men to bed as many women as they could while avoiding entangling relationships. By the early 1960s, Helen Gurley Brown matched Hefner in her best-selling *Sex and the Single Girl*, in which she reasoned that young working women should receive as many gifts, dinners, and vacations as possible in return for their sexual favors. Later in the 1960s, Brown would turn *Cosmopolitan* magazine into a female version of *Playboy* (sans pinups, however). The *Playboy* man and the *Cosmo* "girl" represented a new mainstream type: hard-bargaining "sexual swingers." They were also the original yuppies: Hefner and Brown asserted that hardworking young urban professionals (well-paid men) and young, independent pink-collar workers (poorly paid "girls") deserved all the pleasure they could get. In their vision, good sex and material comfort added up to the good life. This model was not the one the counterculture cared to embrace, but it was an important part of the sexual revolution, and central to the sexually charged national conversation young people joined.

In 1960, the federal government (the Food and Drug Administration) permitted doctors to prescribe oral contraceptives, the Pill. And while very few unmarried women were able to secure the Pill from doctors or clinics until the late 1960s, it, too, contributed to the public debate about premarital sex. Many conservatives and religious people were appalled by the idea of such a casual method of contraception. But others celebrated the sexual freedom the Pill seemed to permit.

By the late 1960s, sex seemed to be everywhere. In 1964 the Beatles had topped the hit list with "I Want to Hold Your Hand."

By 1967, they were wailing, "Why don't we do it in the road!"

Around the hippies' embrace of free love and drug use, a series of institutions grew. Turned-on, sexually explicit "underground" newspapers—*The Great Speckled Bird* in Atlanta, the *Vortex* in Lawrence, Kansas, the Chicago *Seed*, the Austin *Rag*, and dozens of others—mixed local stories on sex, drugs, and music with news about cop hassles, health reports, and a "freak's-eye" view of national events. "Head shops" like the New Consciousness in New York, the Psychedelic Shop in the Haight-Ashbury, and Climax in Chicago sold dope paraphernalia—pipes, rolling papers, and "bongs"—as well as the "hippie" accoutrements of beads, bells, and buttons. Acid-dropping artists churned out posters with words flowing and colors dripping which announced the next party, the newest happening, the next gathering. Acid rock musicians—the Grateful Dead, Janis Joplin, and the Jefferson Airplane in San Francisco, the MC5 in Ann Arbor, and dozens of local bands throughout the country—played at ultra-high volume at weekend celebrations which drew acid freaks and ever larger crowds of fun-loving teenagers who watched with little comprehension of what was at stake on both a personal and a public level.

By 1968, counterculture enclaves like the Haight-Ashbury and Chicago's Old Town were tourist spots, complete with tour buses and fatuous guides. In 1967, *Time* had put the hippies on its cover. Other mass-circulation magazines ran photo spreads of the eye-catching freaks and publicized a forthcoming "Summer of Love." Big-time corporate record companies and ad agencies, a music industry executive argues, "saw that there was money to be made on this new counterculture, so they embraced what they did not even understand." The Levi-Strauss clothing company and their ad agency, for example, selected the acid rockers in the Jefferson Airplane to promote their new "hip" white jeans. National marketers had seized upon the counterculture as a likely spectacle for selling their products.

Unsophisticated and often troubled young runaways flocked to the Haight and other "paisley ghettos," crowding into crash pads. Surrounded by young people extolling the virtue of going "further" and unfettered by any authority, these new arrivals got loaded on anything pushed their way. Hard-hearted, violent men—most infamously Charles Manson—came to prey on the weak and the ignorant. Dope selling became a big business and neighborhood dealers began to be muscled out by career criminals and motorcycle clubs like the Hell's Angels. During the 1967 Summer of Love the San Francisco police estimated that 75,000 young people lived in the Haight-Ashbury and thousands more drifted in over the next year: "the eager, puzzled faces and the denim and department store shirts of the nation's high schools."

According to one scholarly study, by 1968 about 15 percent of the young people drawn to the Haight were "psychotics and religious obsessives," and about 45 percent were dropouts, lowlifes, and hard livers, most of them young men looking to find sex and get stoned as often as possible. A minority of true-believing freaks tried to build their alternative community in what was fast becoming an out-of-control mess in which no one felt they had the right or the authority—"do your own thing" being the watchword of the community's faith—to tell the crazies and the heroin addicts and the violent criminals to go away.

Writer Joan Didion, fierce observer of anomie in the 1960s, respected the antic behavior of the Diggers and other counterculture visionaries but pitied the "pathetically unequipped children" she watched streaming into the Haight. In *Slouching Towards Bethlehem*, she wrote:

> At some point between 1945 and 1967, we had somehow neglected to tell these children the rules of the game we happened to be playing. Maybe we had stopped believing in the rules ourselves, maybe we were having a failure of nerve about the game. These were children . . . less in rebellion against the society than ignorant of it, able only to feed back certain of its most publicized self-doubts, Vietnam, Saran Wrap, diet pills, the Bomb.

The children she is mourning are not the Diggers but those with whom the Diggers had dreamed of building a "new civilization." The Diggers, at least the core group, had thought long and hard about the corporate culture they had the capacity to help lead. But an increasing number of the young people in the counterculture enclaves, lured into the hippie life by the mass media and, indeed, by the underground newspapers of the young, knew only their discomfort and anger with the old fly-apart, TV-screen go-go nowhere world of Mom and Dad.

Many counterculturalists understood the problem and worried about it. They had hoped to transcend the problem of the "pathetically unequipped children" by working through the strength of a self-selecting organic community rather than through the inevitable weakness of a mass-mediated spectacle that drew thousands of dropout youths. Many hated the publicity their experiments received in the mass media and called it "media poisoning."

Indeed, the Diggers and others felt overwhelmed by both the numbers of young people who flocked to the Haight-Ashbury in 1967—the Summer of Love—and the massive media coverage. With other veterans of the community, the Diggers (by then calling themselves simply Free City) held a "Death of Hippie" ceremony. The very word "hippie," they felt, had become a means for turning the hard kicks of their community into the domesticated sidekick of frozen-food America.

The media cast nets, create bags for the identity hungry to climb in. Your face on TV, your soul immortalized without soul in the captions of the *Chronicle* . . . The FREE MAN vomits his image and laughs in the clouds because, he, the great evader . . . flexes his strong loins of FREE and is gone again from the nets.

Many thought it was time to move on. A few thousand young people did move on from the glory days of the counterculture to other experiments in community building. They formed communes in New Mexico, southern Illinois, Colorado, the Big Island of Hawaii, northern California, elsewhere. They experimented with group marriages, communal child rearing, and self-sufficiency. Some of them, and others, too, in out-of-the-way places, began growing crops of high-quality marijuana. Thousands of these rural communards, dope farmers, and up-country folks still meet once a year in the unpublicized Rainbow Family Peace Gatherings.

Stewart Brand, Merry Prankster and Trips Festival organizer, founded *The Whole Earth Catalog* in 1968 with the psychedelic slogan "If we're gods, we might as well get good at it." The *Catalog* provided a wealth of information on how to set up a rural commune or homestead. By 1971, the book had become a national best-seller, entrancing hundreds of thousands of people who fantasized what it would be like if . . .

Many other committed freaks and hippies, in search of the spiritual kick acid had provided, joined or created a variety of mystical, religious movements. A variety of rock stars lent credibility to some of the gurus who trolled turned-on youth's troubled waters, most famously the Maharishi Mahesh Yogi, who hooked the Beatles for a short time. The Hare Krishnas, a mantra-chanting group of religious ecstatics, had a great deal of success in enrolling young men and women who'd had their "minds blown" by acid. Many new religious and spiritual movements, vaguely based on "Eastern" teaching and often focused on finding "the god within" and/or on achieving spiritual states without the aid of drugs, emerged out of the counterculture and formed the basis of what came to be called the New Age movement.

By the later 1960s and early 1970s, even as almost all of the original countercultural enclaves had devolved into combination tourist traps and hard-drug, runaway-dropout scenes, the trappings and some of the practices of freak culture had made their way into mainstream culture. The free concerts that the Grateful Dead and others played for their communities became mega-rock festivals drawing hundreds of thousands, most famously at Woodstock in the summer of 1968 and most infamously at Altamont in 1969 (where the Hell's Angels beat a young man to death). Acid rock musicians like the Jefferson Airplane, Jimi Hendrix, and the Doors sold millions of records to apolitical, spiritually disinclined suburban teenagers, who adopted the "trippy" clothes, beads, and long hair of their idols. Drug use, too, had spread far outside the counterculture. Acid dealer extraordinaire Owsley alone had distributed an estimated 12 million doses of LSD by the end of the decade. The fact that by the time the tail end of the baby boom generation became high school seniors (in the late 1970s) about 40 percent of them affirmed that they "regularly" smoked marijuana indicates how broad a swath illegal drug use had cut among America's youth. The counterculture, defined most broadly, had a greater personal effect on both young white Americans and national public life than did the better-publicized political activities of student radicals.

The counterculture also had a powerful impact on the student and radical political movements of the 1960s. Many movement activists, especially young whites—most of whom had at first dismissed the counterculture as an antipolitical dead end—were challenged by the burgeoning drug scene and "love one another" ethos of the freaks. But the most politicized young people of the late 1960s were radicalized by far more than an occasional drug trip or hippie rap. By 1968, the war in Vietnam had turned white-hot, black urban neighborhoods were on fire, and America's political mainstream had started to rupture. Young political activists had moved, as the radical vanguard of the antiwar movement said, "from dissent to resistance." Black militants and white radicals, their faith in American justice and democracy lost, had begun talking about making a revolution.

9. STORMY WEATHER

~~~~~~

IN 1968, Americans on all sides of the issues believed they had reached a political impasse and many had turned to other means to carry their fight forward. Small but vocal components of the antiwar movement, the New Left student movement, and the African-American movement for social justice had lost faith in the American political and judicial system. The radicals' flirtation with a revolutionary political stance had become, by 1968, an embrace. White radicals waved Vietcong flags in the faces of the American people. Many seriously considered Cuba, China, and even North Korea as models for a good society. Todd Gitlin, among the most sophisticated and thoughtful of the young white radicals, explains the tortured logic that drove them:

> It no longer felt sufficient—sufficiently estranged, sufficiently furious—to say no to aggressive war; we felt driven to say yes to revolt. . . . If the American flag was dripping napalm, the NLF flag was clean . . . if the American Christ turned out to look like the Antichrist—then by this cramped either-or logic the Communist Antichrist must really have been Christ. . . . The Manichean all-or-nothing logic of the Cold War was conserved, though inverted, as if costumes from Central Wardrobe had been rotated.

By 1968, the leadership of Students for a Democratic Society, the most visible white radical organization with approximately 100,000 members scattered across the nation's college campuses, had gone over to "the other side." The *New* Left remained hostile to the Soviet Union and a strict Marxist-Leninist ideology, but by the end of the 1960s many called themselves revolutionaries. The relentless horror of the war in Vietnam played an essential role in the radicalization of many young whites, but it was not the war alone that drove them ever leftward toward revolutionary violence.

Though most student protesters never took that journey, by the end of the decade roughly three-quarters of a million students (out of more than 7 million) identified themselves as "radical or far left." For these self-described radicals, and for others who hopped onto the radical express only briefly, the trip made sense only because of what they believed they had learned about America's failures to live up to its own high standards of liberty and justice for all.

Some of the seeds of the white radical student movement of the late 1960s were planted in the spring of 1962, when a few dozen white young people, most from the nation's best schools, gathered in Port Huron, Michigan, at an AFL-CIO summer retreat to draft a political manifesto for their tiny, nascent organization, Students for a Democratic Society. They dreamed of creating a new left-wing political movement, untethered to either Marxist ideology or the labor union politics of the small non-Communist American left.

Tom Hayden wrote much of *The Port Huron Statement*. He had grown up in the white middle-class Detroit suburb of Royal Oaks. His divorced parents were Irish Catholics but in tune with the postwar suburban ethos neither religion nor ethnicity played major roles in his upbringing. Like millions of other 1950s teenagers, he identified with Hollywood's *Rebel Without a Cause*, which starred James Dean as a middle-class "juvenile delinquent" trapped in a stifling, boring suburban dystopia. Intellectually gifted, charismatic, a proto-bohemian and a good athlete, Hayden went to the University of Michigan, where he joined the student newspaper and started to live out his inchoate desire to explore, in Kerouac-inspired terms, "the emotional and intellectual wilderness."

The opening paragraphs of *The Port Huron Statement* reflected the mixed feelings of disquiet and then excitement that animated a small but vital group of white college students in the early 1960s:

We are people of this generation, bred in at least modest comfort, housed now in universities, looking uncomfortably to the world we inherit. . . .

Many of us began maturing in complacency. As we grew, however, our comfort was penetrated by events too troubling to dismiss. First, the permeating and victimizing fact of human degradation, symbolized by the Southern struggle against racial bigotry, compelled most of us from silence to activism. Second, the enclosing fact of the Cold War, symbolized by the presence of the Bomb, brought awareness that we . . . might die at any time. We might deliberately ignore, or avoid, or fail to feel all other human problems, but not these two.

Hayden, first as a student journalist, then as a committed activist, was an eager participant in the civil rights movement. As with most of the core group of SDS stalwarts who also participated in the Movement, his experiences in the South working alongside mainly poor, relatively uneducated black people helped him to see the world anew: "Mechanics, maids, unemployed people taking things into their own hands." It was, he enthused, "a creative, revolutionary period."

The democratic ethos of SCLC administrator Ella Baker and young SNCC leaders like Robert Zellner, Diane Nash, and John Lewis captivated the SDS founders. They dreamed of bringing that democratic energy to a white student movement dedicated to racial justice but also to a radically reoriented foreign and domestic political agenda. SDS's founders, based in part on the writings of the non-Marxist radical sociologist C. Wright Mills, argued that a "power elite," composed of "the upper circles of the corporate, political and military worlds" (alternatively described as the "system" in Paul Potter's 1965 anti-Vietnam War speech or as "corporate liberals" according to SDS theoretician Carl Oglesby), interested mainly in promoting their own interests and maintaining their own power, had directed the American people into a spiraling arms race, a hysterical Cold War standoff, and a system of fundamental economic inequality. In *The Port Huron Statement*, Hayden and the few dozen others challenged conventional wisdom

on the Cold War, outlined a vast domestic program of reform
aimed at eradicating poverty, and most of all insisted that democracy itself had to be reinvented if the American people meant
to determine their collective fate. Inspired by the civil rights movement, they wanted to create a "participatory democracy":

> In participatory democracy, the political life would be based in
> several root principles: that decision making of basic social conse-
> quences be carried on by public groups; that politics be seen posi-
> tively, as the art of collectively creating an acceptable pattern of
> social relations; that politics has the function of bringing people out
> of isolation and into community.

This vision of an engaged citizenry forging their own collective
fate, without need of domineering leaders or cumbersome bureaucracies, ruled the New Left until the very end of the 1960s.
And while most white radicals were more involved in grass-roots
organizing against the war in Vietnam or on behalf of campus
issues, the ideal of participatory democracy proved to be immensely appealing to hundreds of thousands of white college
students.

Between 1962 and 1964, SDS chapters, loosely connected to the
"national" SDS, popped up on college campuses. In 1964, the core
group of SDS—about 125 in all—decided to focus on organizing
poor people, white and black, off campus in Northern cities. SDS
leader Sharon Jeffrey, when interviewed by historian James Miller,
recalled the decision as personal and political—a hallmark of the
New Left: "I mean, on some level, it was stupid . . . we were
going after people who were totally disenfranchised and disem-
powered and disorganized on a personal level. But we wanted to
be independent . . . so we had to carve out an arena in which there
wasn't yet any organization." While SDS members' attempts to
organize America's poorest people had limited success, the young
people themselves were further radicalized by their experiences (as
had been true for many SNCC organizers who had worked among
poor blacks in the Deep South). Even before Vietnam turned off
many young whites, and before SNCC activists pushed their white

peers to take more radical positions, the core group of SDS was becoming further estranged from mainstream American politics. In a near-endless stream of pamphlets, newsletters, speeches, and in-person harangues, they attempted to convince other young people of the moral necessity of their increasingly radical positions. SDS and allied New Left organizations played a key role in politicizing students throughout the 1960s. But other, more powerful forces were at work, too.

The first big student explosion came at Berkeley in 1964. If SDS was the organizational center for white student radicals in the 1960s, Berkeley was the geographical locus. As early as 1960, Berkeley had become, in Tom Hayden's words, "the mecca of student activism."

Berkeley had an established radical tradition that preceded the 1960s. The relative freedom radicals enjoyed in Berkeley, protected, in part, by its dominant freethinking academic community, attracted leftists from around the country, some of whom came to Berkeley after being blacklisted or expelled from prestigious private schools. In May 1960, a large group of Berkeley students protested against the "Red-hunting" House Un-American Activities Committee, which was holding hearings in the Bay Area. The protests demonstrated both McCarthyism's unpopularity and its inability to intimidate students in Berkeley. Committed student leftists, many tied to "old" left organizations like the Communist Party and the Young Socialist Alliance, would provide a strong cadre of leaders and organizers on the Berkeley campus. But without thousands of new activists the "old" left organizers would have remained a relatively insignificant factor in Berkeley student life.

The civil rights movement, on most campuses, played a critical role in politicizing students from nonleftist, nonpolitical families. Berkeley, more than most university towns, had a large black population and the city council and university administration publicly debated a variety of antidiscrimination measures. A small group of students staged local protests against job discrimination and in support of other civil rights issues (especially after Berkeley residents voted in 1963 to reject an open-housing ordinance). By

1964, a small group of white students, many who'd participated
in the Movement in the South, were actively proselytizing on
campus on behalf of the civil rights struggle. These politicized
students would become campus leaders. And as one observer
noted: "A student who has been chased by the KKK in Mississippi
is not easily scared by academic bureaucrats."

Demographic factors swelled the number of students prepared
to join a student movement. By 1964—the year the first postwar
baby boomers went to college—the Berkeley campus had exploded to over 25,000 students. More than a third of them were
graduate students, who were even more likely to be concerned
with political issues than young undergraduates.

At Berkeley, like many other big state schools, students were
crammed into classrooms, dorm rooms, and cafeterias. Some students had to watch their professors on closed-circuit television.
Senior professors had little time for undergraduates. Most under-
graduate teaching, in fact, was done by poorly paid graduate as-
sistants, often in their early twenties. University administrators,
dealing with tens of thousands of students, acted less like nurturing
educators and more like corporate systems managers. To manage
the herd, the university insisted on maintaining a host of anachronistic *in loco parentis* rules, from parietals that restricted student
visiting hours to regulations that limited students' freedom of
expression. In order to keep track of the tens of thousands of
matriculants, Berkeley became the nation's first computerized
campus: students were numbered, registered by computer, and
issued a punch card. Many students (in those distant days) found
this computerized information dehumanizing. In mock recognition of life in the "mega-versity," the school paper offered this
welcome to new students: "Welcome to lines, bureaucracy and
crowds . . . the incoming freshman has much to learn—perhaps
lesson number one is not to fold, spindle or mutilate his IBM
card."

In September 1964, Berkeley students' floating alienation came
to ground when a police patrol car drove onto campus to arrest
a small band of students who were breaking school policy by
passing out political leaflets from tables they had set up on uni-

versity property. As police attempted to arrest the first student, Jack Weinberg, hundreds of others spontaneously surrounded the patrol car. For the next thirty-two hours students maintained a sit-in around the police car. Any who felt they had something to say climbed atop the cruiser (after taking off their shoes) and spoke out. Students complained about their lack of freedoms, over-crowding, their sense of powerlessness. This unorganized exercise in "participatory democracy" led to the Free Speech Movement (FSM).

Over the next few months, FSM leaders negotiated with ad-ministrators over students' right to political freedom on campus. As the debate went on, the administration became more ham-handed, punishing FSM leaders for minor infractions; as a partial result, the FSM "martyrs" became more popular. Many FSM leaders were experienced leftists or civil rights activists but most of the rank-and-file rally-goers and supporters were new to po-litical engagement.

On December 2, 1964, Mario Savio, the FSM's most powerful speaker, addressed thousands of rallying students:

> There is a time when the operations of the machine becomes so odious, makes you so sick at heart, that you can't take part; you can't even passively take part, and you've got to put your bodies upon the gears and upon the wheels, upon the levers, upon all the apparatus and you've got to make it stop. And you've got to indicate to the people who run it, to the people that own it, that unless you're free, the machines will be prevented from working at all.

Savio's speech was perfectly pitched to many students' vague feel-ings of alienation against the computerized, mega-university which seemed to demand of them complete obedience as it pre-pared them to become America's future technocratic managers. Folksinger Joan Baez followed Savio with Bob Dylan's genera-tional anthem, "The Times They Are a-Changin' " and ended the rally with "We Shall Overcome." Over a thousand students then walked into Sproul Hall and sat in against the university's refusal to grant them political freedom. The administration allowed the

Berkeley police to come in and arrest the students; 773 young
people were roughly hauled away. It was the largest mass arrest
in California history. The police action infuriated and further politicized many of the protesters.

The Berkeley protesters shared certain characteristics. In general, their grades were higher than the university average. Most
of them majored in history, English, anthropology, philosophy,
or speech (none majored in business administration). Few belonged to fraternities or sororities. Almost a third of them were
from Jewish backgrounds, while only 6 percent were Catholic (the
Berkeley student body was approximately 20 percent Jewish and
15 percent Catholic). Most came from politically liberal families.
Unlike the young men and women who led the FSM, they were
not, yet, radicals. A great many student protesters in the 1960s
shared this general profile.

Over the next year, supported by the faculty, FSM's main
demand—that students be allowed political freedom—was
granted. The Free Speech Movement died away, but its influence
on Berkeley students and on the development of a large radical
student movement was intense. Berkeley historian W. J. Rorabaugh argues that the FSM "led many students to challenge the
status quo . . . they became feisty and contentious. . . . The Free
Speech Movement unleashed a restless probing of life."

Berkeley's FSM was only the first of many such mass student
protests around the country. Except for the Deep South, student
protests over housing issues, curriculum, parietals, mandatory
ROTC, and other school-specific issues took place throughout the
country, at big public universities and at small private colleges.
Issues raised by the war in Vietnam, particularly war research
carried on by faculty members, informed and popularized many
campus protests. In general, such protests did not drive most
students to embrace a radical critique of the United States. But
few students who participated in campus protests were not moved
to at least consider the larger issues and bigger stakes involved in
their questioning of authority.

By 1968, a network of activists were trying to connect campus
issues to national and international events and to radicalize stu-

dents. Increasingly, student governments and student newspapers
were dominated by politicized students: draft resister David Harris
was elected student president of Stanford; leading campus dissident
David Awbry became student president of the University of Kansas; New Left stalwart Marshall Bloom was editor of the Amherst
student paper. A series of radical, student-oriented off-campus
underground newspapers popped up around the country, mixing
a New Left editorial stance with youth culture news and an uncensored look at campus events. The *Berkeley Barb* was the model
for these papers. In the Los Angeles *Free Press*, one of many underground papers that reached out to both the counterculture and
politicized students, Jerry Farber published a seminal article in
March 1967 that captured the imagination of many young people
and displayed both how radical students tried to draw connections
and, somewhat ironically, how often those connections focused
on the students rather than the outside world. "Students are niggers," he wrote hyperbolically. "When you get that straight, our
schools begin to make sense. . . . What school amounts to, then,
for white and black kids alike, is a twelve-year course in how to
be slaves." Reprinted and widely circulated by student radicals
around the country, Farber's underground screed was an evocative
organizing tool. By late 1967, the Liberation News Service distributed radical news stories (often written by leading white student activists) to dozens of school and off-campus underground
newspapers. By the late 1960s, many young people were wired
in to each other by more than the Beatles and the Rolling Stones.

American student protests in the 1960s were matched by student
protests in almost every other major industrial nation, including
Japan, Germany, England, Italy, and France. None of these countries was involved in the Vietnam War; none faced racial turmoil.
W. J. Rorabaugh argues that despite their many differences, all
the young protesters looked out at "a world created and then
frozen into place in 1945. . . . For students born just before, during,
or just after the war, the projection of twenty years of stasis in-
definitely into the future promised the inheritance of a sterile world
without any chance to alter it." Many American students, a majority at most of the country's elite universities, tried to change

that static world, at least a little bit, by reforming their own schools. Race issues, and then even more the war in Vietnam, gave many white students pressing reasons to become further involved in challenging the world they were to inherit. Pushing them particularly hard in this direction was the militant turn of the young black activists to whom many whites had long looked for inspiration.

Black students and young black activists by 1967 rarely focused their energies on the general campus protests or burgeoning anti-war movement. More and more, young black activists chose to go it alone in blacks-only organizations. SNCC, the most prominent black student organization, had purged all whites by early 1967. Black student organizations, agitating in the name of Black Power, grew on almost every campus. By the late 1960s, many young black activists had lost all faith in white society and preached a vague doctrine of revolutionary violence. Black separatism and Black Power extremism, coupled with the riots breaking out across America's cities, transformed America's racial politics.

A majority of young black activists in SNCC had also essentially given up on white America by 1966. The violent attacks they had suffered while organizing in the Deep South, the soul-wrenching poverty their people endured, the failure of the Democratic Party to accept fully their moral claims, and the modest impact of civil rights legislation drew them away from both nonviolent protest and democratic reform. The Watts riot of 1965 and the many smaller ghetto riots of 1966 proved to them and to a minority of other black activists that masses of African-Americans were ready for a more militant course. Young black activists felt propelled toward new solutions to one of America's oldest problems.

The spirit of Malcolm X was there waiting for them. He offered African-Americans embittered by generations of racism a stark alternative to Martin Luther King's nonviolent, integrationist path. From the time of his release from prison in 1952 until early 1964, Malcolm X preached the gospel of the Nation of Islam, a religion born during the Great Depression. Led by Elijah Muhammad, Black Muslims combined elements of traditional Islamic doctrine with a set of racially inspired beliefs. They believed that Negroes were a superior race and that whites were literally subhuman devils created by Yacub, "the big-head scientist." Some day soon, the doctrine decreed, "the Mother Ship" would come to Earth and rescue all Negroes before killing all the white devils. No one in America in the early 1960s could preach the apocalyptic "whites are devils" orthodoxy more powerfully than Malcolm X.

Some accused Malcolm X of preaching a gospel of hate. To them his reply was as uncompromising as it was searing:

> How can anybody ask us do we hate the white man who kidnapped us four hundred years ago, brought us here and stripped us of our history, stripped us of our culture, stripped us of our language, stripped us of everything you could have used today to prove that you're part of the human family, bring you down to the level of an animal, sell you from plantation to plantation like a sack of wheat, sell you like a sack of potatoes, sell you like a horse and a plow, and then hung you up from one end of the country to the other and then you ask me do I hate him. Why, your question is worthless!

If Martin Luther King offered whites a doctrine tailor-made to bridge the racial gulf and calm those who feared change, Malcolm X gave black Americans a vision of the oppressor called to justice for his evil and mocked for his baseless self-righteousness.

Malcolm offered his black listeners far more than hatred of whites. Building on the foundations of black nationalism set by past champions—most notably Marcus Garvey—he gave followers a vision of racial dignity and self-pride restored. At a time when African and African-American history and culture were essentially untaught at American schools, Malcolm X gloried in Africa's past and its cultural richness. He insisted that African-Americans live up to their African heritage and take pride in their dark skin and in their own communities. "Stand yourself up and look at yourself—with your eyes not the white man's," he preached to crowds in Harlem's streets. He argued fiercely against integration, calling it a sham and insisting it was no solution to racism or to black Americans' need for economic development. He saw nonviolence as undignified and attacked Martin Luther

King as an Uncle Tom. Though he expended far more energy urging his black audiences to open their eyes to the myriad ways in which whites held them down than in describing racial solutions, Malcolm X insisted on the long-term need for a separate black nation. He told black listeners they must establish economic, political, and cultural control of their collective lives. He called for Black Power.

Many black Americans delighted in Malcolm X's abuse of the white man and his vision of black pride and strength. A non-Muslim follower, a young rank-and-file activist in Georgia, recalled Malcolm's forceful appeal:

> Sure, King was a significant figure in the civil rights movement, but he was too soft. . . . Malcolm X was more my hero than King was because he touched deep into my heart and soul when he talked about black unity and black pride. . . .
>
> If change was to come about, we had to respect ourselves as well as one another and have pride in ourselves as black people. That pride meant to stop thinking of ourselves as inferior. . . . It was only natural that blacks thought of themselves as second-rate because we were treated as such for so long. We also had to stop kissing up to white folks . . . they were the cause of all our problems.

Malcolm X was assassinated on February 21, 1965, killed by members of the Nation of Islam for apostasy after he left the faith. Before his death, after a pilgrimage to Mecca, Malcolm X had begun to modify his absolute condemnation of all whites. Many of his closest followers abhorred this racial moderation. As black nationalist Charles Kenyatta charged: "Why, the average black in this country *lives* on hatred. . . . Good gracious, they had been told for twelve years that the white man was the devil, and then you turn around and say some of them was *different?*" Most activists looked to Malcolm's legacy not for signs of moderation but for his fiery rhetoric of liberating rage against white injustice, for a rekindled pride in their African heritage, and with an inchoate desire to forge a black nation on the rock of Black Power.

In June 1966, SNCC leader Stokely Carmichael, just released

from jail, where he had been imprisoned for leading a peaceful civil rights rally, stood before a crowd of three thousand angry black men and women in Canton, Mississippi, and declared the time had come to change the direction of the movement to which he had dedicated his young life. "This is the twenty-seventh time I have been arrested, and I ain't going to jail no more!" he announced. "The only way we gonna stop them white men from whuppin' us is to take over. We been saying freedom for six years—and we ain't got nothin'. What we gonna start saying now is 'Black Power'!" The crowd took up the chant with a roar of approval: Black Power! Black Power! Black Power!

Martin Luther King, Jr., urged Carmichael and other SNCC militants to rethink their rhetoric. He argued that the cry of Black Power would "confuse our allies, isolate the Negro community and give many prejudiced whites . . . a ready excuse for self-justification." But neither Carmichael nor most of SNCC's organizers would back down. They were frustrated and angry and many felt they had come as far as they could—which in their minds was not nearly far enough—with nonviolence and narrowly cast civil rights protests. They wanted to be a part of the psychologically liberating, revolutionary fervor many of them had seen firsthand in newly independent African countries like Ghana and in other Third World nations like Cuba. They believed that the Movement as a vehicle for mass participation and mass empowerment had begun to stagnate. It wasn't appealing to poor ghetto blacks or to young students.

In the late 1960s, the notion of Black Power won over black students, a majority of whom were living and studying in predominantly white schools for the first time (about 330,000 black students attended predominantly white schools by 1970 and about 170,000 attended traditionally black colleges; in 1960 only 234,000 black students had attended any college). Many felt isolated. Almost all were angry about the level of racism, deliberate or otherwise, they confronted. Black Power and black nationalism offered many students both a way to confront racism and a means to empower themselves in what often felt like alien territory.

For example, Preston Washington (who as the Reverend Dr.

Washington would become a prominent Harlem leader) was one of a few dozen African-American students to attend Williams College in the late 1960s. When he arrived in 1966, administrators scattered black students throughout the school's dormitories—integrating them. Few to no courses focused on the black experience. Williams had almost no black faculty members. Washington, influenced by Malcolm X, believed that black students should at the least have the right to live together and to learn about their heritage. As head of the Williams Afro-American Society, he led a three-day sit-in at the administration building demanding that the college create a "Black House," recruit more black students, and hire more black professors to teach black-oriented courses. The Afro-American Society-sponsored sit-in was a blacks-only affair (though heavily supported by whites). The Williams sit-in was similar to the great majority of such protests around the country: racially separatist in practice, peacefully run, and a success. During the sit-in, the Williams administration held a series of workshops on racism. They acceded to black students' demand for separate housing and also announced that the college would end the antiblack and anti-Jewish fraternity system, in which most Williams students participated. In addition, administrators assured students that they would more aggressively seek out black students and black faculty.

In the North by the late 1960s, almost always in direct response to black (and, in the West, Chicano) students' demands, colleges and universities began changing admission practices to ensure higher black and, to a lesser extent, Hispanic student enrollment. Black students often demanded and got a black cultural center and racially separate housing. Most major Northern and West Coast colleges and universities added courses, programs, and sometimes entire departments devoted to "Black Studies" or "Afro-American Studies," usually taught by black professors. While a very few well-publicized violent or militant black student protests—especially one by gun-toting radicals at Cornell—spooked conservative faculty members around the country and made many white families skittish, most black student protests in the late 1960s and early 1970s were settled in a fairly amiable manner. Nonetheless, they

did represent a radical change. Increasingly, black students, organized in blacks-only groups or centers, were pursuing a separatist agenda at the cultural and political level. Politically motivated
white and black students were for the most part not working
together. Many nonpolitical white students, who were coming
into contact with black people their own age for the first time,
were met with Malcolm X-like anger.

The radical reorientation of the black movement away from
integration, assimilation, and improved race relations and toward
separatism, racial pride, and group power was not restricted to
college campuses. It spread like wildfire through black America.
While the NAACP leadership fought all forms of the Black Power
movement that was counterproductive to its integrationist agenda,
by the end of the decade even the leading conservative black newspaper, *The Pittsburgh Courier*, editorialized in favor of a narrow
version of cultural "nationalism": "How great can the American
Negro become in self-esteem and personal dignity if his history
and culture are lost, both to him and to his white colleagues?"
Overall, the black pride aspect of the Black Power movement was
most enthusiastically embraced within black communities and organizations. African-American parents and community activists
pushed school administrators to develop a curriculum that taught
black history and culture. Young men and women stopped
straightening their hair and let it grow out into what became
known as an Afro. People started wearing African-styled clothing
and jewelry. Black-oriented magazines like *Ebony* helped promote
slogans like "Black Is Beautiful," and soul singer James Brown
hammered home the message: "Say it loud, I'm black and I'm
proud." A great many African-Americans who had never been
allowed to enter "the melting pot" or "climb the corporate ladder"
or buy a "California ranch house" in the new suburbs began de-
nouncing the whole enterprise of assimilation and integration as
a fraud not worth pursuing. While few African-Americans saw
their exclusion from the economic mainstream as unimportant, at
the cultural and social level many African-Americans chose to
begin celebrating and developing the separate world they had both
voluntarily and involuntarily created. Flying in the face of con-

temporary conventional wisdom, they insisted on cultural pluralism rather than cultural assimilation.

Black militants saw this cultural process as a first step in a larger process in which African-Americans would gain a politically powerful group identity. Stokely Carmichael offered the simplest and most compelling critique of the prevalent American belief that individual advancement produced by hard work lay at the core of the American dream and was the African-American's greatest hope and opportunity. Before a mainly white audience of Berkeley students, he argued: "We are oppressed as a group because we are black, not because we are lazy, not because we are apathetic, not because we're stupid . . . and in order to get out of that oppression, one must feel the group power one has. Not the individual power."

Carmichael also explained the logic that had compelled SNCC to throw all whites out of the organization and which had directed most radical and Black Power-oriented groups to insist that white people had no business working, even as volunteers, in black communities:

> We've been saying that we cannot have white people working in the black community and we've based it on psychological grounds. The fact is that all black people often question whether or not they are equal to whites because every time they start to do something white people are around showing them how to do it. . . . Black people must be seen in positions of power doing and articulating for themselves.

Carmichael concluded this speech as Black Power militants almost always did when speaking to whites, with a threat: "Brothers and sisters, we have no choice but to say very clearly, move on over or we're going to move on over you."

Carmichael's remarks reflect both the central ideas and, just as importantly, the heated emotions that drove Black Power militants. Race, they decreed, not class, gender, or any other identity, was what divided Americans. To overcome that divide, they argued, black people must work together.

In theory, this notion was unexceptional—and even in accord with the "liberal pluralism" model many mainstream political scientists used to explain how politics actually functioned in America. In cities like Gary, Cleveland, and Newark, relatively mainstream black politicians moderated a rhetoric of Black Power to inspire black voters to turn out in large numbers to elect black mayors and other city officials for the first time. This ethnic voting was basic to urban politics. However, even the most modest forms of Black Power horrified whites who clung to traditional racism. But white Americans did have good reasons, too, to fear some champions of Black Power.

In Cambridge, Maryland, in August 1967, new SNCC chair H. Rap Brown spoke to a crowd of angry young blacks. "Burn this town down," he told them. "When you tear down the white man, brother, you are hitting him in the money. . . . Don't love him to death, shoot him to death." A few hours later, downtown Cambridge was in flames. Writer Amiri Baraka urged black people to "smash the windows . . . take the shit you want. Take their lives if need be." Rather than seeking to cool ghetto youths' tempers, as Martin Luther King had, Black Power advocates at the local and national level often urged them, in the most explicit language, to explode. Conservative white politicians like Governor Ronald Reagan and House minority leader Gerald Ford, as well as many other white Americans, saw Black Power advocates as the cause of the riots that swept America between 1965 and 1968. They were not. Decades of poverty, neglect, and racism coupled with rising and unfulfilled expectations were. But Black Power advocates were, in several incidents, the catalyst for riots and so contributed to the arson and violence that ensued.

Incendiary, revolutionary black militancy crystallized with the formation of the Black Panther Party in Oakland in October 1966. Huey Newton and Bobby Seale created the Panthers to embody Malcolm X's doctrine of community self-defense. Above all, the Panthers believed that the black community needed to arm in order to defend itself from the brutality of the white police: "only with the power of the gun can the black masses halt the terror and brutality perpetuated against them by the armed racist power structure." In a Ten-Point Program, Newton and Seale articulated a set of radical demands that included the release of all black prison inmates and a massive redistribution of property and wealth from whites to blacks.

The Panthers were superb self-promoters. They wore an intimidating uniform of black berets and leather jackets. In military formation they chanted: "The Revolution has co-ome, it's time to pick up the gu-un. Off the pigs!" They did their best to be the "baddest on the scene" and largely succeeded in appealing to the imagination both of "brothers on the block," young angry ghetto black kids, and of white radicals looking for new black allies. Their first major action, taken when the party had a few dozen members, was to stroll into the California state capitol fully armed in order to protest gun-control laws aimed mainly at their tactic of following white policemen while openly carrying guns. This protest resulted in Bobby Seale going to jail and the Panthers becoming instant celebrities throughout the world. The Panther's élan and their heated rhetoric which focused on "offing the pigs" (killing white policemen) brought them widespread publicity and recruits. Despite their prominence, however, the Panthers never had more than a few thousand members.

Uninterested in legislative or political reform, the Panthers called themselves armed revolutionaries and it wasn't just rhetoric. In October 1967, Panther leader Huey Newton went to jail for killing a police officer. In April 1968, thirteen Panthers ambushed an Oakland police car, hitting it with 157 shots and badly wounding one officer. Subsequently police subdued the ambush party and in retaliation, it seems, executed a seventeen-year-old Panther. Panther recruits, many of them ex-convicts, relished the image and reality of being armed blacks waging war on white America. By 1970, the Panthers had killed eleven police officers. Some of the Panthers also used their political front to rip off and terrorize their own black neighbors.

After Newton and Seale were jailed, Eldridge Cleaver headed the party. Cleaver had spent years in jail for violent crimes, but he was also a brilliant writer whose *Soul on Ice* became a 1968 bestseller. Cleaver reached out to both white radicals and SNCC militants, enlisting both Stokely Carmichael and Rap Brown as Panther "ministers." He forged a loose coalition of radicals in which the Panthers figured (in the words of an SDS communiqué) as "the vanguard of the black liberation struggle." White radicals relished having black militant allies after having been scorned by SNCC and most other campus-based black separatist organizations.

Beyond their rhetoric and their shoot-outs with the police, a few committed Panthers, many of them women, set up free breakfast programs, medical clinics, and other community-based programs in several cities. For some Panthers (most notably Bobby Rush, who was elected to Congress from Chicago in 1992) this hands-on struggle led to a long-term commitment to political change. But many Panthers simply became caught in their own rhetoric of violence. To the degree that white radicals tried to follow the Panthers' "vanguard" leadership, they left reality behind: most people, white and black, had no interest whatsoever in revolution and saw armed militants as a personal threat to their safety and well-being.

FBI director J. Edgar Hoover took almost perverse pleasure in the rise of the Black Panthers. Their call for revolution and "offing the pigs" gave him practically carte blanche to destroy the organization. In particular, the FBI mounted an effort called COIN-TELPRO (already in use against SNCC, SCLC, and the Nation of Islam), which involved attempts to trick various Panthers into believing that other militants were gunning for them or were police informants. And of course, the FBI and many police departments really did have informants, undercover agents, and agents provocateurs working inside the Panthers.

Local police departments, not surprisingly, were particularly antagonized by the Panthers' promise of violence: "Off the pigs!" They harassed the Panthers, tore up their local headquarters, and jailed them whenever they could. The Chicago police on December 4, 1969, in a 3 a.m. raid fired over eighty shotgun rounds and dozens of bullets, seemingly without provocation, into an apartment in which several Panthers lived, concentrating their fire on the bedroom where an informant had told them Illinois Panther leader Fred Hampton slept. The police succeeded in executing Hampton and another young Panther.

At the dawn of the 1960s few Americans would have dreamed that Black Power revolutionaries would be shooting it out with the police by the end of the decade. But by 1970, such violence —while not commonplace—was an agonizing reality. The worst plague of domestic violence, however, was caused neither by Black Power revolutionaries nor by retaliating armed agents of the government.

On April 4, 1968, Martin Luther King, Jr., was assassinated. He was shot in Memphis, seemingly by a white man, probably in league with others still unknown. King had come to Memphis to support the city's striking garbagemen. Through all the uproar over Black Power and calls for violent revolution, King had remained faithful to nonviolence and the transforming power of love. But in the face of racist intransigence and slow progress, his vision had expanded, too, and he was groping toward what Jesse Jackson would later call a Rainbow Coalition. Just before his death, he and SCLC were laying the foundation for a "Poor People's Campaign" that would rally in Washington, D.C., that summer to seek economic justice for all Americans. The night before he died, depressed by the violence tearing at his movement, King told his followers, "I may not get there with you. But we as a people will get to the promised land."

In bungalows and housing projects, on front stoops and in alleyways, black Americans wept for King. And then some let their tears boil over into rage: a white man had killed Martin Luther King, Jr.

In the black ghetto neighborhoods of Washington, D.C., 700 fires broke out as cordons of police surrounded the Capitol. Chicago's West Side black ghetto erupted after hundreds of schoolchildren broke away from a memorial service and began tearing up their neighborhood in an uncontrolled fury; by the end of the day almost every business up and down Madison Street, the main commercial thoroughfare, was looted and torched. In the next week an orgy of destruction swept through over 130 towns and cities. Militant activists hurled Molotov cocktails, laughing teenagers carried looted television sets on their heads, and drunken men and women paraded booty-filled shopping carts down flaming streets. They had turned their own neighborhoods into funeral pyres.

Only a few months earlier a presidential commission investigating the riots of 1965–67 had concluded: "White racism is essentially responsible for the explosive mixture which has accumulated in our cities." During the "King riots" in the spring of 1968, many terrified whites, even in distant suburbs, had barricaded their homes, certain that they would be attacked by rioting blacks. After this wave of riots, on top of all the others, they were even less ready than they had been before to accept what the then archconservative *Chicago Tribune* called "the wave of sentimentality and assumed guilt that has swept the country." With order restored and with fear having often turned to anger, many whites demanded that the chaos engulfing their world be stopped. They listened attentively as Richard Nixon, running again for the presidency, told them: "Until we have order, we can have no progress."

In the face of militant antiwar demonstrators, Black Power revolutionaries, student radicals, and dope-smoking hippies, whites around the country called out for Law and Order. Mainstream politics and national policy were imploding. Many Americans felt that the good lives they had made for themselves and their families had been taken from them before they had ever really had a chance to enjoy them.

A minority of white and black radicals gloried in the fear and anger they produced in most Americans. In June 1969, SDS fragmented into rival factions—all of which declared themselves revolutionary—and rapidly began to lose members. The most publicized faction, the Weathermen (named after a Bob Dylan line about not needing "a weatherman to know which way the wind blows"), composed mainly of the sons and daughters of the well-to-do, dedicated themselves to armed revolt. By early 1970, about 100 Weathermen, locked in fantasies about waging war on America in the name of "Third World People," went "underground." In March 1970 three Weathermen killed themselves when they accidentally detonated a bomb they were manufacturing. The roofing-nail bombs they were making, seemingly, were to be exploded at Columbia University.

Between September 1969 and May 1970 approximately 100 mostly unconnected white revolutionaries set off or attempted some 250 bombings around the country, most of them targeted against ROTC buildings, induction centers, draft board offices, or other Vietnam-linked government buildings. Late one night, at the University of Wisconsin, one small group bombed a building used for an Army math research project; a graduate student was killed. As Todd Gitlin writes: "In the illumination of that bomb, the movement knew sin."

In their horror over the war in Vietnam, in their often ignorant and misplaced enthusiasm for revolutionary struggles abroad, and in their zealous attempt to repudiate their own "white skin privilege" in a society that had been built on racism, a tiny group of extremists lost their grip on political, social, and global realities. They and their black revolutionary allies managed to inject a poison into American political life which only served to weaken the antiwar movement and all other progressive forces struggling for social justice. Their fanaticism gave credibility to the hard-line forces that wanted to put a stop to all forms of dissent in America.

10. RN AND THE POLITICS OF DECEPTION

~~~~~~

PRESIDENT JOHNSON WITHDREW from the 1968 presidential race even before the riots that followed the assassination of Martin Luther King, Jr. On March 31 he told the nation: "I shall not seek, and I will not accept, the nomination of my party for another term as your President." Looking far older than his fifty-nine years, Johnson promised to devote his last days in office not "to any personal partisan course" but to negotiating a peace settlement with the North Vietnamese.

Twentieth-century America's greatest political infighter wanted out. In part, he quit because his health was failing him. His heart was bad, and his wife had been begging him to step down before the pressures of the job killed him (he died less than five years later). But Johnson's health had been bad for years; the proud Texan might have risked "dying with his boots on" if the presidency had not become a nightmare for him. From retirement, Johnson explained:

> I tried to make it possible for every child of every color to grow up in a nice house, eat a solid breakfast, to attend a decent school and to get a good and lasting job. I asked so little in return, just a little thanks. Just a little appreciation. That's all. But look at what I got instead. Riots in 175 cities. Looting. Burning. Shooting. . . . Young people by the thousands leaving the university, marching in the streets, chanting that horrible song about how many kids I had killed that day ["Hey, hey, LBJ, How many kids did you kill today?"]. . . . It ruined everything.

Also pushing Johnson out of the White House was his precipitous drop in public support and the growing rebellion against him within his own party. An antiwar Democrat, Minnesota senator Eugene McCarthy, had announced his presidential candidacy on October 20, 1967. McCarthy, a pensive, ironic sort, as far from the bear-hugging, lapel-grabbing Johnson as a major politician could be, explained that as much as anything he campaigned to fight the "sense of political hopelessness" he saw overcoming too many young people who were, in their "discontent and frustration" with Vietnam, turning to "extralegal if not illegal actions to manifest protest." As historian Allen Matusow argues, McCarthy hoped he could restore antiwar students' faith in the political process.

McCarthy's candidacy, given next to no chance by the pundits and political insiders, received a boost by tragic events in Vietnam. On January 30, 1968, at the start of Tet, the lunar New Year, some 80,000 Vietcong and North Vietnamese regulars launched a major military offensive, invading more than 100 South Vietnamese cities and towns, and even attacking the U.S. embassy in Saigon. The Communist troops mercilessly slaughtered South Vietnamese civilians, massacring some 3,000 people in Hue alone. The offensive went on for day after bloody day.

For months before Tet, in response to the growing antiwar movement, the Johnson administration had been telling the American people that the war was being won, that the enemy was weak, and that there was "light at the end of the tunnel." The American people expected a war of attrition in which their "boys" steadily mopped up the enemy. They had been led to believe that the enemy was incapable of a major offensive; they had not been prepared for a Communist escalation of the war.

South Vietnamese troops and American air and ground forces beat back the enemy offensive in every town and city. While American and South Vietnamese losses were high, Vietcong losses, in particular, were massive. The Communists had suffered a major military defeat. Despite the military victory, powerful figures in America saw Tet as a sign that despite what the Johnson administration claimed, the war was not ending; it was spiraling out of control.

Americans *were* told that Tet was an American military victory. CBS news anchor Walter Cronkite flew to South Vietnam and reported: "First and foremost, the Vietcong suffered a military defeat." But Cronkite and the rest of the media elite focused less on this victory and much more on the "credibility gap" it exposed. ABC news analyst Joseph C. Harsch told viewers that Tet flew in the face of "what the government had led us to expect." In an image that haunted many Americans, NBC and ABC news showed South Vietnam's national police chief put a gun to the head of a Vietcong captive, his hands tied behind his back; the networks cut away just as the trigger was pulled. This image appeared on the front pages of most major newspapers in the country, signifying a truth few Americans had wanted to know: their Vietnamese allies were not the democratic, freedom-loving people portrayed to them by their President. The news media might have pointed out that Communist atrocities during Tet exceeded those of the South Vietnamese. But the televised coverage of Tet was focused not on the relative merits of America's allies and enemies but on the course of the war itself.

CBS news anchor Walter Cronkite put the most powerful spin on Tet in a special report aired after the Communist offensive had been beaten back: "To suggest that we are on the edge of defeat is to yield to unreasonable pessimism. To say that we are mired in stalemate seems the only realistic, yet unsatisfactory conclusion." After Tet, America's media elite, which had struggled to stay on board the Johnson administration's war, began shifting their coverage. They portrayed America's fighting men less "heroically" than they had before and showed the war not as a victory in progress but as a quagmire in process. While Tet turned only a few more Americans completely against the war, public approval of Johnson's Vietnam policy dropped from 39 percent in January to 26 percent by late March and only a third of the nation, down from half, believed that the war was being won.

Not just the public was losing faith in the war. A majority of LBJ's key advisers and Senate supporters had begun to reject their

President's war policy. Outgoing Secretary of Defense Robert McNamara told the President that while Tet had resulted in "very heavy" enemy casualties, "after they absorb the losses they will remain a substantial force." Seemingly, America was no closer to defeating the enemy after this battlefield victory than it had been before. When incoming Secretary of Defense Clark Clifford and other "old hands" met with LBJ on March 4 to discuss General Westmoreland's request for a massive increase in troops, they told him that American military strategy was bankrupt. It was time, Secretary of State Dean Rusk said, to negotiate with the Communists. Uncertainties about the United States' role in Vietnam reverberated around the world, causing a run on gold that threatened America's balance of payments and which forced the London gold market to close on March 16.

By mid-March, Johnson appeared to be politically vulnerable. McCarthy's underdog campaign had been inundated with volunteers, overwhelmingly drawn from the peaceful majority of campus antiwar protesters. Their efforts were focused on the first primary in New Hampshire. With a barber operating right in McCarthy headquarters, long-haired young men cut their locks while young women traded in ragged jeans for girl-next-door frocks. Having gone "clean for Gene," some 3,000 student volunteers went door to door asking New Hampshire voters to reject President Johnson's war in Vietnam. On March 12, the nearly unknown McCarthy shocked the experts by receiving 42 percent of the vote, narrowly losing in a conservative state to the sitting President of the United States. Four days later, seeing the possibilities, Robert Kennedy announced his candidacy: "At stake is not simply the leadership of our party and even our country, it is our right to the moral leadership of this planet."

Bobby Kennedy was, as a campaigner, everything McCarthy was not. Kennedy was electric; he seemed to hold nothing in reserve. Though slow to accept the civil rights movement while serving as Attorney General for his brother, by 1968 he cared viscerally about inner-city poverty and frustration. And yet the onetime "Commie-hunting" assistant to Senator Joe McCarthy was no "bleeding-heart" liberal. As historian Allen Matusow argues: "Kennedy could walk through the streets of both white working-class and black neighborhoods and be warmly cheered by each." Bobby Kennedy was the only candidate running who could credibly call out for "law and order" while also demanding that America pay its moral debt to the poor and the underprivileged. Kennedy had a magic about him, call it charisma, that no other candidate running for the presidency in 1968 possessed.

Despite Tet, New Hampshire, and then Johnson's withdrawal from the race, the chances for either McCarthy or Kennedy winning the nomination were slim. Vice President Hubert Humphrey had taken up Johnson's fallen mantle, and President Johnson (who had hated Bobby Kennedy since his days as Attorney General) threw all his support behind Humphrey. Overwhelmingly the party bosses and mainstream Democratic politicians fell in with the President behind the Vice President and against the antiwar insurgents. These party bosses controlled the nomination. Only a minority of the delegates to the presidential nominating convention were then determined by the state primaries; back in 1952 Senator Estes Kefauver had won 12 of 13 Democratic primaries and had still lost the nomination to Adlai Stevenson. Robert Kennedy knew that he would have to demonstrate massive national support if he was to convince the party bosses that, his disloyalty to the President notwithstanding, he had earned the nomination. Humphrey, counting on traditional party loyalty, was not even running in the primaries.

Over the next two and a half months the two antiwar candidates slugged it out over the campaign trail, running against each other and a variety of "favorite son" candidates and place holders for Humphrey. Tens of thousands of people, young and old, who opposed the war joined the traditional political process to work for McCarthy or Kennedy as grass-roots volunteers. On June 4 in the California primary, Kennedy and McCarthy won a combined total of 87 percent of the vote, with Kennedy the narrow victor. If Kennedy could somehow convince the party boss supreme, Chicago's mayor, Richard Daley—who had so ably championed his brother's candidacy—that the California victory was an electoral mandate not to be ignored, maybe, just maybe, he could start a bandwagon that would win him the nomination. It was possible.

As Kennedy made his exit from the California postvictory celebration, as Theodore White wrote, "at once broker of power, magic leader, desired sexual object, protagonist of aspirations, liberator and hero," he was shot dead. A lone assassin, seemingly infuriated by Senator Kennedy's pro-Israel stance, had clawed his way through the admiring throng and fired a bullet through Robert Kennedy's brain. For the third time in less than five years, Americans had to ponder the meaning of another assassination of one of their leaders.

California governor Ronald Reagan, running unsuccessfully for the Republican nomination, used Kennedy's death to escalate his strident calls for a crackdown on lawlessness. And despite Reagan's known propensity for making up stories to illustrate his points and prejudices, people listened. They listened because, despite his exaggerations, Reagan was on to something. Violent crime was exploding—since 1960, statistics showed murders up 34 percent and assault up a staggering 67 percent. Many factors contributed to the increase in violent crimes: a bulging population of young people, the endemic overcrowding and frustrations of inner-city life, the increased use and sale of illegal drugs, and the decreasing influence of stabilizing institutions like church and family among the poor. But despite the crime wave, fewer criminals were actually going to jail. As political analyst Michael Barone states, the decrease in jail time was not the result of a few "liberal theorists" but represented "the widely decentralized decisions of thousands of prosecutors, judges, legislators, and voters." Still, whoever or whatever was to blame, Americans worried and with good reason.

Republican presidential candidate Richard Nixon, his political antennae ever sensitive, zeroed in on the law-and-order theme. He castigated the Supreme Court for the legal safeguards it had provided criminal defendants—especially in the *Escobedo* (1964) and *Miranda* (1966) decisions, both of which attempted to create a fair national standard of justice by mandating that police inform criminal suspects that they had the right to an attorney during questioning and that they had the right to remain silent in order

to avoid self-incrimination. Nixon also blasted the Justice Department for not prosecuting rioters and protesters to the full limit
of the law. "Today, all across the land," Nixon intoned, "guilty
men walk free from hundreds of courtrooms. Something has gone
terribly wrong in America." With the riots, "crime in the streets,"
the war, the assassinations, and angry protesters turning up night
after night on the evening news, public life had stopped making
sense for many Americans. They were looking for answers, not
sure where to turn.

Alabama governor George Wallace, running in 1968 for the
presidency as an independent candidate, tried to provide suitable
scapegoats. His credentials as a racist segregationist already well
known, Wallace ran in the North less as an opponent of the civil
rights movement and more, as he put it, as the people's champion
against the "pointy heads, the long hairs, the anarchists, the bureaucrats, [and] the intellectuals."

Wallace told Americans that the reason they felt powerless and
scared was that a bunch of snobs and college brats and big-shot
know-it-alls who'd never done an honest day's worth of work in
their lives had taken over America. To an enthusiastic audience
of white working-class families in Cicero, Illinois—a town known
for greeting Martin Luther King, Jr., and his supporters with
bricks and racist epithets when they marched to protest the community's segregated housing—Wallace vented his brand of populist politics:

> We're talking about domestic institutions, we're talking about
> schools, we're talking about hospitals, we're talking about the se-
> niority of a workingman in his labor union, we're talking about
> the ownership of property. . . . We don't need guidelines to tell us
> and we don't need half a billion dollars being spent on bureaucrats
> in Washington of your hard-earned tax money to check every school
> system, every hospital, every seniority list of a labor union . . . let
> them know a man's home is still his castle.

Wallace thought he understood something about the white
working class. The average American, he believed, desperately

wanted to maintain control of the small parts of life still left to him by the giant corporations and the federal government and the other outside forces that seemed to be grabbing greater and greater power and authority. At the same time, people were appalled by the pictures flashed at them on television of demonstrators shouting against their government and flouting traditional morality and trying to turn their own children against them. George Wallace knew that a great many white Americans in 1968 felt themselves caught between the faraway elites in places like New York and Washington, D.C., who seemed to run the economy, the culture, and national politics and the protesters, black and white, who took to the streets angrily demanding something better for the people —a group which never seemed to include all the day-in-and-day-out folks who took simple pride in doing what needed to be done to make ends meet. By the end of the summer, the meanspirited George Wallace had the support of about 20 percent of the electorate and 53 percent of Americans said that "Wallace would handle law and order the way it ought to be handled." While his main support was in the Deep South, Wallace had a considerable following in much of the industrialized Midwest.

While Wallace rallied his supporters, the antiwar movement struggled to maintain its pressure on the Johnson administration. President Johnson's decisions to partially halt bombing in Vietnam and not to seek reelection in order to concentrate on peace negotiations had convinced many moderate antiwar movement participants to adopt a wait-and-see attitude. The McCarthy and Kennedy campaigns had also siphoned off thousands of antiwar rank-and-file activists. Against these moderating forces, more militant antiwar activists tried hard to spread the message: "The war is not over!" After much internal debate, antiwar organizers associated with the National Mobilization to End the War in Vietnam, known as the Mobe, decided to push ahead with their long-planned protest at the Democratic National Convention in Chicago. The protest was to be a continuation of the national antiwar leadership's vow to militantly "confront the war makers."

By the summer of 1968, tens of thousands of Americans had turned to more radical means of opposing the war in Vietnam. A group called Resistance urged young men to burn their draft cards in public. Thousands did. In Oakland, waves of protesters tried to shut down an Army induction center. The police responded by beating the demonstrators bloody. In universities, small groups of students sat in to protest weapons research projects and military contracts, and blocked recruiting efforts by defense contractors. Many of the most radical students, often associated with SDS, believed that in order to "bring the war home" they should take advantage of any possible political issue to disrupt "business as usual" on their campuses. This plan resulted in a number of spectacularly confrontational protests. At Columbia University, for example, students took over a number of buildings to protest against a small war-related campus research project and a proposal to build a school gym on public parkland mainly used by black neighborhood residents. The Columbia protest, which came to a climax with a bloody police attack on the students, took place just a few miles uptown from the headquarters of the mass media, and so received extensive coverage—enough to convince many Americans that universities were being taken over by revolutionaries.

In a further sign of the radicals' efforts to bring the war home and to confront the war makers, in October 1967, some 50,000 protesters had marched on the Pentagon and more than 600 people were arrested for trespassing, and some 47 protesters were hospitalized after being tear-gassed or beaten up. The Pentagon march was also notable for being the first major protest to consist of a sizable counterculture contingent, which had, tongue in cheek and one eye on the TV cameras, tried to levitate the Pentagon in order to rid it of evil demons. By 1968, conservative critics were right; the line separating the antiwar movement and the counterculture had blurred. Increasingly, young antiwar protesters were in rebellion against both their government's policies in Vietnam and their society's established values. That many of the protesters had been beaten by police (sometimes at the behest of university administrators) while participating in peaceful protests or had been harassed by various authorities because of their long hair or countercultural style of dress fueled their political alienation. The McCarthy and Kennedy campaigns had reconnected some young

Americans to more traditional avenues of political expression, but Kennedy's death, McCarthy's fast-fading chances, and the fact that the war in Vietnam was not any closer to ending left many others bitter and frustrated.

In late August 1968, a few thousand of the most committed and most militant antiwar demonstrators massed in Chicago to protest against the Democratic convention that was poised to nominate prowar candidate Hubert Humphrey. Originally the protest organizers had hoped to have well over 100,000 demonstrators in Chicago. But Mayor Daley, without interference from Johnson or Humphrey, had taken a hard line against the demonstrators, refusing until the very last minute to grant parade or rally permits and making it very clear that his police would come down hard on protesters. Chicago police, FBI, CIA, and military intelligence agents had infiltrated all branches of the protest movement in an attempt to use whatever means they could to discredit and legally prosecute protest leaders. Finally, the mayor let Chicago's black leaders know that they would be held responsible if any black Chicagoans demonstrated in a manner the mayor's people thought ill-advised. The lack of permits, the intimidation, the muscle, the threats, and the infiltration worked to scare away tens of thousands of nonradical, law-abiding antiwar protesters.

Mayor Daley's threats had not scared away Jerry Rubin and Abbie Hoffman. Rubin had been a Berkeley antiwar organizer in the mid-1960s with close ties to both the "old" and New Left. Hoffman had a background in the early civil rights movement and had been an early activist against the war in Vietnam. But by 1968, both men, though in their early thirties, had become convinced that the future of radical change in America lay in blending counterculture freedoms with New Left political ideology. They dreamed of convincing turned-on youth that only through radical politics would the freedoms inherent in sex and drugs and rock 'n' roll be fully realized. They created the "Yippies," the Youth International Party, as the organizational vehicle for their dream. To get their message out to young people they pulled off Digger-inspired guerrilla theater stunts, like burning money and nominating a pig for President, which a fascinated mass media covered in detail. The convention protest in Chicago was to be the first big Yippie event—a "Festival of Life" confronting the "Convention of Death."

Mayor Daley had also failed to scare away Tom Hayden and Rennie Davis, project directors for the National Mobilization to End the War in Vietnam. That New Left militants Hayden and Davis, who openly supported the Communists in Vietnam, were the head organizers for the protest revealed a growing split within the antiwar movement. Hayden and Davis had been selected by Mobe head David Dellinger, a veteran radical pacifist who had gone to jail for three years during World War II rather than register for the draft. Dellinger believed that the antiwar movement had to accept more confrontational tactics and a more openly pro-Vietcong position in order both to stop the war and to discredit the Cold War logic that produced it. Dellinger, as well as Davis and Hayden, were far more politically radical than the overwhelming majority of rank-and-file antiwar protesters.

When the Democrats convened in Chicago in late August 1968, security forces in and around Chicago outnumbered the demonstrators almost two to one. This massive security blanket did not, however, prevent a series of violent confrontations between the protesters and the Chicago police department.

Just a couple of hours before the roll-call vote in which party loyalists would easily defeat antiwar insurgent Eugene McCarthy, the police launched a punishing attack on approximately 7,000 protesters. The protesters had massed in confusion in downtown Chicago after city officials had refused their request to march to the convention hall, which was more than six miles away. In specific response to shouted obscenities, a few rock throwers, and the blocking of Michigan Avenue, dozens of police officers went berserk and physically expressed the rage millions of Americans had built up against America's dissidents.

Mayor Daley, an Irish-Catholic machine pol of the old school, had essentially given his police a green light to attack the protesters, or what he called "the hippies, the Yippies, and the flippies." Like most Americans, the mayor saw little difference among well-dressed, middle-aged antiwar demonstrators, long-haired dope-sters, and those who sought to mix counterculture pleasures with radical politics. In his mind they were all the same: troublemakers. And the mass media, always so willing to make news of the rebels' demands and their attacks on the "traditional" American way of life, the mayor had told reporters publicly, was no better than the boat-rocking dissidents.

When the police attacked on the night of August 28, a few of the most militant or anarchistic protesters fought back, meeting the charging police with bricks and bottles. But overwhelmingly the violence ran in one direction. Police clubbed protesters un-conscious, shoved them through plate-glass windows, sprayed them with Mace, and beat them until the blood flowed. Bystanders often got the same treatment. Reporters and cameramen, in line with Mayor Daley's view of the mass media as co-participants in the protests they reported, were singled out by some officers for particularly brutal treatment.

Senator George McGovern, who had tried and failed to pick up the pieces of Robert Kennedy's tragic bid for the nomination, could see the confrontation from his hotel room. He was enraged: "Do you see what those sons of bitches are doing to those kids down there?" At the convention, Connecticut senator Abraham Ribicoff used his televised nominating speech for McGovern to tell his party and the American people: "With George McGovern we wouldn't have Gestapo tactics on the streets of Chicago." The Democrats were divided for all of America to see.

The American people—about 89 million watched the conven-tion that night—got a powerful view of violence on Chicago's streets. Because of an electricians' strike in Chicago, live coverage outside the convention hall was limited. So the networks had to tape footage and then send it to the convention production center, where it was spliced into the live convention coverage. CBS, as a result, could not show riot-in-the-streets footage as it was ac-tually happening. Instead, it was used hours later, interspersed with live shots of the roll-call vote which gave Hubert Humphrey the Democratic presidential nomination. While Humphrey dele-gates whooped and hollered, police were shown beating protesters bloody; back and forth the producers cut, creating some very dramatic and devastating television—even if it wasn't quite literally happening the way it seemed. For Hubert Humphrey and the Democratic Party the convention was an unmitigated disaster.

The convention protest also further split the antiwar movement. A minority of antiwar advocates—including many who had been beaten in Chicago—saw the government-supported police violence as a sure sign that America was becoming a fascist state, and the experience in Chicago strengthened their belief that only through violent confrontation and even revolution could the country be directed to a more just and democratic path. Yippie stalwart Stew Albert spoke for the extremists when he called Chicago "a revolutionary wet dream come true." The most militant leaders of SDS left Chicago convinced that armed revolt was both necessary and possible. The radicals' extremism was fueled further a few months later when the U.S. Attorney General put a group of Chicago protesters—the "Chicago 8"—through an elaborate show trial charging them with conspiracy to incite riot.

Todd Gitlin, increasingly estranged from the radical movement he had helped to found, called the extremists' new vision "fetishism of the streets." But like many committed radicals, he ended 1968 unsure where the antiwar movement should go and thus unable to speak out strongly against those howling for armed revolt. Arthur Waskow, an older antiwar organizer, spoke for many committed but more moderate activists when he argued: "Our armies of the night need new recruits—to get them we must invent a political course of action, not street tactics." Over the next year, moderate antiwar activists worked at separating themselves from the violence-prone radicals and created a plan to mobilize the American people against the war in Vietnam.

The only clear winner of the Democratic convention was the Republican nominee for the presidency, Richard Milhous Nixon. He was the main political beneficiary of the revulsion most Americans' felt for the violence in Chicago—which they overwhelmingly, if inaccurately, blamed on the protesters. Through sheer grit, political genius, and a flair for the cynical, Nixon had come back from political near-death. After losing to Kennedy in 1960 he had lost a bid for the California governorship in 1962, telling reporters afterward that they wouldn't have him "to kick around" any longer. In 1968 he was the odds-on favorite to win the presidency.

Since 1960 Nixon had been stewing over his incompetent use of the media. He was ready now. In carefully scripted TV appearances he assured voters that he had a secret plan "to end the war and win the peace" but said that it would be unpatriotic to reveal it while President Johnson was negotiating with the North Vietnamese. Later, Nixon admitted that he had "no way to win the war. But we can't say that of course. In fact, we have to seem to say the opposite." By rigidly controlling press and public access, Nixon allowed reporters and his political opponents little opportunity to query him on the subject. With the war issue finessed— while it weighed on Humphrey like a lead shroud—Nixon was free to concentrate on exploiting white America's resentment against all the "clamorous voices" demanding change. Nixon, ex-Wall Street lawyer, portrayed himself as spokesman for the great Silent Majority.

Nixon told one reporter that, unlike President Johnson, who "just doesn't listen to anybody," "I like to listen" (the meaning of which would become perfectly clear later in his presidency). Nixon vowed to the American people that he would hear their "quiet voices." He would dedicate his presidency not to the protesters or the naysayers but to the "great, quite forgotten majority—the nonshouters and the nondemonstrators, the millions who ask principally to go their own way in decency and dignity and to have their own rights accorded the same respect they accord the rights of others."

Hubert Humphrey and his union supporters struggled to win back the white working-class voters who were drifting toward George Wallace and Richard Nixon. Organized labor sent out some 20 million pieces of literature pointing out that Wallace's Alabama was one of the most antiunion states in the country. Humphrey emphasized that Nixon offered the workingman nothing but failed Republican economic policies (raising the ghostly image of Herbert Hoover). Finally, Humphrey appealed to the conscience of white voters, declaring that, unlike the racist Wallace or Nixon, whom he called Wallace's "perfumed, deodorized" imitator, he believed in "the principle of human equality and human opportunity . . . for every American, regardless of race, color, or creed."

According to voter surveys, Humphrey trailed Nixon by 15 percent just a few weeks before the election and was barely leading Wallace. But by early November most Northern white working people who had considered supporting Wallace had decided that his brand of hate was too hard to swallow. Humphrey had also convinced liberals—who really had nowhere else to go with their support—that his Vietnam policy was different enough from Johnson's to deserve their vote. Finally, Humphrey ran an energetic, emotional campaign in which he pledged to maintain social order but also racial progress and economic growth. By election eve Humphrey had fought his way back into contention.

Nixon still won. As Allen Matusow concludes, in 1964 Lyndon Johnson had run as an unabashed liberal and pulled in 43.1 million votes; in 1968 liberal Hubert Humphrey received just 31.2 million votes. Three of ten white Johnson supporters had rejected Humphrey. He received less than 35 percent of the white vote overall. But at the same time, Nixon won by just half a million votes, and in winning captured fewer votes than he had in losing to John F. Kennedy. He was the first President since Zachary Taylor in 1848 to win the presidency and face a House and Senate still controlled by the opposition party.

George Wallace ended up with just 13.5 percent of the vote, though he did win the states of Louisiana, Mississippi, Alabama, Georgia, and Arkansas. In the North, Wallace carried 8 percent of the vote. Wallace's Northern sympathizers, though appreciative of his populist rhetoric, were not in the end racist enough to vote for such a strong symbol of segregation. Wallace would try to win the Democratic presidential nomination in 1972—toning down his racist rhetoric and emphasizing his antiestablishment, anticosmopolitan populism—but he was badly wounded by a would-be assassin and his campaign ground to a halt.

All through the 1960s the number of whites in the North and

South willing to express racist thoughts to pollsters and takers of surveys had greatly declined, while whites' stated support for racial equality continued to grow. Still, by the late 1960s, many whites blamed all African-Americans for the riots and criminal violence that plagued America's cities. And by the end of the 1960s, a rising proportion of whites asserted that black Americans wanted too much too fast and that the federal government, too often, gave in to their radical demands. Many whites were particularly upset by civil rights organizations and the federal government's use of "group remedies" to fight racial discrimination.

In 1969, the group-remedy that most rankled whites was mandatory busing of students across school district lines to achieve racially balanced schools. Richard Nixon played to one of the building blocks of his nascent Republican majority, white ethnic urban voters, by arguing strongly against such busing. He also worked at pushing civil rights enforcement as far from the White House as he could and into the hands of the judiciary.

At the same time, in order to appease moderate suburban voters, the Nixon White House successfully pursued desegregation of Southern schools—so much so that by the end of 1972, Southern schools were less racially segregated than their Northern counterparts. While journalists at the time portrayed Nixon's racial policies as determined by his "Southern strategy"—a coordinated effort to turn the South permanently Republican—Nixon only rarely pandered to the hard-core racist element of the South (as he arguably did with his Supreme Court nomination of the incompetent, racist-tinged Southern jurist Harrold Carswell, whom the Senate rejected). Nixon actually targeted white Southern moderates, especially those living in the Southern border states, by portraying himself as the standard bearer of the reasonable center, standing firm between Wallace extremism and Black Power militants.

Nixon's inconsistent views toward racial justice are perhaps best understood in the light of his administration's unexpected embrace of affirmative action—a powerful example of what historian Hugh Graham calls Nixon's lack of a "philosophical gyroscope" when it came to most domestic policy issues.

Civil rights leaders had been urging some kind of economic affirmative action since the early 1960s. At the 1963 March on Washington for Freedom and Jobs, as national columnist James Reston quietly reported, several speakers had insisted that in order to combat centuries of racial discrimination they would need not only "equal opportunity in the field of civil liberties, but . . . preferential treatment on jobs." In 1965, Lyndon Johnson seemed to philosophically endorse this position when he spoke at Howard University:

> Freedom is not enough. . . . You do not take a person who for years has been hobbled by chains and liberate him, bring him up to the starting line of a race and then say, "You are free to compete with all the others."
>   . . . We seek not just freedom but opportunity—not just equality as a right and a theory but equality as a fact and as a result.

Johnson was not really thinking about preferential hiring or admissions when he spoke; he was promoting his War on Poverty plans. But his statement that "equality as a right and a theory" was not enough, that only "equality as a fact and as a result" would prove that racially nondiscriminatory opportunity existed, challenged the prevailing American wisdom.

By 1965, officials in the EEOC and other civil rights agencies were struggling to apply the idea of racial "equality as a result" to the labor market—but with very limited success. It is ironic that Nixon's economically conservative Secretary of Labor, George Shultz (later Secretary of State under Reagan), would orchestrate the implementation of a national policy of preferential hiring of minority workers based on "visible measurable goals to correct obvious imbalances" in the labor force.

Richard Nixon greeted his cabinet officer's plan with admiration. As Nixon's senior adviser and hatchet man, John Ehrlichman, wrote:

> Nixon thought that Secretary of Labor George Shultz had shown great style in constructing a political dilemma for the labor union

leaders and civil rights groups. The NAACP wanted a tougher requirement and the unions hated the whole thing. . . . Before long the AFL-CIO and the NAACP were locked in combat and the Nixon administration was located in the sweet and reasonable middle.

By 1970, affirmative action plans, in which minorities—at first mainly African-Americans, but later women and other targeted groups—were given preferential treatment in hiring and promotion, began to disturb white workers and raise their ire. By the mid-1970s, the issue of affirmative action would become the most polarizing racial issue in America. But despite the centrality of racial themes in the 1968 presidential campaign, race was not the focal point for either Nixon or the American people as the 1960s came to a close.

Between 1968 and 1971, the war in Vietnam continued to tear apart the country. Nixon had no plan to win the war but he did want to end it. He called his war policy "peace with honor." He believed that he could increase pressure on the Communists to negotiate a satisfactory peace settlement by massively escalating the American air war. At the same time, he could reduce American domestic tensions through Vietnamization: a plan to turn the war over to the South Vietnamese and bring American troops home. The reality was four more bloody years of war, 20,000 more American deaths, and a peace that, in historian George Herring's words, was "neither honorable nor lasting."

Nixon hoped that the North Vietnamese would fear him as they never feared the liberal Democrats. He told a key adviser (speaking of himself in the third person, as was his tendency): "They'll believe any threat of force Nixon makes because it's Nixon. We'll just slip the word to them that, 'for God's sake, you know Nixon's obsessed about Communism . . . and he has his hand on the nuclear button." This was the Nixon-as-madman strategy.

As Nixon plotted, a loose coalition of antiwar activists, many of whom had been active in the McCarthy, Kennedy, and

McGovern campaigns, formed the Vietnam Moratorium Committee. On October 15, 1969, their work culminated in a national teach-in against the war. Americans countrywide took time off from their regular routine to participate in public discussions on Vietnam. As many as 10 million Americans were involved in the largest public protest ever held in America.

Nixon was enraged by the expanding peace movement. He believed, with reason, that the peace movement strengthened North Vietnam's resolve to reject any peace settlement that did not offer them complete victory. He vowed to ignore the peace movement and accused protesters of being little more than traitors. Shortly after the October 1969 Moratorium, the President spoke on national television: "To you, the great silent majority of my fellow Americans—I ask for your support. . . . North Vietnam cannot defeat . . . the United States. Only Americans can do that."

The Vietnamese had been fighting for decades—first against the French and then against the Americans—and Nixon had no way of defeating them. Still, he chose to further polarize the nation by blaming the stalemate not on the nature of the war but on the antiwar movement. To prowar Americans he held out the hope that he could brutalize the North Vietnamese into a settlement that had the appearance, if not the reality, of an American victory.

The North Vietnamese in 1969, in large part due to their Tet defeat, pulled back into a defensive posture. They were prepared to wait the Americans out, "no matter what additional suffering," Vietnam war historian George Herring argues, "it might entail."

In the years after Tet, more and more of the men charged with fighting the war lost heart and an angry GI antiwar movement grew. According to historian Terry Anderson, in 1967 only three GI antiwar underground papers existed; by March 1972 about 245 had been published. Tens of thousands of other fighting men suffered a devastating loss of faith in the war. By 1970, half or more of the soldiers in Vietnam were using drugs. Reenlistments plummeted; desertion and AWOL rates soared. The number of "combat refusal" incidents skyrocketed and by 1972 the Army reported over 800 cases of suspected or actual "fragging"—soldiers shooting or blowing up unpopular, "gung ho" officers—and feared that another 1,400 officers or noncommissioned officers might have been killed by their own troops. As Congressman Pete McCloskey noted in 1971: "We're asking a few individuals to make a tremendous sacrifice for the dubious goal of peace with honor. No one wants to be killed on the last day of a war."

At home, thousands of military men joined antiwar organizations. Several thousand war veterans participated in protests organized by the Vietnam Veterans Against the War. In late April 1971, veterans marched—some in wheelchairs, others on crutches—in Washington, D.C. They chanted, "Bring 'em home. Bring our brothers home." On April 23, thousands of Vietnam veterans gathered at the U.S. Capitol, took the medals they had won for bravery and service to their country in war, and threw them away. The nation watched and was stunned. But most Americans would not listen to these men; their voices were too painful and their conclusions too devastating.

The vast majority of veterans did not protest against the war. Most came home and got on with their lives. That same majority hated the antiwar protests. Most veterans did not so much disagree with arguments made against the war; they simply could not stand to hear them coming from those who had not suffered as they had. As one vet said: "The only test we had was: were you there?" In a war without victory, the men who fought were too often blamed by all sides. The prowar side offered them little to nothing in the way of glory or thanks and many on the antiwar side scorned the soldiers for a war they had only fought out of a sense of patriotic duty and obligation.

The soldiers' commander-in-chief, Richard Nixon, year after bloody year, kept searching for a way out of the morass that would bring his talismanic "peace with honor." He forced the South Vietnamese government to build up their fighting capacity and turned over to them billions of dollars in weapons, ships, helicopters, tanks, planes, and vehicles. As Vietnamization proceeded, Nixon pulled U.S. troops out. But in order to protect the Vietnamization process, to be assured of a friendly government on

Vietnam's border, and to demonstrate his resolve, as he put it, to be "tough," in April 1970 Nixon ordered American troops to invade North Vietnamese bases in Cambodia.

The military results in Cambodia were mixed but the domestic reaction was tragic. Protests exploded around the country. The President had said he would end the war. Instead he had expanded it.

Nixon responded characteristically: "Don't worry about the divisiveness," he told his aides. "Having drawn the sword . . . stick it in hard." As Nixon biographer Stephen Ambrose explains: "Nixon, sadly, was a man who all too often gave in to an impulse to hate."

At a demonstration at Kent State University in May, Ohio National Guardsmen panicked and shot into an angry crowd, killing four students. A few days later, state police and National Guardsmen in Mississippi fired on students at Jackson State College and killed two of them.

Vice President Agnew (forced to resign his office in October 1973 for income-tax evasion and having accepted bribes while he was governor of Maryland), whom Nixon used as a kind of attack dog, blamed the students for their own murders. In a logic a majority of Americans found compelling, he argued that if the students hadn't been protesting they wouldn't have been shot.

At least 1.5 million students went on strike, closing down campuses nationwide. While most of the post-Cambodia invasion protests were nonviolent, some, of course, were not. At Stanford, for example, demonstrators trashed the campus, and at the University of Kansas the student union was burned down. Over the next months more than two dozen ROTC buildings were set ablaze or bombed.

Nixon responded to the turmoil by ordering the CIA, the FBI, and his own clandestine operatives within the executive branch to further target the antiwar movement for infiltration, persecution, and sabotage. Increasingly Nixon felt himself under siege by protesters, by a Democratic Congress, by an increasingly hostile press, and even by his own government bureaucracy.

Nixon had built his political career by lashing out against those he perceived as enemies. The virulently hostile political realities of the early 1970s pushed him well over the blurry line dividing legal if abusive use of presidential power and gross illegal use of presidential power. Most blatantly, the President crossed that line after *The New York Times* began publishing excerpts from the top-secret Pentagon Papers—the study of the war in Vietnam that had been commissioned by Secretary of Defense McNamara in 1967. The documents had been leaked to the *Times* by a disillusioned Pentagon analyst, Daniel Ellsberg. Nixon was enraged; he believed that the excerpts—which detailed the pattern of deception that characterized past presidential administrations' portrayals of the war to the American people—together with the continuing leaks, would severely damage his ability to wage the war. On July 17, 1971, the White House created a secret team of "black bag" operatives, called the Plumbers, composed of ex-CIA, ex-FBI, and eventually CIA-trained anti-Castro Cuban émigrés—to stop government leaks and to discredit Nixon enemies. One of the Plumbers' first acts was to break into the office of Ellsberg's psychiatrist in hopes of finding material that might discredit Ellsberg. Exactly eleven months after they were founded, a group of Plumbers, by then working directly for the Committee to Reelect the President (CREEP), was caught breaking into and "bugging" the offices of the Democratic National Committee at its Watergate office complex. From the moment Nixon learned of his operatives' capture, he would seek to obstruct justice by illegally using the CIA and the FBI to "cover up" the White House's connection to the Plumbers and the Pandora's box of illegal activities to which the Plumbers and CREEP were connected. For this cover-up, he would be tried for impeachment by the Senate. On August 9, 1974, a low-water mark in the decade of disillusionment—the 1970s—Nixon became the first President to resign from office.

Even as Nixon perpetrated his sordid corruption of the presidency, he was both ending the war in Vietnam and fundamentally transforming the structure of the Cold War. Through secret negotiations carried on by Henry Kissinger, his National Security Adviser, Nixon began to normalize relations with China, which the United States had refused to recognize since the Communist revolution of 1949. Nixon bettered relations with China, primarily to put pressure on the Soviet Union. By "triangulating" foreign policy among China, the Soviet Union, and the United States, Nixon believed he could play the co-belligerent Communist giants off against one another to American advantage in Vietnam and other hot spots around the world, especially in Asia. It was a pragmatic strategy which, ironically, Nixon and other rabid anti-Communists had successfully prevented past American leaders from pursuing.

In February 1972, Nixon became the first President to visit China. In a public speech, he told the Chinese leadership that they should "start a long march together . . . on different roads to the same goal. . . . There is no reason for us to be enemies." A few weeks later, Nixon was in Moscow, "China card" in hand, ready to negotiate. The two superpowers successfully negotiated a complex nuclear arms reduction treaty and also a large trade agreement focusing on Soviet purchases of U.S. wheat. Nixon, whose rise to political prominence was based on his unyielding anti-Communism, had successfully changed the tenor of the Cold War by visiting China and reaching "détente" with the Soviet Union. Just as the 1960s began with Nixon and Kennedy dueling over who would be tougher on Communism, so the 1960s ended with Nixon and his Democratic rival for the 1972 presidency, "peace candidate" Senator George McGovern, arguing about how best to establish peaceful coexistence with the Communist superpowers.

By 1972, the American people had turned overwhelmingly against the war in Vietnam. According to polls, a majority of Americans had even concluded that America's role in the war was "immoral." At the same time, the steady withdrawal of American troops from Vietnam—from 536,000 at the end of 1968 to 156,800 by the end of 1971—had most Americans convinced that Nixon was getting the country out of the war. In essence, they were right.

In March 1972, with American troop strength down to 95,000 (of whom only 6,000 were combat troops), the North Vietnamese again launched a military invasion of South Vietnam. Nixon, still

unwilling to let South Vietnam fall, responded with massive retaliation: Haiphong Harbor was mined, the Navy blockaded
North Vietnam, and North Vietnam was to undergo sustained,
massive bombing. "The bastards have never been bombed like
they're going to be bombed this time," Nixon told aides. Because
of his diplomatic efforts, Nixon was confident that neither China
nor the Soviet Union would come to their ally's aid. Roughly
125,000 Vietnamese died in the fighting and bombing and North
Vietnam's offensive was stopped. A little bit more time was bought
as the Americans and the Vietnamese negotiated in Paris over peace
terms.

Just a few days before the 1972 election, Henry Kissinger announced to the world that "peace is at hand" in Vietnam. But the
South Vietnamese government, painfully aware that the North
Vietnamese and the United States were fast coming to an agreement that would result in total U.S. withdrawal and the almost
certain end of an independent South Vietnam, threw up roadblocks
to the agreement. The north refused to accept the south's terms
and the war dragged on.

As a final measure to force North Vietnam to accept at least
some U.S. face-saving measures and probably also to so devastate
the north that the South Vietnamese would have, again, time to
build up its defenses, Nixon ended 1972 with the so-called Christmas bombing. Planes dropped 36,000 tons of bombs on the north,
more than had smashed into North Vietnam between 1969 and
1971. Hanoi and Haiphong each became "a mass of rubble"; at
least 2,200 civilians died.

On January 27, 1973, the Americans signed a peace treaty with
the Communists. The American negotiators had made key conces-
sions: North Vietnamese troops would stay in position in the south
and the Vietcong's Provisional Revolutionary Government had
been formally recognized. The treaty allowed the American-
backed government in South Vietnam to stay in place. The North
Vietnamese agreed to return all American prisoners of war. In
exchange, the American military would be withdrawn from Vietnam. This was "peace with honor."

Nixon's pursuit of "peace with honor" had cost the United

States another 20,553 American lives. It had cost the Vietnamese another 600,000 battlefield deaths and the destruction of vast areas of their country.

America left South Vietnam with a world-class supply of military hardware, including the fourth-largest air force in the world. But it was not enough, as everyone knew. After the North Vietnamese rebuilt after the destruction of Nixon's last air strikes against them, and with the Congress having nearly cut off military aid to the South Vietnamese, the Communists launched a final offensive. On April 30, 1975, the United States helicoptered the last Americans out of South Vietnam as Saigon fell and the Vietnamese reunified their country. After thirty years of brutal war in which the humanity of all sides had suffered, the Communist victors unleashed a bloody hell on their country.

America's withdrawal from Vietnam in early 1973 marked another end of "the sixties." But if the close of the war and the antiwar movement signaled an obvious passage in American history, other, more subtle but, in some ways, more powerful changes were also signaling the end of "the sixties."

The 1960s had been born of economic affluence. Great national wealth and global economic interests had made waging a war in the distant lands of a nation peripheral to American national security seem reasonable to both policymakers and the public. Then, too, President Johnson predicated his War on Poverty and his government-financed Great Society on an ever expanding revenue that he believed was his to direct. Young people's consumer revolt—which created a booming illegal drug market, an expansive youth culture, and even the multifaceted counterattack on materialism—was underwritten by economic boom times. Good times had helped to give college students, in particular, a faith that they had the luxury of exploring and questioning because the good jobs would be there waiting for them when they were needed. Even the civil rights movement was helped by the expanding national economy, which allowed racial problems to replace liberal Democrats' long-term focus on labor-capital issues. And, ironically, the economic good times had permitted working-class voters who had supported the Democratic Party for decades to feel secure enough economically to begin supporting Republican candidates for cultural and social reasons. The list could go on.

By the end of the 1960s and into the early 1970s, the good times, while not ending, were under increasing threat. America's economic house was in disarray. Though few Americans noticed, the signs were everywhere.

Lyndon Johnson's guns-and-butter policy was one cause of economic weakness. In order to pay for Vietnam and his Great Society domestic programs without raising taxes, the Johnson administration had begun running federal budget deficits and pumping a great deal of money into the economy. The result was economic overheating and inflation. In the early 1960s, inflation had stayed generally under 2 percent. By 1971 it had crept up to 4 percent. President Nixon knew what he had to do to squeeze out inflation, but because of his need to continue the war in Vietnam and his fear of putting the economy into a recession before the 1972 election, he lacked the political will. Instead of choosing the hard medicine of reducing government spending or raising taxes or pushing hard for higher interest rates, Nixon ran a then record budget deficit; at the end of 1973 the inflation rate had taken off at an annual level of 10 percent.

Johnson's guns-and-butter policy and the inflation it caused occurred at the same time as a complex array of factors related to the international gold market, America's deteriorating balance of payments (again due in part to the overseas costs of waging the war in Vietnam), and the international stability of the dollar. As a result of these relatively undiscussed and complex international economic pressures on the U.S. economy, America's policymakers had to face an unpleasant reality: the era of economic limitlessness was over and the nation had to start thinking about global economic realities. Such an approach would affect domestic and foreign policy. By 1970, America was no longer the world's singular economic juggernaut. Between 1955 and 1970 America's share of the major industrial countries' global exports had declined from 32 percent to 18 percent. Japan and Western Europe, especially West Germany, were back on economic track.

The American car market was indicative of the changes. In 1960, foreign car manufacturers had 4 percent of the American new car market; by 1970 they had 17 percent. A large part of the problem was that American autos were, by and large, no longer as good a value for the money as foreign-made cars. American car companies' relative lack of concern for manufacturing quality was partially to blame. Between 1966 and 1973, manufacturers had to recall 30 million American cars and trucks because of serious defects. In addition, both labor and management had become complacent about their jobs and together had become far less productive manufacturers. Assembly-line workers were earning far more than the median national wage for manufacturing work. Their unions had succeeded in winning them an awesome array of fringe benefits and accommodating work rules. As a partial result, American cars cost a great deal more than their foreign competitors. In 1972, when GM had attempted to get the workers in their new state-of-the-art assembly plant at Lordstown, Ohio, to work faster and better, the workers had staged a wildcat strike. The strike, dubbed an "industrial Woodstock" by the press, stood as a stark symbol of managerial ineptitude and America's high-wage union employees' fierce resistance to becoming more productive. In too many of the main economic sectors in which American affluence had been produced, both managers and workers had lost their world leadership.

To some extent, this decline was inevitable. One sector of the American economy, the postwar big-unit manufacturing sector, had matured. U.S.-dominated industries like steel, autos, and electronics were bound to be emulated and overtaken by other countries which benefited, at least at first, from low labor costs, new industrial plants, and their ability to get a free ride piggybacking on American research and development. And in the 1970s the seeds of a new economy—built in part on information technologies, especially the computer business, and a new complex service sector—were sprouting. But by the early 1970s, the strains of economic transformation had begun. The oil crises of the mid-1970s, recession, and a stagnating wage rate would make that transformation extremely painful and dramatically change the temper of the American people.

11. A NEW WORLD

~~~~~~

IN MAY 1961, President Kennedy had vowed that "before the decade is out" the United States would land a man on the moon. "That goal," he told Americans, "will serve to organize and measure the best of our energies and skills." We will go to the moon, Kennedy concluded, " 'because it is there.' " On July 20, 1969, Americans once again united in front of their televisions. They watched Neil Armstrong step out of the Apollo 11 lunar landing module and onto the surface of the moon. One grand promise had been kept.

If Vietnam revealed one aspect of America's pursuit of global power, the space program represented another. While it, too, was propelled by Cold War competition with the Soviet Union, it also was, as historian Walter McDougall argues, "a model for a society without limits, an ebullient and liberal technocracy." As Americans watched the near-miracle of a moon landing live on their televisions, they could again imagine embracing a boundless future.

But by 1970 the sense of boundlessness and the ebullient spirit that underwrote it, was under attack. Congress signaled the change when soon after the successful Apollo moon mission it cut NASA's projected budget (NASA had received some $33 billion in congressional appropriations in the eight years between Kennedy's promise and Neil Armstrong's moon walk). Even the images of the conquest of outer space were ambivalent; some Americans looked at the dramatic pictures of the earth brought back from the moon voyage and saw not the United States, Colossus of the Free World, but Spaceship Earth, floating alone and vulnerable in the vast black emptiness of the universe.

A few Americans began the 1970s by arguing forthrightly for a new age of limits. On April 22, 1970, the first Earth Day was held at the Washington Monument. More than 10,000 Americans nodded in agreement as speaker after speaker argued that unbridled economic growth and an ethic of material abundance were destroying the planet. In 1962, Rachel Carson had introduced the idea of ecology and ecological degradation to a widening circle of Americans in her best-selling *Silent Spring*. By the end of the decade, liberal Democrats had enacted a series of laws to fight polluters' uncaring and often unthinking degradation of the air, land, and water. In 1969, an oil spill off the coast of Santa Barbara (which befouled beaches and killed huge numbers of seabirds and aquatic creatures) turned the nation's attention, if only briefly, to the costs of their energy-intensive consumer lifestyles. The Nixon administration, ever unpredictable, responded to growing public concern over environmental issues by creating the Environmental Protection Agency (1970) over the objections of much of the business community and many congressmen.

In the early 1970s, ecological activists wrote best-selling books, made headlines with dramatic congressional testimony, and forged powerful lobbying groups. Sometimes they sounded like prophets of old, foretelling doom, but while their jeremiads might stretch credulity, their larger ecological vision was cogent. Millions of Americans began moving toward a more thoughtful and caring concern about the environment.

While the two largest mass movements of the 1960s—the antiwar protests and the African-American struggle for social justice —had by and large come to a close by the end of 1972, other mass movements, including concerns for the environment, grew stronger in the early 1970s.

The women's liberation movement was perhaps the most radical "sixties" political and social movement, and only in the early 1970s did it develop national attention and broad support. The women's movement challenged basic premises of mid-twentieth-century conventional wisdom: that men should control political and economic life and that women should participate in these public spheres, if at all, as men's subordinates; that men had the right to head their households and that women should serve them as helpmates responsible for housekeeping and day-to-day child rearing; and finally, that women were best measured by their beauty, charm, and sexual restraint and men by their accomplishments, power, and sexual prowess. The incarnation of the women's movement, beginning in the 1960s but increasing dramatically in the 1970s, revealed that a complex system of legal, social, and cultural forces worked to restrict women's opportunities and to rigidly cast gender roles.

Feminists argued fiercely among themselves about the nature of masculinity and femininity and about whether there was such a thing as a feminine way of knowing, seeing, and acting. Some proponents of the women's movement had come to believe that gender identity was not an absolute biological fact of life or all-encompassing essential identity, but was instead largely a cultural construction that could be changed. All women's liberationists, regardless of where they stood on the question of the biological or cultural construction of womanhood, agreed that society was organized, at a fundamental level, to restrict the power of women to control their own lives and to act meaningfully in the world.

The women's movement, like the civil rights movement, had roots deep in American history. Unlike the civil rights movement, however, neither World War II nor the Cold War revitalized the almost invisible remnants of a mass movement that had last flowered in the 1910s and which in 1920 had won a constitutional amendment guaranteeing women the right to the vote. In the immediate post-World War II years, women's societal roles, sense of autonomy, and economic opportunities were all reduced or diminished. Most obviously, in the postwar years labor unions, employers, and the federal government all pressured women to put their well-paid war work behind them and clear the way for returning veterans. About 3.25 million women were let go or quit their wartime jobs between September 1945 and November 1946.

Of course, other women, mostly the young and unmarried, entered the work force, but once the war was over they were hired for poorly paid "women's jobs." In the words of historian Cynthia Harrison, "Rosie the Riveter became a file clerk." Women were told by countless voices in the mass media and from almost every pulpit and lectern to embrace their "natural" roles as family nurturers and housewives.

Most men and women, after the turmoil of the war and the Great Depression, and in the midst of the Cold War nuclear weapons race, readily accepted socially prescribed gender roles. They found such roles, in which the rules were clear, stabilizing, comforting, and satisfying. Many "fifties" couples found that gender-specific behavior was a harmonious means of accommodating all the other differences (regional, ethnic, rural/urban, class background, or religious) which were being deliberately and rapidly collapsed in the postwar rush to create a white middle-class suburban ethos. Finally, the combat service of millions of men during World War II and the Korean War stood as a powerful reminder of the real difference between the experiences of men and women.

While women's lives—especially those of black women and Latinas—in postwar America rarely matched the gender roles to which they were or felt they were assigned, few people spoke out publicly against the foreclosing of women's options or against men's open discrimination against women who worked outside the home. Instead, men and women seemed to embrace their narrow, socially prescribed gender roles. They married in record numbers, and the mass media celebrated "togetherness," as millions of Americans did their best to raise their large families according to a narrow code of conventional gendered behavior.

By 1960 the word "feminist" was almost never used publicly as anything but an epithet and only a tiny group of activists kept alive issues of equality and social justice for women. Between 1945 and 1960, the political establishment did nothing to protect women against rampant job discrimination or legal inequities. The bipartisan view from Washington was summed up by Adlai Stevenson, the liberal Democrat who twice ran against Dwight Eisenhower for the presidency. Speaking at Smith College, one of the nation's

most prestigious women's schools, Stevenson told the graduating
senior women:

> Women, especially educated women, have a unique opportunity to
> influence us, man and boy. This assignment for you, as wives and
> mothers, you can do in the living room with a baby in your lap or
> in the kitchen with a can opener in your hand. . . . I think there is
> much you can do about our crisis in that humble role of housewife.
> I could wish you no better vocation than that.

Stevenson's patronizing of the "humble" housewife reflected social
reality: little opportunity for influence outside the home, little
career advancement or economic mobility existed for women. In
1960, just as want ads in Southern newspapers were racially segregated, so want ads throughout the nation were segregated by
sex. Almost every single decent-paying job—be it accountant,
attorney, boilerman, electrician, or even wholesale bra and girdle
sales representative—was exclusively for men. Newspapers did
not even list jobs for which either men or women could apply.
Between 1920 and 1960, the status of women relative to men had,
by many educational and professional measures, actually declined,
as the percentage of women attaining advanced degrees or becoming professors, lawyers, or doctors fell in relation to men.
     Most men and women took their gender-stereotyped roles in
life for granted. Women's struggle for equality, which had been
heated in the 1840s and the 1910s, had essentially disappeared from
history books. Overwhelmingly, housewives told pollsters that
they were happy with their role in life. Despite most women's
expressed contentment with the American gender system and the
lack of public protest against it, a variety of factors were laying
the ground for both reform and a radical attack on what nobody
in 1960 yet called sexism.
     Despite the decline of women working outside their homes
immediately after World War II, the long-term trend of increasing
labor market participation by woman continued. Between 1940
and 1960 the proportion of married women who had jobs doubled,
from 15 percent to 30 percent. By 1960 about 38 percent of women

were wage earners. Even about 25 percent of suburban housewives
held full- or part-time jobs. Throughout the 1960s (and after) more
and more women, especially married women with small children,
worked outside the home.

Women worked for different reasons. Most worked because
their income was vital to supporting either themselves or their
families. Many married women worked to boost their family income in order to buy the new consumer "necessities" like washer-
dryers, a second car, a home entertainment system. From 1945 to
1960 the percentage of Americans who approved of a married
woman working, even if "she has a husband capable of supporting
her," rose from around 15 percent to over 40 percent. By 1975
the approval rate stood at 71 percent. Increasingly, men and
women saw the need for a two-income household.

In 1960, a woman who worked full-time, year-round, earned
on average 60.6 percent of what men, on average, did. While
paying women less than men for the exact same job had become
atypical by 1960, and while most men and women worked in
gender-specific jobs, it was not uncommon for men and women
working in the same company to do comparable work but, for
example, for the woman to be titled "clerk" and to have no possibility of promotion while the man was a promotable "assistant
office administrator" with a significantly higher salary. The blatant
inequalities of the labor market nettled working women.
Throughout the 1960s, as labor trends continued, more women
spent more time wrestling with a system which unapologetically
excluded them from almost all well-paying jobs and which treated
them as second-class humans.

Working women did not face the labor market completely alone.
They had a few champions scattered throughout the national political system, most important the Women's Bureau, which had
been permanently established in the federal Department of Labor
in 1920. The Women's Bureau, even into the 1960s, focused on
ensuring that special protective labor legislation for women—
mainly regulating hours and working conditions in industry—was
being enforced. Another group of reformers, many linked to
the National Women's Party, the onetime suffrage organization,

single-mindedly worked Capitol Hill in pursuit of the Equal Rights Amendment (ERA) for women. This proposed constitutional amendment was first introduced in Congress in the 1920s; in 1946 a majority in the Senate voted to approve the measure, though not by the required two-thirds. Between 1946 and 1960, the ERA made little progress.

ERA supporters in the early 1960s tended to be middle-class and professional women, members of such groups as the American Federation of Business and Professional Women, whose careers and lives had been rigidly circumscribed by discrimination against women. Most women players in national politics, especially those involved with the Women's Bureau, opposed the ERA. They argued that absolute equality between the sexes would be detrimental to most working women, who benefited from protective labor laws which had been passed early in the twentieth century. Class issues came before gender solidarity for the majority of women operating at the margins of Washington power in the early 1960s.

The election of John Kennedy did not offer much opportunity for change. Kennedy was indifferent to women's issues, and the Democrats, following the lead of the labor unions, had been less interested in the ERA than had the Republicans. But as partial payoff to women activists within the Democratic Party, Kennedy did approve a President's Commission on the Status of Women. Headed by a savvy political insider, Esther Peterson, who as head of the Women's Bureau and an Assistant Secretary of Labor was the highest-ranking woman in the Kennedy administration, the commission successfully launched an Equal Pay Act, which outlawed in most cases paying men more than women for the same job. Since segregation by sex, not unequal wages for identical jobs, was at the root of women's pay problems, the 1963 bill had little direct effect. But as historian Hugh Graham argues, the measure did help labor union and Democratic Party women to move from "the protectionist tradition to the equal rights tradition." Slowly, a political coalition, within liberal circles, was forming around issues of sexual discrimination.

How slowly that coalition was growing became apparent in

1964, when, as detailed in Chapter 5, archsegregationist and conservative congressman Howard Smith added the word "sex" to the 1964 Civil Rights Act. Esther Peterson, for example, led the Women's Bureau in the fight against including women in the equal employment aspects of the act. On the House floor, Democratic liberal Edith Green similarly fought Smith's amendment, on the ground that it would cost women the special employment protection they received under federal law. But conservative Republican representatives, as well as younger Democratic women, joined in supporting the bill, arguing that modern working conditions no longer made "special privileges" for women worth the price they were paying, ubiquitous legal employment discrimination. With most men bemused by the issue, their focus on the racial implications of the legislation made it possible for the one-word amendment to pass. Women, suddenly, had the legal right to equal employment opportunities. However, the real meaning of the amendment was unclear.

Congress had held hundreds of hours of committee hearings on the racial aspects of the 1964 Civil Rights Act. They had held no hearings and had issued no reports on gender discrimination. No organized feminist movement existed to make sure that the government implemented the law. No voices in the mass media were raised in support. Instead, the gender discrimination aspects of the bill were widely ridiculed.

Equal Employment Opportunity Commission (EEOC) chair Franklin Roosevelt, Jr., laughingly dismissed a reporter who asked him, "What about sex?" Roosevelt snickered, "Don't get me started. I'm all for it." *The New York Times* ran a satirical editorial on the EEOC and the "Bunny problem," asking what would happen when a man applied to be a Playboy bunny or when a woman applied to work on a tugboat: "Bunny problem, indeed! This is revolution, chaos. You can't even safely advertise for a wife anymore."

Behind the scenes, the EEOC was shocked to discover that about one-third of the complaints they received were gender-based. They chose, in general, to ignore them in order to focus their limited resources on racial issues. In 1965, EEOC staffer

Frances Cousens concluded: "To include sex as a provision . . . undermine[s] efforts on behalf of minority groups. . . . Complaints about sex discrimination . . . diverted attention and resources from the more serious allegations by members of racial, religious and ethnic communities." Representative Martha Griffiths, activist lawyer Pauli Murray, Esther Peterson (who had come around on the issue), as well as a few EEOC officials, did try to push anti-gender discrimination efforts forward—and with some success—but without more help from Congress or outside pressure groups progress was limited.

Betty Friedan, who had been contacted by several "pro-women" EEOC officials, decided to form a pressure group. Friedan was the author of the 1963 surprise best-seller *The Feminine Mystique*. In it, Friedan described the lives of well-educated women who had at age twenty or twenty-five voluntarily, happily, and singularly devoted themselves to home and family but who found themselves a decade or so later feeling depressed and unfulfilled. Friedan had called this middle-class housewife's predicament "the problem with no name," and she had concluded: "We can no longer ignore that voice in women that says: 'I want something more than my husband and my children and my home.' " Friedan had broken ground, in the mid-twentieth-century United States, by arguing in a popular work that women's unhappiness was not caused by individual shortcomings or neuroses but by social forces.

Friedan began organizing women in mid-1966 to lobby the EEOC. She began by talking with representatives of the state commissions on the status of women that had emerged out of the 1961 national commission. At a lunch meeting, Friedan scribbled on the back of a napkin: ". . . to take the actions needed to bring women into the mainstream of American society, now, with full equality for women, in fully equal partnership with men, NOW, the National Organization for Women."

In October 1966, about 300 women and men held the founding conference of NOW. Betty Friedan was elected president. NOW's board of directors was narrowly drawn from the academic world, the government, and other well-connected elites. With no mass movement yet to draw on, NOW's leaders aimed to work as

political insiders, lobbying the executive branch to fully implement
existing statutes which outlawed sex discrimination. But NOW
was not formulated to be just another inside-the-Washington-
beltway lobbying group. While their immediate aims were simply
to force full compliance with the law, their larger goals were, in
the context of the mid-1960s, a powerful challenge to the status
quo:

> We reject the current assumptions that a man must carry the sole
> burden of supporting himself, his wife and family . . . or that
> marriage, home and family are primarily a woman's world and
> responsibility—hers to dominate—his to support. We believe that
> true partnership between the sexes demands a different concept of
> marriage, an equitable sharing of the responsibilities of home and
> of the economic burdens of their support.

NOW's charter members publicly declared themselves to be feminists in revolt against the postwar cult of domesticity. They fought
for the right to break free of long-standing gender-ridden social
roles in pursuit of equality between the sexes.

In 1966, few women were prepared to join NOW and attack
the notion of fixed gender roles or to enlist in a mass movement
dedicated to equal rights for women. However, far more than a
changing labor market and NOW's legal and political campaign
against inequality within it were working to make women angry
and frustrated. Throughout the 1950s and 1960s two other major
changes in American society caused women to reconsider their
status and the possibility of expanding their opportunities.

The first of these changes was the one brought about by Betty
Friedan's *The Feminine Mystique*. Many middle-class women, especially the well-educated, were not satisfied with their lives. As
family historian Stephanie Coontz notes, by 1960, three years
before *The Feminine Mystique* appeared, almost every major news
magazine in the country featured stories about "trapped" housewives. When the housewife-oriented magazine *Redbook* asked
readers to send in examples of "Why Young Mothers Feel
Trapped," some 24,000 women responded. What made these re-

ports of "trapped" wives and mothers politically portentous was that in large numbers unhappy women were not simply stewing at home but were actively seeking solutions to their discontent.

Many unhappy women looked for therapeutic answers. Their faith that therapy could help them deal with their discontent was consistent with the ever increasing emphasis twentieth-century middle-class Americans placed on a psychological framework for understanding their lives. To put it bluntly, many middle-class Americans were shifting from the view that duty and obligation were paramount to a belief that personal happiness was both possible and an acceptable goal in life. Millions of women in the 1950s and 1960s flocked to therapists and family doctors in search of psychological help that would end their unhappiness and bring them personal satisfaction.

Many housewives were told by their doctors and therapists that their unhappiness was caused by their inability to embrace their natural feminine role of passivity, domesticity, and placidity. Freudian therapists talked about "penis envy" while less rigorously trained family doctors spoke of women suffering from an "intense striving for masculinity." To help women to banish unhappiness while they struggled to overcome their supposedly inappropriate "masculine" desires to have more varied lives, millions of women were dosed with tranquilizers. By 1960, tranquilizer consumption, most of it by women, had soared to over a million pounds a year. While many women "got better" and learned to accept their prescribed gender roles, many remained discontented and continued to search for an answer to their unhappiness. By the end of the decade many middle-aged women, a large portion of whom had read *The Feminine Mystique*, would turn to the women's movement for that answer.

Unhappy housewives would become a vital part of a reanimated women's movement, but in a kind of Catch-22 their isolation and circumscribed lives made it difficult to be at the forefront of the fight. The women who did the most to bring a feminist consciousness to national attention were neither the NOW insiders nor discontented housewives. Women college students and movement activists led the way in forming a mass women's movement.

In large part they had the courage and the faith to build a mass movement because they had come of age when "rights talk" was common.

Many white students first participated in protests not against the war in Vietnam or for civil rights but over their schools' *in loco parentis* rules which established limits on students' campus freedoms. Most of these rules aimed at curbing not student free speech (as in Berkeley) but sexual behavior. Given the prevailing wisdom of the early 1960s, which placed sexual responsibility almost completely on women, such rules almost always prescribed women's behavior and not men's. The University of Michigan student handbook in 1962, for example, devoted nine of its fifteen pages to curfews and late-minute penalties for women. Men had no such limits or penalties. At the University of Kansas in 1965, a woman wrote in the second SDS campus newsletter: "Women . . . are regulated in the most minute aspects of everyday existence. . . . If the university experience is to be meaningful, girls as well as boys ought to decide that they are here for something . . . and that such limits and goals as they are to have must be conceived of and imposed by them."

At Kansas, student protesters were supported on this issue by the feminist Dean of Women, Emily Taylor, who stated, "I believe in equality and our sole function is to produce as many autonomous adults as we can." Equal rights to come home late from a date sounds frivolous. But young women fighting for that right often came to see other rules and social practices that discriminated against women. And many a young woman began to ponder why various authorities (usually men) had the right to control her own life and sexuality. In Emily Taylor's view (which she made sure Kansas women knew), "relaxing parental rules removed a windmill to fight. We could pay attention to the larger issue—sex discrimination."

Many of the women who were most active in movement politics in the early to middle 1960s never worked on issues directly related to women's rights or feminism. In fact, many of the women most instrumental in founding the women's liberation movement had participated in protest movements that were, to varying degrees

and in reflection of the larger society, what is now called sexist.
And while women, especially black women in the civil rights
struggles, played critical roles as organizers and activists, almost
always the men in the movement treated them as subordinates.
As the movements grew in size, these problems worsened. In the
1970 best-seller *Sisterhood Is Powerful*, editor Robin Morgan stated:

> Thinking we were involved in the struggle to build a new society,
> it was a slowly dawning and depressing realization that we were
> doing the same work *in* the Movement as out of it; typing the
> speeches men delivered, making coffee but not policy, being ac-
> cessories to the men whose politics would supposedly replace the
> Old Order.

As historian Alice Echols has concluded, both the New Left and
the civil rights movement "were dominated by men who were,
at best, uninterested in challenging sexual inequality."

At a 1964 SNCC conference in which two women, Casey Hayden and Mary King, had presented a pathbreaking paper protesting
women's subordinate position within the Movement, many men's
attitudes toward women were exposed. Responding to the wom-
en's concerns, SNCC leader Stokely Carmichael asked: "What is
the position of women within SNCC? The position of women in
SNCC is prone." Carmichael was joking but he was also revealing
a harsh truth; many women, especially white women in SNCC,
were thought of by the men more as sexual objects than as political
partners.

But participating even in a male-centered movement gave
women tremendous opportunities. By 1967, a small but vital
group of Movement women had begun to discuss how ideas such
as participatory democracy, equality, liberation, and oppression
might apply to women in the United States.

Many politically radical men in the New Left and the antiwar
movement were appalled, at first, by the women's liberation cau-
cuses forming in their midst. Many of these male radicals held the
same unthinking, sexist view of women that most of their fathers
did. They simply found it ludicrous that "chicks," in the widely

accepted parlance of the time, thought themselves capable of exercising power and authority. When Shulamith Firestone spoke out against the oppression of women at a political rally in 1969, some male radicals heckled her with shouts of "Take her off the stage and fuck her!" More often, radical men tried to patronize their feminist peers, accusing them of being selfish for focusing on "chick lib" when the Vietnamese and poor people of color around the world suffered from far greater oppression. But radical feminists were able to turn this kind of attack around by applying a militant-styled analysis to their own condition. One group of SDS women, for example, retorted: "As we analyze the position of women in capitalist society and especially in the United States we find that women are in a colonial relationship to men and we recognize ourselves as part of the Third World."

Such rhetoric was a powerful tool in converting radical men—and it, along with other arguments, worked—but it was a poor method for reaching out to the vast majority of American women. Politically savvy women of NOW found the radical women's revolutionary political vocabulary alienating and dangerous to the larger cause and so kept their distance. This distance was fine with most of the radical women, who saw NOW as a reformist group focused on narrow questions of equal opportunity. As radical activist Jo Freeman saw it: "Women's liberation does not mean equality with men . . . [because] equality in an unjust society is meaningless." It would take time and a great deal of rethinking for NOW's political insiders, the young radical feminists, politicized but nonfeminist students, and the millions of mainly older men and women who were unpoliticized but discontented with their gender-circumscribed roles to find common political ground.

One path to that common ground, though it was not at first seen as such, was laid at the Miss America pageant in Atlantic City in September 1968, when, in the words of writer and activist Robin Morgan, the women's liberation movement "announced our existence to the world." On the boardwalk outside the pageant hall, a group of about a hundred women nominated a sheep as their candidate for Miss America and set up "a freedom trash can." In the can they piled "instruments of torture," including high heels, bras, girdles, hair curlers, false eyelashes, typing books, and copies of *Playboy* and *Cosmopolitan* magazines. They intended to burn everything in the can but were prevented from doing so by a fire ordinance. Nonetheless, from this theatrical protest came an enduring term for the new-style feminists—"bra burners." Inside the auditorium, the protesters unfurled banners reading: "Women's Liberation," and chanted: "Freedom for women" and "No more Miss America."

Most of the women involved in the Miss America protest had worked in other protest movements. They knew what it took to win the attention of the mass media. They also believed that to get women to rethink their social position, they had to capture their imaginations. While many people found the attack on Miss America and the American ideal of femininity abrasive, the protesters succeeded nonetheless. They made headlines around the country. They also got many men and women thinking, as historian Alice Echols argues, about the ways in which society promoted "physical attractiveness and charm as the primary measure of women's worth." Judging women above all by their beauty, these radical feminists argued, was just one way, the most obvious perhaps, in which men "colonized" women's bodies in order to exploit them.

While many of NOW's leaders found, at this time, the word "colonized" to be off-putting in this context, and a cultural critique of beauty a politically ill-advised tactic, most of them were coming to agree with the logic of the Miss America protest. Men did, in fact, control women's bodies, as well as their labor power, in the most basic ways. Overwhelmingly, male gynecologists and obstetricians had made childbirth a technological exercise in which neither the mother nor the father was allowed to play any substantial, decision-making role. Male legislators in the nineteenth century, at a time when women could not even vote, had taken from women the legal right to decide for themselves whether or not they wanted to carry a pregnancy to term. And a male-dominated judicial system had made it seem that, in all but the most exceptional cases, a woman who had been raped had only herself to blame; if she was dressed "provocatively," or had been out alone at night, or had accepted a drink, or had been sexually active sometime in the past, she was "fair game" and therefore "deserved what she got." For the radicals, these issues pointed to what feminist theorist Kate Millett called "sexual politics," or what another theorist, Adrienne Rich, called "patriarchy":

> . . . the power of the fathers: a familial-social, ideological, political system in which men—by force, direct pressure, or through ritual, tradition, law and language, customs, etiquette, education and the division of labor—determine what part women shall or shall not play and in which the female is subsumed under the male.

Between 1968 and 1975, dozens of articles and best-selling books spread the feminist message. Terms such as "patriarchy," "male chauvinist pig," and "sexism" entered the American vocabulary. On college campuses, in exclusive men's clubs, in women's magazines, at construction sites, anywhere where feminists detected "male supremacy," women carried their fight for equal rights and, more radically, their campaign to overthrow the social view that, when it came to the roles of men and women in a society, "biology is destiny." Radical feminists, while alienating a large majority of Americans, had also succeeded in focusing the nation's attention both on gender inequality and on the immense cultural and political forces that constructed and constrained gender roles in America.

By 1970, millions pondered the radical feminists' messages. In 1970, when Kate Millett's *Sexual Politics* was published, *Time* magazine put her on the cover. Less than two years later, *Ms.*, a feminist women's magazine, sold out all 250,000 copies of its first issue in eight days. By the early 1970s, NOW and dozens of small radical feminist groups were joined by the Women's Equity Action (focused on gender discrimination in universities), the National Women's Political Caucus (which aimed to elect more women to office), and Human Rights for Women (an abortion rights group). According to historian Rosalind Rosenberg, by the late 1970s, thousands of women's groups were fighting at the local and national level for social change.

Rank-and-file members of these groups, financial supporters, and other sympathizers were primarily college-educated, middle-class white women. Many had read books like Betty Friedan's *The Feminine Mystique* (1963), Robin Morgan's *Sisterhood Is Powerful* (1970), Kate Millett's *Sexual Politics* (1970), Shulamith Firestone's *The Dialectic of Sex* (1970), the Boston Health Collective's *Our Bodies, Our Selves* (1971), Germaine Greer's *The Female Eunuch* (1972), and later Susan Brownmiller's *Against Our Will: Men, Women and Rape* (1975), a searing indictment of how the police and court systems treated rape. But many women were pulled into the women's movement by more than reading a book, no matter how eye-opening it was.

What came to be called "consciousness-raising groups" were integral to the rise and development of the movement. These women-only rap sessions began informally within the radical movement. Women talked to each other openly about intimate details of their lives, often for the first time. But instead of treating these things as psychological issues to be individually resolved, they considered the broader social implications of their personal feelings: why do I, and so many women, someone might ask, feel under constant sexual pressure from men; or why do I, and so many women, get so nervous about talking to large groups of people; or why am I, and so many women, unable to confront a man when wronged by him? One early participant, feminist author Susan Brownmiller, wrote that in consciousness-raising groups "a woman's experiences at the hands of men were analyzed as a *political* phenomenon." Politically radical and astute women were turning the therapeutic ideal on its head and asking not why am *I* unhappy, but what do my personal feelings and experiences say about how society is organized to make women politically, culturally, and economically subordinate to men?

By the early 1970s, these consciousness-raising groups were springing up in cities and suburbs around the country. Many of the women who participated were married and had children; many were the "discontented" housewives of the early 1960s who had been searching for years for answers to their frustrating sense of being unfulfilled by the traditional gender role they had embraced. Gloria Cohen, for example, saw a note for a women's group pinned up on the bulletin board at her daughter's elementary school. She called up her sister and they decided to go. As her sister recalled, the meetings were "just so eye-opening":

> . . . We talked about our marriages, and what we wanted and just about being women in a way I had never done before even with my closest friends. It wasn't just whining, it was trying to figure out *why*, why we felt things and what we could do to make our marriages more equal and our lives better. Mainly, it was just so eye-opening to realize that other women had the same problems as you and that it wasn't your fault that you felt angry and wanted more for yourself.

Many women, for the first time, shared stories about being raped or abused. They told about the illegal abortions they had endured: "I went with another woman who was also having an abortion. We didn't know each other. We met at a restaurant and then we followed a woman to a car; she blindfolded us in the car. I was fine. . . . I bled the whole next day. But I was fine. The other woman died." Such terribly private stories, when shared, moved many women to public action.

Ms. magazine publicized the consciousness-raising groups and even provided a how-to article. No organization oversaw these informal groups and no national membership rolls existed, but it is likely that throughout the 1970s millions of women participated in or had a close friend or relative who went to such groups. The groups worked to link radical feminists, NOW's reformers, and a great many previously unpoliticized women. By the early 1970s, the women's liberation movement, once composed of a few political insiders and small cadres of radicals, was becoming a mass movement.

Throughout the 1970s, the women's movement gained in power and mainstream acceptance. NOW activists and their allies won a series of sweeping court decisions that essentially ended legal discrimination against women. And while they failed to achieve passage of the Equal Rights Amendment, they succeeded in solidly enlisting the federal government in their cause.

In 1973, the Supreme Court ruled in *Roe* v. *Wade* that women had a constitutional right to control their own bodies and have an abortion. What had once been dismissed as radical nonsense, that men should not have the right to "colonize" women's bodies, had, in one critical instance, become the law of the land.

Despite great legal and political victories, the women's movement remained extremely controversial and was not just opposed by "male chauvinist pigs." While some black women became feminists, many black women active in the civil rights struggle and the Black Power movement felt that matters of racial justice had a prior claim on their energies and that the women's movement hurt their cause by diverting resources and attention from it. In addition, they were suspicious of what they saw as the mainly middle-class desires of the new feminists. As one activist said wryly: "Black women . . . could not understand why these white women were so gung ho about working and being the same as men. Black women . . . had been working all of their lives. They would have been glad to sit at home and not work. . . . For the black women it was a question of liberating black men and not women."

Many women, a clear majority at least through the early 1970s, opposed the movement because they felt it did not recognize or respect their lives. They feared the economic consequences of a gender-blind society in which a man's legal and moral responsibility to support his wife and children would be weakened. They worried about seeing their daughters sent off to war or into dangerous work environments. Many women, in then Congresswoman Barbara Mikulski's words, did not want to see their daughters have to go back to the factories or rough-and-tumble times they had escaped: "They wanted to be 'ladies' . . . and they wanted their daughters to be 'ladies.' " Being "just" a housewife, many American women believed, was a whole lot better than any real-life alternative. Not surprisingly, many women were also appalled by radical feminists' well-publicized arguments that marriage, monogamy, and motherhood were all traps that essentially reduced women to men's chattel and that housewives were little more than unpaid servants. These bald arguments, regardless of their heuristic value or even their accuracy, were not likely to win most women over to the side of feminism. Finally, many men and women were horrified by the women's movement's increasingly close identification with lesbianism.

The women's movement had long wrangled over that issue. In part, radical feminists' political analysis and support of lesbianism stemmed from their overall concerns about how sex and sexuality were used by men to oppose women. Much of what made the women's liberation movement radical was its analysis of how men reduced women to sexual objects and the ways in which women cooperated in their own objectification. Women could not achieve real equality, many feminists argued, until they could stop men from seeing them primarily as sex objects. Provocatively, and not unreasonably, radical feminists argued that until women took more responsibility for their own sexual fulfillment—in part by focusing their sexual partners' attention on clitoral rather than vaginal stimulation—they could not expect to achieve sexual parity, let alone gender equality with men. Lesbianism offered a profound response to the intertwining problems of sex and sexuality. As one radical argued: "The lesbian rejects male sexual/political domination . . . lesbianism puts women first while the society declares the male supreme. Lesbianism threatens male supremacy at its core." For a committed radical feminist, dedicated to fighting women's dependence on men at its root, lesbianism made a certain amount of ideological sense. In addition, the women's liberation movement really did attract the support of many lesbians, who without husbands to rely on for economic support, had more reason than most straight women to actively pursue gender equality.

Reform-minded feminists like Betty Friedan were, at first, very much opposed to incorporating lesbians and lesbianism into the women's movement. Friedan went so far as to call lesbians "the lavender menace." The reformers, quite simply, recognized that an overwhelming majority of Americans were unapologetically prejudiced against lesbians and homosexual men and they feared conflating the idea of feminism and lesbianism in the public mind—something that conservatives and many provincial Americans did anyway. Not until well into the 1970s did nonradical, straight feminists decide that it was simply wrong to allow political expediency to dictate morality; homophobia should have no place in their fight for an egalitarian society.

The rise of the lesbian question within the women's movement was part of a larger struggle that emerged at the very end of the 1960s: the gay liberation movement. Semi-secret, reform-minded homosexual rights and discussion groups had begun forming soon after World War II and a large and vital gay movement would not emerge until well into the 1970s. But in at least symbolic terms gay liberation burst onto the public stage very early in the morning on June 28, 1969, after police officers raided the Stonewall Inn, a gay bar in Greenwich Village.

A police raid on a gay bar was nothing new in New York City or elsewhere; gays were seen by most authorities as deviants who deserved to be harassed periodically. Traditionally, patrons of gay bars did their best to quietly walk away from the police raiders, knowing that they could lose their jobs and reputations if their homosexual activities were made public. But at the Stonewall that night something almost unprecedented occurred. As *The Village Voice* reported: "Limp wrists were forgotten. Beer cans and bottles were heaved at the windows and a rain of coins descended on the cops. . . . Almost by signal the crowd erupted into cobblestone and bottle heaving." In a fury, gay men, many of them working-class, several of whom were Hispanic, torched the Stonewall and a riot broke out. A defiant call to arms was spray-painted all over the Village: "Gay Power."

The new Gay Power activists were fueled by all the other civil rights, liberation, and protest movements that had preceded them. Many had gained organizational experience and a radical perspective working in such movements. Gay and lesbian activists were also building from the tiny "homophile" movement which had, in the 1960s, begun publicly lobbying government officials in Washington, D.C., New York, San Francisco, and elsewhere, asking for an end to discrimination and legal oppression. And by the late 1960s and early 1970s, in New York City and San Francisco, and to a lesser extent several other American cities, homosexuality was no longer "the love that dares not speak its name." Gay bars and other gay-oriented establishments, while under constant threat of police harassment, had begun to increase in number as gay men and women from around the country began to form semi-underground communities in the big cities. A series of books and articles, dating from the 1948 and 1953 Kinsey reports on American sexual behavior, while often far from sympathetic, had made it clear to many, gay and straight, that homosexuality was a far from rare phenomenon. This public knowledge, the increasing numbers of gays living in the big cities, combined with the less rigid sexual mores that prevailed by 1970 (at least on college campuses and among more cosmopolitan Americans), gave gay and lesbian activists a cultural and social platform from which to work.

Like the women's movement, the new gay activists fought on many fronts. At a fundamental level, they fought to turn around the society-wide certainty that homosexuality was, in the words of a brutal 1966 *Time* magazine article, "a pathetic little second-rate substitution for reality . . . a pernicious sickness." Many homosexuals, according to historian John D'Emilio, "absorbed [these] views of themselves as immoral, depraved, and pathological individuals." Part of the activists' fight, then, was to convince gay men and lesbians that they were not sick or bad people simply because of their sexual preference. They urged gay men and lesbians to "come out of the closet" and take pride in being gay. To this end they organized social events, fought to remove the stigma and danger attached to going to a gay bar or event, and on college campuses and elsewhere organized openly gay groups. To change heterosexual attitudes, activists targeted the American Psychiatric Association's official position that homosexuality was a mental disorder. In 1973, they succeeded in getting the APA to remove its stigmatizing label.

The new, militant activists continued the work of earlier reformers by fighting for simple civil rights. In New York City, for example, gay groups struggled to get the city government to pass a bill which would make discrimination by reason of sexual preference illegal—a bill which was finally passed in 1986. By

1973, nearly 800 openly gay organizations fought for the rights of homosexuals at both a local and national level. By the late 1970s, gay liberation had become a vital, multifaceted political movement increasingly accepted as a legitimate interest group by many big-city political establishments. Simultaneously, the relatively sudden visibility of openly gay men angered and frightened less tolerant Americans. Many people were appalled by those gay men who rejected what most Americans considered traditional sexual morality by practicing and publicly promoting sexual promiscuity, anonymous sex, and a more openly erotic way of life. The gay rights struggle was the most controversial civil rights or liberation movement to emerge out of the 1960s; by the late 1980s, conservative politicians would successfully use the question of homosexual rights to inflame and polarize Americans.

By the mid-1970s, most Americans' sense of economic security, which had influenced both liberals and radicals to believe that the times were right for fundamental political and social change, was gone. But it is incorrect to think that social activism came to an end with the 1970s. Throughout the 1970s, the women's movement, the gay movement, the environmental movement, as well as rapidly expanding movements of Chicanos, American Indians, disabled Americans, and others, gained adherents and power. In fact, much of what people remember as (or call pejoratively) "sixties" activism or "sixties" challenges to "traditional values" occurred in the first half of the 1970s. Just as most of the social activism and cultural rebellion Americans experienced in the 1960s had roots in previous decades, what activist Abbie Hoffman called "a sixties state of mind" continued to grow in new directions into the 1970s and after.

CONCLUSIONS

~~~~~~

BY THE EARLY 1970s, Americans of all political persuasions understood that their country had gone through a cultural and political sea change. Some people celebrated, but in the almost palpable national exhaustion that followed the 1960s, more people pointed fingers: at Vietnam, at the riots and the assassinations and the bloody confrontations, at the radicals, at Nixon and Johnson, at the mass media and the universities and the government, at the police and the FBI and the Army . . . at each other. People then and now make lists of what went right and what went wrong, of how much changed and how much stayed the same. For better and for worse, none of the most vital dreams of the 1960s— whether they were of a beloved community, a color-blind society, a Great Society, a "higher consciousness," an end to patriarchy, or freedom for the people of Vietnam—came to pass. But despite the failures much did change, and most of the changes were for the better, even if they were never quite enough, even if they sometimes brought new difficulties in their wake.

In the 1960s many Americans stripped away the Cold War blinders most had forgotten they even wore. Fervid anti-Communism lost much of its domestic political potency, even as the Cold War endured and clear answers to global realities remained elusive. President Eisenhower's America, in which "nigger" jokes could be told behind closed doors of whites-only, men-only citadels of power and prestige, was, if by no means destroyed, under furious attack. And overall, the cultural landscape in which Americans searched for meaningful lives had radically expanded by the early 1970s: freedom of expression had

become practically limitless, gender roles were open for reex-
amination, and spiritual and religious enthusiasms multiplied.
Many Americans relished the freedom and even the confusion they
had wrought in the 1960s; others saw a cultural upheaval that
threatened to destroy them and their families.

America's defeat in Vietnam and the disunity the war had produced shattered the near-consensus that had ruled American foreign policy in the postwar years. The Vietnam experience also
made millions of Americans aware of the multitude of secretive
agencies and apparatuses that managed their government's global
activities. In the early 1970s, Congress would try, with some small
successes, to reestablish a more aggressive role for itself in making
and monitoring foreign policy. The mass media and a variety of
newly formed public-interest watchdog groups also began to scru-
tinize American foreign policy and American political elites more
carefully. Because of Vietnam the "establishment" media, as well
as a variety of alternative sources of global news, were far more
aggressive in their reporting on the CIA and other covert operations around the world, reducing the secrecy with which many
of America's international missions had been performed. Polls and
surveys taken in the early 1970s showed a majority of Americans
had grown skeptical and even cynical about their government's
ability to execute foreign policy successfully and were extremely
wary of using American troops abroad.

While the war in Vietnam had severely damaged the Cold War
consensus of the 1950s, its legacy left most of the hardest questions about America's mission in the world unanswered. How
Americans understood their national interests and their global responsibilities in the aftermath of the Vietnam debacle was unclear.
President Eisenhower's warnings about the power of the "military-industrial complex" still went largely unheeded and no new
foreign policy consensus had emerged that defined what America's
role in the world should be. Into this confusion, in 1980, stepped
Ronald Reagan. He pledged—John Kennedy-like—that America
would be first again, no matter where, no matter when, and maybe
even no matter why. In the 1980s, even as America's position
in the international economy grew less secure, "the military-

industrial complex" would receive well over a trillion dollars, and the national debt seemed to grow out of control. The Reagan and Bush administrations worked to convince Americans that they had gotten over the "Vietnam syndrome." They looked backward and focused on fighting the old Communist menace, even as they largely ignored the real "new world order" in which economic juggernauts fought for global markets.

At home, racism and sexism had been undermined, if not completely eradicated, by the mid-1970s. American government at all levels, along with most major corporations and other leading institutions, fought (with varying degrees of commitment) racist and sexist practices which only a few years earlier had been widely accepted. To ensure that new talk did not mask old deeds, the federal government, as well as many state and local governments, mandated a variety of affirmative action programs aimed at guaranteeing greater racial and gender equality. Because of grass-roots activism and subsequent inside-the-beltway lobbying, racism and sexism had moved from politically peripheral issues, at best, to America's center stage.

But much more was at stake in the domestic fallout of the 1960s than simply opening the door to greater opportunity for all. By the early 1970s, a number of Americans claimed they didn't even want to join the mainstream. Vocal African-American activists not only scoffed that the melting pot was a myth; they openly denigrated the entire ideal of a national culture, insisting that they had the right and the duty to live by and to teach their young according to their own values and traditions. In the early 1970s, American Indians, too, called for Red Power, while Chicanos in the West and Southwest demanded Brown Power. In partial response, many European-Americans began reclaiming and asserting their ethnic heritages. They joined ethnic associations, revitalized traditional holidays and customs, and proudly displayed buttons and bumper stickers proclaiming, for example, Irish Power or Italian Power. In the 1970s, "identity politics"—in which many organized groups worked not for a common national purpose but for their group's right to control political territory or to organize a separate set of cultural institutions or to gain a share

of jobs or contracts by virtue of their race, ethnicity, or gender—
became commonplace, even as it became politically explosive.
What it meant to be an American became a hotly debated topic.

Especially for people who had been, by virtue of their group
identity, denied fundamental individual freedoms and opportunities, identity politics was a vital, even essential means by which
they could struggle for greater political legitimacy, economic
power, and cultural authority. However, in part because of this
kind of identity politics, many white Americans distrusted the
government's efforts to foster economic opportunity, seeing group
remedies for past discrimination as unfair to them and to their
children. Because most Americans also saw most of the liberal
policies of the 1960s—especially the War on Poverty—as having
failed, many Americans by the 1970s essentially lost faith in the
ability of government to uplift the poor or to create more equitable
economic opportunities or outcomes.

The America that emerged out of the 1960s was, in fact, a more
egalitarian society, one in which far more Americans had opportunities to rise economically and exercise political power. But this
new America was also visibly polarized and fragmented. Racial,
ethnic, and gender identities were often treated, by all sides, as
essential markers of group interests which fundamentally and ir-
reversibly divided the American people. Many white Americans
who had embraced an ethic of national assimilation and an ethos
of individualism felt that "minorities" had lost any claim on the
nation when they refused to fully accept the superiority of "mainstream" culture, the desirability of fitting into "white" society,
and the faith that a person succeeds or fails by virtue of his or her
individual merits. In the fierce political fighting that surrounded
"group-based remedies" for centuries of de jure and de facto discrimination, the needs and plight of the poor were, once again,
often ignored.

As a result of the cultural and political struggles of the 1960s,
social elements and ideas that had long been in society's closet or
under siege, emerged in the 1970s with striking vitality. Feminism
became a hot, if often misunderstood, topic of conversation. Gays
and lesbians came "out of the closet." People argued about the

difference between an acceptable lifestyle and an unacceptable way of life. While tolerance for people different from oneself was among America's most traditional values, many clearly felt (as Americans traditionally and unfortunately had) that in practice tolerance had narrow limits.

In the 1980s conservative Americans, led by President Reagan, exacerbated a growing sense of national divide and cultural confrontation. Reagan and others asserted that unless people were willing to live by what they called "traditional family values" and to accept that economic difficulties were the problem of the individual, not society, they were not truly Americans, and so deserved to be excluded from the body politic and punished by respectable society. In the 1980s a politics of unity—in which "every American counted" and in which every citizen felt a part of the national whole—was in short supply, even as, ironically, the nation faced nearly unprecedented international economic challenges. By the election of 1992 a majority of Americans seemed to be looking toward their political leaders for new answers to what already had become the old problem of creating national unity while respecting social diversity.

In the 1960s, Americans also spotlighted—as they indulged in —the moral chaos an unbridled consumerist ethos could produce. In the 1970s, increasing numbers of Americans joined in the relatively uninhibited search for individual pleasures and self-indulgent lifestyles that consumer capitalism seemed to promise and which many young people had so publicly explored in extralegal and often amoral fashion in the 1960s. It was in the 1970s, I would underline, not the 1960s, that drug use and sexual promiscuity exploded. In the economically frightening years of the late 1970s and early 1980s, especially among aging "baby boomers," body drugs like cocaine—which offered little in the way of "mind-expanding" properties but a good deal of simulated energy and ego boosting—became a risky middle-class passion and a scourge among the poor. In the 1980s a great deal of political and legal muscle went into fighting—or scapegoating—this drug use. In many ways, punishing users of illegal drugs and blaming "the sixties" for any and all of the nation's moral and spiritual wounds became a way for many Americans to avoid thinking about how and why our market-driven and market-obsessed society had helped to turn consumerism and hedonism into the nation's most vital "traditional" values. We still ponder—as many did in the 1960s—the meaning of virtue in a society which places its highest value on the marketplace of goods and services, which in turn exists to excite ever new and ever greater desires.

In our public and private conversations the phrase "the sixties" has become a beguiling, shorthand way for either casting aspersions or offering praise—depending upon who is speaking. But as I hope I have made clear, the 1960s left no simple legacy. We owe the people who lived through those frightening and exhilarating times, who made the history of the 1960s, a debt of understanding. By stripping away the myths that cloud the 1960s and thinking hard about what Americans faced in those times and what they did in response, we may gain some clarity in thinking about who we were then, who we might have become, and even whom we wish to be.

BIBLIOGRAPHIC ESSAY

While this book is primarily a synthetic one, I have drawn on material housed at the John F. Kennedy and Lyndon B. Johnson presidential libraries. I have also made use of a good deal of archival research done over the last ten years for a variety of scholarly projects. For this book I have also read on microfilm hundreds of issues of underground newspapers, several years of *Time* and *Newsweek*, and many pages of *The New York Times*.

For the three years prior to writing this book I had Columbia College and Barnard College students enrolled in my courses "America in the 1960s" and "The Civil Rights Movement in America" prepare oral history reports. I read about 900 of these oral histories and found them vital in thinking about the 1960s and in understanding how people felt about those times; I received permission to quote from many of these oral histories and have made frequent use of them, usually not to prove a point but rather to illustrate one. I have also talked with hundreds of people about their memories of the 1960s and found many of their accounts helpful in making the literary leap from the 1990s to the 1960s.

Rather than provide an exhaustive survey of sources in this bibliographic essay, I have included only those books and articles that I found most useful or important.

For historical overviews I relied on: Michael Barone, *Our Country: The Shaping of America from Roosevelt to Reagan* (1990), a hardheaded, trustworthy chronicle of political and economic history; William H. Chafe, *The Unfinished Journey: America Since World War II* (1986), most useful for its sympathetic accounts of social change movements; Charles R. Morris, *A Time of Passion: America 1960–1980* (1984), a smart, skeptical appraisal of public policy and the conventional wisdom; *The Rise and Fall of the New Deal Order*, eds. Steve Fraser and Gary Gerstle (1989), a collection of essays most useful in explaining the role of the state in the life of the American people over the last several decades; *Major Problems in American History Since 1945*, ed. Robert Griffith (1992), a historiographically sophisticated collection of useful documents and essays; James Gilbert, *Another Chance: Postwar America 1945–1985* (1986), a superb overview of the nation's large-scale social and cultural changes; and Godfrey Hodgson, *America in Our Time: From World War II to Nixon—What Happened and Why* (1978), a beautifully written, insightful account of postwar "establishment" thinking and cultural upheaval in the 1960s.

Other histories of the 1960s include: John Morton Blum, *Years of Discord: American Politics and Society 1961–1974* (1991), which is particularly astute on events in Washington, D.C.; Todd Gitlin, *The Sixties: Years of Hope, Days of Rage* (1987), a fascinating and fruitful mélange of memory and history; Allen Matusow, *The Unraveling of America* (1984), a riveting, biting account of liberalism and its radical critics in the 1960s; and the scholarly collection *The 1960s: From Memory to History*, ed. David Farber (1994).

For overviews of the Cold War period, I balanced the very critical Thomas J. McCormick, *America's Half Century: United States Foreign Policy in the Cold War* (1992) with the always wise John Gaddis, *The Long Peace* (1987). Lawrence H. Fuchs, *The American Kaleidoscope: Race, Ethnicity and the Civic Culture* (1990), provided a brilliant examination of American identity. Andrew Ross, *No Respect: Intellectuals and Popular Culture* (1989), offers a superb reading of postwar American culture. Tom Wolfe, *Tom Wolfe: The Purple Decades* (1982), is a funny and telling portrait of America.

Other important overviews for understanding specific aspects of the 1960s include: Beth L. Bailey, *From Front Porch to Back Seat: Courtship in Twentieth Century America* (1988); James T. Patterson, *America's Struggle Against Poverty 1900–1985* (1986); *The New American State: Bureaucracies and Policies Since World War II*, ed. Louis Galambos (1987); Warren I. Susman, *Culture as History: The Transformation of American Society in the Twentieth Century* (1984); Edward D. Berkowitz and Kim McQuaid, *Creating the Welfare State: The Political Economy of 20th Century Reform* (1992); James J. Flink, *The Automobile Age* (1988); Steven Mintz and Susan Kellogg, *Domestic Revolutions: A Social History of American Family Life* (1988); Stephanie Coontz, *The Way We Never Were* (1992); Kenneth Jackson, *Crabgrass Frontier: The Suburbanization of the United States* (1985); Robert Wuthnow, *The Restructuring of American Religion* (1988); Bruce J. Schulman, *From Cotton Belt to Sunbelt: Federal Policy, Economic Develop-*

ment, and the Transformation of the South, 1938–1980 (1991); Jack R. Gold-field, *Black, White and Southern* (1990); and Benjamin I. Page and Robert Y. Shapiro, *The Rational Public: Fifty Years of Trends in Americans' Policy Preferences* (1992).

1. GOOD TIMES

This chapter draws heavily on Robert Collins, "Growth Liberalism in the 1960s: Great Societies at Home and Grand Designs Abroad," in *The 1960s*, ed. Farber. My analytic frame is influenced by Daniel Bell, *The Cultural Contradictions of Capitalism* (1976). To capture America at the cusp of the 1950s and 1960s, I found the following particularly helpful: Douglas T. Miller and Marion Novak, *The Fifties* (1977); Elaine May, *Homeward Bound: American Families in the Cold War Era* (1988); John Patrick Diggins, *The Proud Decades: America in War and Peace, 1941–1960* (1988); William O'Neil, *American High: The Years of Confidence, 1945–1960* (1986); *Recasting America*, ed. Lary May (1989); Thomas Hine, *Populuxe: The Look and Life of America in the 50's and 60's* (1986); and Roland Marchand, "Visions of Classlessness, Quests for Dominion: American Popular Culture, 1945–1960," in *Reshaping American Society and Institutions, 1945–1960*, eds. Robert Bremner and Gary W. Reichard (1982).

The Kitchen Debate is well described by Stephen Ambrose, *Nixon: The Education of a Politician* (1987).

For car culture and corporations: James Flink, *The Automobile Age* (1988), and Louis Galambos and Joseph Pratt, *The Rise of the Corporate Commonwealth* (1988). For poverty: James T. Patterson, *America's Struggle Against Poverty* (1986). For an understanding of American culture in the late 1950s and early 1960s, I draw on Beth Bailey, "World Without Limits," unpublished paper.

2. THE WORLD AS SEEN FROM THE WHITE HOUSE 1960–1963

I was very much influenced in this chapter by Mary Sheila McMahon, "Naming the System: Foreign Policy and Political Culture," in *The 1960s*, ed. Farber.

The literature on John F. Kennedy is voluminous. The best insider account remains Arthur M. Schlesinger, Jr., *A Thousand Days: John F. Kennedy in the White House* (1965); for a more balanced portrait, consult

Herbert Parmet, *JFK: The Presidency of John F. Kennedy* (1983), and the pithy biography by David Burner, *John F. Kennedy and a New Generation* (1988). The most evocative account of the Kennedy-Nixon race is by Theodore White, *The Making of the President 1960* (1961), the first and, I think, best of his election books. For an account of Kennedy's domestic record, more positive and richer than my own: Irving Bernstein, *Promises Kept: John F. Kennedy's New Frontier* (1991).

For Kennedy-era Cold War events, I have relied heavily on Michael Beschloss, *The Crisis Years* (1991); also Richard Ned Lebow, *Between Peace and War* (1981).

The letters mourning JFK's death come from the condolence mail collected at the Kennedy Library.

3. The Meaning of National Culture

The most useful overview of the mass media in the postwar years is by James L. Baughman, *The Republic of Mass Culture* (1992). Other important works include: *Private Screenings: Television and the Female Consumer*, eds. Lynn Spigel and Denise Mann (1992); Todd Gitlin, *The Whole World Is Watching: Mass Media in the Making and Unmaking of the New Left* (1980); Cecelia Tichi, *Electronic Hearth: Creating an American Television Culture* (1991); and Erik Barnouw, *Tube of Plenty* (1982).

Rock 'n' roll: Jon Weiner, *Come Together* (1983); Lawrence Grossberg, *We Gotta Get Out of This Place* (1992); Robert Pielke, *You Say You Want a Revolution* (1985); Robert Pattison, *The Triumph of Vulgarity: Rock Music in the Mirror of Romanticism* (1987); Steve Chapple and Reebee Garofalo, *Rock and Roll Is Here to Pay* (1977); and George Lipsitz, " 'Who'll Stop the Rain'—Youth Culture, Rock 'n' Roll and the Social Crises of the 1960s," in *The 1960s*, ed. Farber. For a sprightly and informative history of the baby boomers: Landon Jones, *Great Expectations: America and the Baby Boom Generation* (1980).

4. Freedom

The civil rights movement has earned a rich historical literature. I am indebted to Robert Weisbrot, *Freedom Bound: A History of America's Civil Rights Movement* (1990); Harvard Sitkoff, *The Struggle for Black Equality*, Rev. ed. (1992); Manning Marable, *Race, Reform, and Rebellion: The Second Reconstruction in Black America, 1945–1982* (1982); Taylor Branch,

Parting the Waters: America in the King Years, 1954–1963 (1988); Hugh Davis Graham, *Civil Rights and the Presidency: Race and Gender in American Politics 1960–1972* (1992); Jack Bloom, *Class, Race and the Civil Rights Movement* (1987); the documentary film series *Eyes on the Prize*, Blacksides Production 1986–1987; *Black Leaders of the Twentieth Century*, eds. John Hope Franklin and August Meier (1982); William H. Chafe, *Civilities and Civil Rights: Greensboro, North Carolina, and the Black Struggle for Freedom* (1980); Clayborne Carson, *In Struggle: SNCC and the Black Awakening of the 1960's* (1981); David Garrow, *Bearing the Cross* (1987); David Garrow, *The FBI and Martin Luther King, Jr.* (1983); Michael R. Belknap, *Federal Law and Southern Order: Racial Violence and Constitutional Conflict in the Post-Brown South* (1987); Goldfield, *Black, White and Southern*; and Schulman, *From Cotton Belt to Sunbelt.*

5. The Liberal Dream and Its Nightmare

For the March on Washington, Branch, *Parting the Waters*, and for SNCC and its discontents, see Carson, *In Struggle*. The best short survey of the 1964 Civil Rights Act is found in Graham, *Civil Rights and the Presidency*. Doug McAdam, *Freedom Summer* (1988), is an excellent account of the white volunteers active in Mississippi.

LBJ's memoirs are a valuable source: Lyndon Baines Johnson, *The Vantage Point* (1971). See also Vaughn Roberts, *The Presidency of Lyndon B. Johnson* (1983); Paul K. Conkin, *Big Daddy from the Pedernales: Lyndon Baines Johnson* (1986); Harry McPherson, *A Political Education: A Washington Memoir* (1988); and for the early years, Robert Caro, *The Path to Power* (1982) and *Means of Ascent* (1990). The Great Society is intelligently discussed in Matusow, *The Unraveling of America*; Morris, *A Time of Passion*; Nicholas Lemann, *The Promised Land* (1991); *Exploring the Johnson Years*, ed. Robert Divine (1981), and *The Johnson Years*, ed. Robert Divine (1987); Patterson, *America's Struggle Against Poverty*. Useful conservative critiques include Charles Murray, *Losing Ground* (1984), and Lawrence M. Meade, *Beyond Entitlement* (1986).

For Hoover, I relied on Richard Gid Powers, *Secrecy and Power: The Life of J. Edgar Hoover* (1987).

Although much was written about the riots in America's cities when they occurred, almost no solid historical treatments of the riots exist except for the story of Detroit done by Sidney Fine, *Violence in the Model City* (1989).

BIBLIOGRAPHIC ESSAY

6. Vietnam

I have based my account mainly on the following works: George Herring, *America's Longest War* (1986); James William Gibson, *The Perfect War* (1986); Marilyn Young, *The Vietnam War: 1945–1990* (1991); James S. Olson and Randy Roberts, *Where the Domino Fell: America and Vietnam* (1991); Neil Sheehan, *A Bright Shining Lie: John Paul Vann and America in Vietnam* (1988); *Light at the End of the Tunnel*, ed. Andrew Rotter (1991); and *Major Problems in the History of the Vietnam War*, ed. Robert J. McMahon, (1990).

For an intelligent defense of the war: Guenter Lewy, *America in Vietnam* (1978). For an immoderate Marxist attack on the U.S. position: Gabriel Kolko, *Anatomy of a War: Vietnam, the United States and the Modern Historical Experience* (1985).

7. A Nation at War

I have been very influenced in this chapter by Richard Immerman, " 'A Time in the Ride of Men's Affairs': Lyndon Johnson and Vietnam," unpublished paper. Christian G. Appey, *Working Class War* (1992), offers a striking portrait and insightful analysis of the men who fought the war. A solid history of the Selective Service System and Vietnam is provided by Lawrence M. Baskir and William A. Strauss, *Chance and Circumstance* (1978). For the hotly argued issue of the mass media and Vietnam, I relied on Chester Pach, " 'And That's the Way It Was': The Vietnam War on the Network Nightly News," in *The 1960s*, ed. Farber. Peter Braestrup, *Big Story: How the American Press and Television Reported and Interpreted the Crisis of Tet in Vietnam and Washington* (1977), is highly critical of the mass media, while Daniel C. Hallin, *The "Uncensored War": The Media and Vietnam* (1986), provides a more nuanced and sophisticated portrait.

I have also drawn on haunting firsthand accounts of the war: Michael Herr, *Dispatches* (1977); Philip Caputo, *A Rumor of War* (1977); Tim O'Brien, *Going After Cacciato* (1978); and dozens of oral histories of Vietnam vets done by my students, often with their fathers or uncles. I have also talked with many Vietnam veterans about their experiences.

For the antiwar movement: *Give Peace a Chance: Exploring the Vietnam Antiwar Movement*, eds. Melvin Small and William D. Hoover (1992); Charles DeBenedetti, with Charles Chatfield, *An American Ordeal: The*

Antiwar Movement of the Vietnam Era (1990); Nancy Zaroulis and Gerald Sullivan, *Who Spoke Up? American Protest Against the War in Vietnam* (1984); Kenneth Heineman, *Campus Wars* (1992); David Farber, *Chicago '68* (1988); and for an important overview on protest in the 1960s, Terry Anderson, "The 'New American Revolution': The Movement and Business During the 1960s," in *The 1960s*, ed. Farber. For the important issue of how much the antiwar protesters affected policymakers: Melvin Small, *Johnson, Nixon and the Doves* (1988).

8. THE WAR WITHIN

Counterculture: Emmett Grogan, *Ringolevio* (1990); *Cows Are Freaky When They Look at You: An Oral History of the Kaw Valley Hemp Pickers*, eds. David Ohle, Roger Martin, and Susan Brosseau (1991); Abe Peck, *Uncovering the Sixties: The Life and Times of the Underground Press* (1985); Charles Perry, *The Haight-Ashbury* (1985); *Digger Papers* (1968); Tom Wolfe, *The Electric Kool-Aid Acid Test* (1969); and Jay Stevens's wonderfully told *Storming Heaven* (1987). For the sexual revolution: Beth Bailey, "Sexual Revolution(s)," in *The 1960s*, ed. Farber; and John D'Emilio and Estelle B. Freedman, *Intimate Matters: A History of Sexuality* (1988); and Arlene Skolnick, *Embattled Paradise* (1991).

9. STORMY WEATHER

For the political and cultural divide separating Americans, see Farber, *Chicago '68*. For the New Left: Tom Hayden, *Reunion* (1988); James Miller, *"Democracy Is in the Streets": From Port Huron to the Siege of Chicago* (1987); Wini Breines, *Community and Organization in the New Left, 1962–1968: The Great Refusal* (1982); Ronald Fraser, *1968: A Student Generation in Revolt: An International Oral History* (1988); and Heineman, *Campus Wars*.

For the Berkeley scene: William J. Rorabaugh, *Berkeley at War: The 1960s* (1989).

The Black Power movement is sympathetically recounted by William L. Van Deburg, *New Day in Babylon: The Black Power Movement and American Culture* (1992). A vivid portrait of Malcolm X is given by Peter Goldman, *The Death and Life of Malcolm X* (1979); see also *The Autobiography of Malcolm X*, as told to Alex Haley (1965); Stokely Carmichael and Charles V. Hamilton, *Black Power: The Politics of Liberation in America*

(1967); and David Colburn and George Pozzetta, "Race, Ethnicity and the Evolution of Political Legitimacy During the 1960s," in *The 1960's*, ed. Farber. For both the New Left and Black Power advocates I have made frequent use of oral histories.

10. RN and the Politics of Deception

Richard Nixon is portrayed sympathetically by Herbert Parmet, *Richard Nixon and His America* (1990). More critical are Stephen Ambrose, *Nixon* (1987), and Joe McGinniss, *The Selling of the President* (1970). Also useful are Kevin B. Phillips, *The Emerging Republican Majority* (1969); Gary Wills, *Nixon Agonistes* (1970); William Safire, *Before the Fall* (1975); Richard Nixon, *RN: The Memoirs of Richard Nixon* (1978); Stanley Kutler, *The Wars of Watergate* (1991); Robert Coles, *The Middle Americans* (1974); and David Farber, "The Silent Majority and Talk About Revolution," in *The 1960s*, ed. Farber.

For the economy of the late 1960s and early 1970s: Peter N. Carroll, *It Seemed Like Nothing Happened: America in the 1970s* (1982); Collins, "Growth Liberalism in the 1960s: Great Societies at Home and Grand Designs Abroad"; Barone, *Our Country*; and Morris, *A Time of Passion*.

11. A New World

I was much influenced in this chapter by Kenneth Cmiel, "The Politics of Civility," in *The 1960s*, ed. Farber.

The environmental movement and policy is discussed by Samuel Hays, *Beauty, Health and Permanence: Environmental Politics in the United States, 1955–1985* (1987).

The women's movement is fast developing a rich historical literature. The best overviews include: Nancy Woloch, *Women and the American Experience* (1984); Rosalind Rosenberg, *Divided Lives: American Women in the Twentieth Century* (1992); and Cynthia Harrison, *On Account of Sex: The Politics of Women's Issues 1945–1968* (1989). For the 1960s and early 1970s the best sources are Sara Evans, *Personal Politics: The Roots of Women's Liberation in the Civil Rights Movement and the New Left* (1980); Alice Echols, *Daring to Be Bad: Radical Feminism in America, 1967–1975* (1989); Alice Echols, " 'Nothing Distant About It': Women's Liberation and Sixties Radicalism," in *The 1960s*, ed. Farber; Jo Freeman, *The Politics* of *Women's Liberation* (1975); and Betty Friedan, *The Feminine Mystique* (1963).

For gay liberation: John D'Emilio, *Sexual Politics, Sexual Communities: The Making of a Homosexual Minority in the United States, 1940–1970* (1983), and D'Emilio and Freedman, *Intimate Matters.*

For both the women's movement and the gay movement I have benefited from oral history accounts.

ACKNOWLEDGMENTS

I wrote this book while a 1992–93 American Council of Learned Societies Senior Research Fellow. As a long-term untenured assistant professor and "gypsy scholar," I am especially grateful to the ACLS for their financial support and scholarly recognition. I thank Stanley Katz for his wise stewardship of the ACLS.

I am also grateful to Barnard College, which granted me a 1992–93 Barnard College Special Assistant Professor Leave. Barnard Dean Robert McCaughey also facilitated a research grant, for which I am most appreciative.

I would also like to thank the many students on whom I tried out much of the material that went into this book. Special thanks to my sorely missed graders Leah Arroyo Peterson and Yanek Mieczkowski.

I am indebted to the scholarship of Terry Anderson, Beth Bailey, Ken Cmiel, David Colburn, Robert Collins, Alice Echols, George Lipsitz, Mary Sheila McMahon, Chester Pach, and George Pozzetta. I am also indebted to Ken Heineman's pathbreaking research on campus protesters at non-elite universities.

Robert Collins's scholarship on "growth liberalism" was particularly influential in shaping sections of this book. And conversations with Mary Sheila McMahon, as well as her many lengthy papers on political culture, have greatly affected my analysis of America in the 1960s.

Political scientist Judith Russell shared with me both her knowledge about the War on Poverty and thousands of pages of Johnson Library material.

Special thanks to Twila Perry for her incisive comments on Chapter 7, and though we agreed to disagree about a few points, it wasn't for her lack of forceful arguments.

My editors Eric Foner and Arthur Wang provided helpful advice and encouragement. I appreciate their professional insights and their openness to my analysis of the era.

Richard Immerman and Beth Bailey read the entire manuscript and did their best to make me see the light. Richard's comments on Vietnam and American diplomatic history saved me from several blunders and made me think harder. He also worked on the prose and tested my history against his memory. His professionalism has long served me as a model and I cherish his friendship.

Beth Bailey read the daily rushes, the first, second, third, and fourth drafts. She marked up the chapters and rewrote some awkward prose. We talked over the moves, debated interpretations, and Beth's scholarly work on the 1950s, television, American identity, and sexuality figures throughout the book. As always, she is my best critic, most loyal supporter, and greatest influence.

Many others have contributed directly and indirectly to this book. Linda Kerber's interest and support have been vital. The long-standing encouragement of Lewis Bateman and Doug Mitchell has helped to get me this far. My Barnard friends Mark Carnes, Ester Fuchs, Richard Lufrano, and Herb Sloan kept the home fires burning. Nancy Woloch's knowing looks and laughter have inspired and instructed me more times than I can count, and Rosalind Rosenberg's good sense and scholarly acumen have kept me thinking and rethinking, too. Friends Ayelet Berman Cohen, David Cohen, Dan Frank, Bill Katovsky, Ian Trondent Miller, Katherine Miller, Ann Schofield, Steve Tilley, and Bill ("Hit 'em where they ain't") Tuttle made the year writing this book a pleasure.

Max Warsaw Bailey/Farber explored the computer with me and took many adventurous trips in the 1967 Kaiser Jeepster to the Waialua library. He was a good helper.

My mother and father shared with me their memories of the 1960s. My mother, Nancy Farber, tried to convey to me her experiences as a young mother yearning for creative outlets for her energy and intelligence, as well as her involvement at the grass roots in the civil rights movement and, later, the women's movement. My father, Donald Farber, talked about the meaning and possibilities economic good times offered him and, thus, his family. My father also involved me in the political energy of "the sixties" when he became a stalwart activist in the independent Democratic Party movement in Chicago. Because of his encouragement and the experiences he gave me, I became the youngest (at least, I like to think so) independent precinct captain in Chicago during the 1972 election. My parents made my 1960s childhood on the North Side of Chicago a rich and happy time. This last year was a scary one for my family and I dedicate this book, in part, to my father for his courage, which I will remember all my life.

DAVID FARBER
Sunset Beach
Oahu, Hawaii
June 1993

INDEX

284

INDEX